Principles of Primary Education Study Guide

PAT HUGHES

David Fulton Publishers
London

David Fulton Publishers Ltd
Ormond House, 26–27 Boswell Street, London WC1N 3JZ

www.fultonpublishers.co.uk

First published in Great Britain by David Fulton Publishers 2000

British Library Cataloguing in Publication Data
A catalogue record for this book is available from the British Library

ISBN 1-85346-725-1

Typeset by Elite Typesetting Techniques, Eastleigh, Hampshire
Printed in Great Britain by Bell and Bain Ltd, Glasgow

Contents

Acknowledgements

Particular thanks are due to Les Hankin who wrote Chapter 13.
The following individuals provided advice, notes and inspiration:

Brenda Bland

Helen Clegg

Kath Cox

Brenda Duncan

Janet Evans

Cath Fairhurst

Amanda Fletcher

Wendy Hall

Les Hankin

John Hawkins

Pat Holden

Hilary Letts

Madeleine Lindley

Linda Richardson

Jean Robb

Eric Smith

Susan Worthington

The following schools provided critical documentation, advice and support:

Ballacottier Primary School

Cheetham Hill, C.E.

Cherryfield CP

Deepdale Infants

Ditton, C.E.

Longview CP

Mosscroft CP

Overdale CP

Prescot CP

Challenging and enthusiastic primary PGCE students have helped to form and develop this ever evolving course over many years.

Introduction

Welcome to the world of lifelong learning!
The purpose of this study guide is to look at some of the aspects of education which ITT students cover. The initial target audience is the growing number of students following distance-learning routes for initial teacher training – in particular the primary part-time PGCE and modular routes. It is intended as the starting point to informed primary teaching. The National Standards for Qualified Teacher Status state that those seeking Qualified Teacher Status (QTS) should 'understand the need to take responsibility for their own professional development and to keep up to date with research and developments in pedagogy and in the subjects they teach'. Good teaching demands constant refinement. It is a lifelong process and teachers are lifelong learners.

For whom is the guide written?

- **Full-time and part-time student teachers**.

- **School mentors** may find it useful to know the type of course their students are undertaking and ways in which the standards are exemplified to support student learning.

- **Experienced teachers** will find it useful to revisit at leisure work they may have touched upon in their teacher-training courses. They will find different elements to draw from it because of their experience, but the guide provides an opportunity for updating reading in the field.

- **Teachers who are considering taking a higher degree** may find it helpful as a gentle means of getting back into academic reading.

- **Pre-service teachers** and those on teacher taster courses can use it to plan their career.

- **New teachers** – they will find it helps them stay on track.

- **Teacher returners** – those hoping to start teaching again after a career break or change of career.

- **Staff development officers** – to identify starting points for courses, particularly those for newly qualified teachers.

- **Colleagues in higher education** and in school-based training schemes who need to devise distance-learning materials for primary teacher training.

- **School governors interested in looking at how primary schools work today**.

- **Secondary teachers** who wish to follow a conversion course for Primary teaching.

How to use the guide

Student teachers will find it most useful to work through the guide a section at a time. Although the text is presented in a linear progression, early units will need revisiting in order to support later ones.

Other readers may prefer to pick out different sections in acordance with need. For example a school govenor with responsibility for Special Needs would look initially at the chapter 'Special children' and then might look at a generic view about pupil behaviour in the chapter 'Working for good pupil behaviour and discipline'. Secondary teachers using the guide to familiarise themselves with primary education might turn first to the chapter 'Curriculum planning'.

To make the most of the guide, you will need to have access to a primary school, preferably more than one, since practice – and children – can differ considerably.

Updates

Education is changing rapidly and readers are advised to consult the educational press and websites to keep informed about changes and developments in primary education. Two useful websites are: The Virtual Teachers Centre – http://etc.ngfl.gov.uk/index.html and the *Times Educational Supplement* on http://www.tes.co.uk

Writing style

The guide has been written informally, in order to convey the personal flavour of a taught course. It is not an academic piece of work, but guides readers to more academic texts to encourage their self-supported learning. Children's names used in examples have been substituted with fictitious ones to avoid offending anyone.

This style of writing presents more of a challenge, because the view of the writer is more obvious and sometimes controversial. So if you do find yourself disagreeing, getting cross or angry with the text, good. This means it's succeeding! There is no teacher-proof method of education, nor are there pat answers, quick fixes or foolproof plans for teaching. We all need continually to try and to learn.

The course

The guide is based on the Principles of Education course taught over two terms to Liverpool Hope's primary PGCE students. It is supplemented by material from the final year of the B.Ed course.

The course aims to give students a flavour of proven, research-based practices employed by thousands of other effective teachers. It links school-based experiences with educational psychology and sociology so that good practice is built on effective school research rather than hearsay, myths or prevailing methods. Educational research is not exclusively theoretical, and the course seeks to improve primary practice by using what the research has identified as the most effective practices. This enables the effective teacher to understand how research is carried out, and to use proven research-based practices.

Educational research is a fluid process, and teachers need to contribute to it as well as update themselves. It has also acquired a powerful new partner: technology. Readers interested in looking at recent research findings in education should consult websites such as: http://www.bera.ac.uk/information.html On this site the British Educational Research Association provide a list of useful web links for educational research in the UK. At a more practical level, websites such as Channel 4's www.4learning.co.uk provides some very useful information for planning curriculum content.

The course requires some background reading in the history of education. This gives a wider perspective to political changes in education and affords the opportunity to learn from the past. A knowledge of educational philosophy and changes to it informs the reflective practitioner and provides choices for his or her own philosophy. The importance of this in promoting good practice can be illustrated by the fact that some governing bodies request statements of personal educational philosophy from prospective teachers.

Additional reading is essential. There is a comprehensive bibliography at the end of this guide. This is divided up into highly recommended (see Bibliography) and useful texts (see Further Reading). There has been a deliberate attempt to refer to a number of commonly available texts which are stocked in public and university libraries. Such texts are frequently updated, so make sure the edition you are borrowing is a recent one.

Organisation of the guide

The guide is divided into four Sections – Learning to Teach, The Curriculum, Whole-School Issues, Consolidation and Planning for Future Development.

Section 1 looks at some very basic elements of learning to teach. It aims to provide a framework for observing and learning in the classroom. (Chapters 1–4)

Section 2 looks more closely at how schools plan their teaching and how assessment and target setting inform planning and teaching. It touches on some of the issues which most concern beginning teachers, such as   maintaining a purposeful working environment and making use of their own subject specialism. (Chapters 5–7)

Section 3 moves beyond the classroom to look at how assessment informs planning so that children make progress as they move through the school. It looks at other whole-school issues such as motivation, curriculum entitlement for all children and home-school-community relationships. (Chapters 8–10)

Section 4 looks forward and provides a framework for the next career stage as a newly qualified teacher. It raises professional issues about legal liabilities as well as how teachers can help other teachers. (Chapters 11–12)

If you dare to teach, then you must dare to learn.

Abbreviations

AA	Above Average	OFSTED	Office for Standards in Education
AV	Average		
BA	Below Average	PGCE	Post Graduate Certificate in Education
B.Ed	Bachelor of Education		
CP	County Primary or Community Primary	PLR	Primary Language Record
		PSE	Personal and Social Education
DfEE	Department for Education and Employment	PSHE	Personal, Social and Health Education
EAL	English as an Additional Language	QCA	Qualifications and Curriculum Authority
EO	Equal Opportunities	QTS	Qualified Teacher Status
ICT	Information and Communications Technology	SAT	Standard Assessment Test/ Task
IEP	Individual Education Plan	SEN	Special Educational Needs
ILEA	Inner London Education Authority	SENCO	Special Educational Needs Coordinator
KS	Key Stage (as in KS1 and KS2)	SMSC	Social, Moral, Spiritual and Cultural
LEA	Local Education Authority	TES	Times Educational Supplement
LSA	Learning Support Assistants		
NLS	National Literacy Strategy	TTA	Teacher Training Agency
NNF	National Numeracy Framework	ITT	Initial Teacher Training
		Y	Year (as in Y2, Y6)
NQT	Newly Qualified Teacher		

Chapter 1

The role of the teacher

Learning objectives
- To identify the changing role of the teacher in today's primary schools.
- To re-examine our own experiences of schooling and teachers.
- To be aware of standards required for gaining qualified teacher status.

Do you remember the Teacher Training Agency's television recruitment advertisement, showing a number of famous people in sport, the media and politics stating the names of teachers who had made a difference to their lives? Several newspapers later used this idea to interview a number of people about their favourite teacher. In some cases, the teacher had been traced and interviewed in turn. It is the idea that the individual can make a difference that guides many people into teaching. They want to be that person who makes a difference to children's lives. Interviewees for initial teacher training often give this as one of their prime reasons for wanting to be a teacher.

 Write down the name of a teacher or teachers who made a difference to you. Why did they make this difference?

Maybe, like me, you didn't immediately think of a good teacher. I remember Mrs A very well. She was my class teacher when I was nine. She once threw chalk at me because I could not do fractions. I feared and hated her and later blamed her for my maths O-level failure because I became frightened of the subject and believed I was no good at it. It took another teacher, at evening class, to convince me that my maths was recoverable and I eventually passed the O level in my mid-thirties. Looking back, I can see a tired, impatient woman, who found the subject easy herself and could not understand why an A-stream child was having problems. She made a difference to me, not only because of my maths O-level failure, but when I did become a teacher, I remembered my fear of her. My favourite teacher of all time was Mrs Crawford, who inspired a love of literature that has stayed with me all my life. Why? She loved it herself and could sell Chaucer and John Donne to a group of cynical sixth-formers. She was also a very happy woman and clearly enjoyed being with us. I knew nothing about teaching strategies then, but the contrast between these two teachers has stayed with me for life.

The mediocre teacher tells
The good one explains
The superior one shows
The great one inspires

We all have a rich experience of teachers through our own schooling, and it is worth thinking through this carefully because we learnt about the role of teachers and schooling with them. Yet schools, teachers and children have changed with the demands of society and the role of the teacher has changed with it.

 Photocopy the sheet on page 3 and fill in what you feel is the role of the teacher. Take a second photocopy and ask someone else to complete it. Compare the differences. Differences may be due to age, experience and culture.

Compare your sheet with the one below, which has been filled in by a primary OFSTED inspector. Schools are inspected to specific criteria and the inspector has linked these criteria to her perception of the role of a teacher in today's society. Some blanks have been left so you can add those things which you feel are missing. Teachers in some other countries might be very surprised at some of the roles suggested for teachers. A friend who trained in Ghana said that he was amazed when he came to England to find that schools expected him to be concerned about the social welfare of his children. He had come from a system where educational knowledge was perceived very differently and children had a different concept both of their role and that of the teacher.

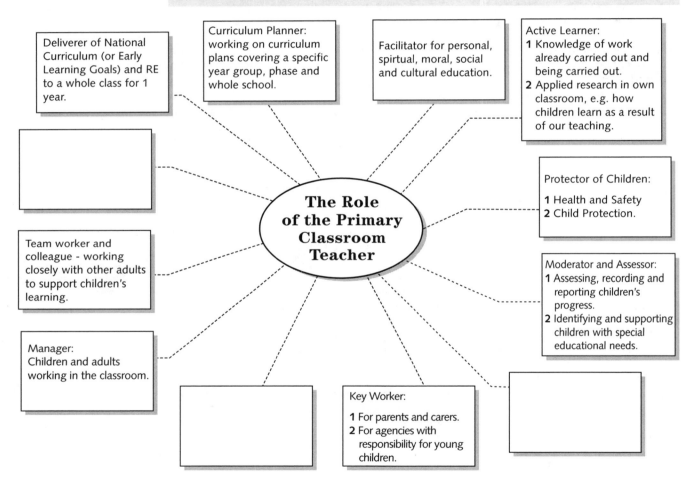

National Standards for Qualified Teacher Status

In 1998, the Teacher Training Agency published National Standards for Qualified Teacher Status (QTS), which identified for the first time the knowledge and skills required by teachers. These standards can easily be seen as forming a central government statement about the role of the teacher. They are divided into four sections.

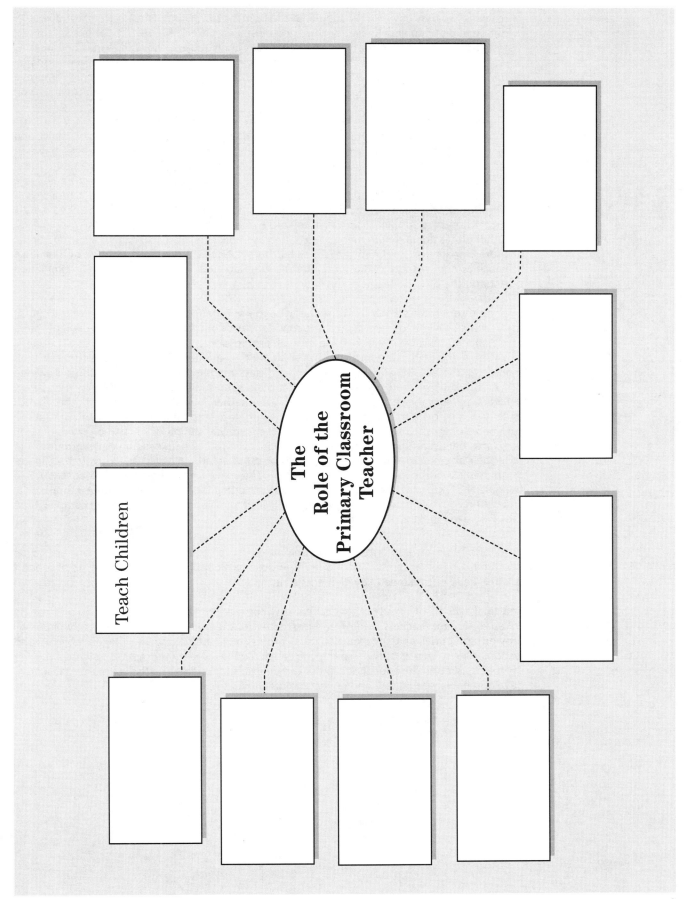

The
Role of the
Primary Classroom
Teacher

Teach Children

1 **Teacher knowledge and understanding:** For primary teachers these are particularly far-reaching, as they cover every subject of the primary curriculum. Most ITT institutions carry out an audit of subject knowledge in the core subjects. Central government has set up skill tests to assess this more formally. Many courses audit subject knowledge in other areas as well. Teacher knowledge and understanding also cover phase knowledge; current research findings on teaching primary children and ways these can be used to inform and improve their teaching. An additional sub-section of knowledge expertise is required for those on courses which cover the under-fives.

2 **Planning, teaching and class-management standards:** These cover very specific competencies, which the trainee teacher must demonstrate, for example, establishing and maintaining a purposeful working atmosphere. Those teaching the under-fives have an additional set of standards linked to planning, teaching and classroom management. These standards also make clear that the role of the teacher must include the ability to evaluate their own teaching and use this to improve their effectiveness in raising children's attainment.

3 **Monitoring, assessment, recording, reporting and accountability:** These are linked closely to statutory responsibilities as well as the more routine monitoring, marking and assessment.

4 **Other professional requirements:** NQTs, and by implication all teachers, must fulfil additional professional roles. It is important for all teachers to have a working knowledge of their legal liabilities and responsibilities in relation to the Race Relations Act, the Sex Discrimination Act and the physical restraint of children.

Looking through the standards at the start of a course is daunting, yet by the end of the course the vast majority of student teachers are confident and competent in what is required of them. This happens because there is some sort of progression through the standards. The initial knowledge and understanding section for students is audited and carried out through their training (1 above). The planning, teaching and class-management section is often subdivided (2). At the start of their course, student teachers spend most of their time looking at how teachers manage their classes and worry about whether they will have a riot on their hands once they take over. In doing this they also need to look at planning and assessment, but the comments of most NQTs are often limited to the 'survival' standards of child behaviour. Later, they look more carefully at how they can exercise their role to help children make progress and raise their attainment. These strategies involve other standards, such as motivating children, establishing a purposeful working atmosphere and exploiting opportunities to contribute to the quality of pupils' wider educational growth, including their personal, spiritual, moral, social and cultural development. The knowledge and skills involved in this are far more complex than those involved in 'keeping the noise down'.

Monitoring and assessment (3) are closely linked to planning, since all planning has to be informed by child progress. There is little purpose in ploughing through a scheme of work if children have not followed key elements of it.

The final section of standards (4) covers a wider breadth of other standards and is closely linked to student teachers reading and re-reading for themselves. Most of the teaching unions provide additional guidance on teachers' professional duties and their legal liabilities and responsibilities. This section is also the one which requires student teachers to get into a routine of looking through the educational press and websites for updates on the law, current research, developments in pedagogy and new community initiatives.

The standards show very clearly how the role of the teacher has broadened considerably and continues to change and develop.

Exemplification of the standards

Several publications are available which look at the standards and 'exemplify' them. Exemplification here simply means providing examples. This enables the student teacher to see what the standard would look like in the classroom or school. They can then use this example, or something similar, to improve their teaching performance. Appendix 1 (pp 156–164) is an example of this form of exemplification, drawn up by three OFSTED inspectors working on a video and CD-ROM exemplification project. A visit to the Teacher Training Agency (TTA) website at www.teach-tta.gov.uk/ gives further information about standards for special educational needs, headship and subject leaders.

It is useful to record systematically, for one lesson, how an effective teacher achieves a particular standard. Some of the most effective teachers do this so well that it is often difficult to work out how it happens.

 Suggest four characteristics of a well-managed classroom which are helping your class teacher to 'establish and maintain a purposeful working atmosphere'. This standard can be found in Section B of the National Standards for QTS: Teaching Approach (h) and Class Management (i). A simple observation schedule might help you to do this. The example on the next page was completed by a student in her first school experience.

Four characteristics which immediately spring to mind are: children deeply involved in their work; knowing what is expected of them; very little wasted time; and a work-orientated classroom environment. Sometimes teachers photograph examples of children at work and put the pictures on the wall as an ongoing reminder of how work is conducted in the classroom. The exemplification in Appendix 1 suggests that a purposeful working atmosphere is created by the teacher communicating the expectation that children will work thoughtfully and conscientiously, ensuring that they understand that they are working to achieve the specified objectives to raise their attainment. Teachers must also maintain a good pace to the lesson and set appropriate targets for children to achieve during the lesson. Provision of meaningful continuation and extension work for those who complete the set tasks early, and presentation of pupils' work, can also be factors in achieving an appropriate commitment to work. The physical environment and resourcing of the classroom will provide the background for a purposeful working atmosphere. This exemplification gives you some criteria against which to observe teaching strategies in the classroom. Ask yourself how the teacher communicates expectations about the way in which children should behave, and how children know what the objectives of the lesson are and the targets they should reach. By the end of the serial attachment you will have the answers to some of these questions. Your primary task now is to raise the questions.

Beyond the classroom

Both educational psychology and sociology look at the role of the teacher in much greater detail. Psychology looks at the different factors involved in the teacher's role and uses role theory to analyse different types of role conflict and strategies which can be used to resolve these. It is often useful to look at this role theory at the start of a course because it can identify and name some of the processes which may be going on in students' lives. Think of some of the roles in your own life – family roles such as parent, daughter, brother, aunt or cousin; work roles such as student, bar person or cleaner; community roles such as charity worker or football coach. For example, the work role may conflict with social or family roles. Role theory enables us to stand back and look at how different elements of the teacher's role may conflict and cause stress. No wonder so many books on teaching finish up with suggestions about relieving stress!

Sociology looks at the role of the teacher much more broadly and often very controversially. Schools can be viewed as microcosms of society and the inequalities within society are not only reflected in schools, but reinforced by the school. How society views the role of the teacher can be expressed locally or nationally and can influence the way in which teachers view themselves and the work they do. This in turn influences the education children receive.

Name of School: Coatley Primary School

Early Observation Schedule		
Date	**Teacher**	**Age Range and Size of Class**
15.2.00	Mrs Jones	Reception/Y1

The Lesson
Introduction (1) Literacy lesson on timetable. Started with children coming in from playtime and having their milk. Completed as routine. Children walked in quietly, had their milk and read quietly at tables. The teacher was hearing a group of guided readers while the majority did this. Guided readers using Kipper's Balloon, asked to predict content, discuss pictures. Read some of text to individual and some as a group. Teacher then asked children to tidy up and come onto carpet. Time 10.50–11.05.
Introduction to Literacy Lesson (2) Mrs J shows ch. flashcards and they have to identify the letter the word begins with. Then she asks about the sound they make.
Development Reception chi. Go to Words and Pictures while Mrs J works with Y1s – consonant blends sp/st/sh/th. How do we get these sounds? Read poem – Blip Blop Blends. What sound can you hear? Fl/sl/pl/etc. Read again altogether. Then move to Read a Rhyme. Mrs J reads first verse and ask ch. to identify the rhyming sounds -ess, -ing, -uff. Brainstorms for words rhyming with snip. Lots of answers, writes a list then uses them to write a rhyme together. Repeats with ack words. Then gives children their 'jobs'. Y1 filling in sheet with gl or cl. Reception return from TV and do sheet related to programme – kicking k. Mrs J also does another guided reading group. Some of the Y3s also write a rhyme of their own using brainstorm words.
Plenary Mrs J reads out rhymes they have done. Praises children for working well and holding their pencils properly. I was surprised at how good some of the rhymes were.
Resources Big Book Phonics, Oxford Reading Tree for guided reading. A's support worker took him and the reception children to TV and supervised them on return to classroom.
Evaluation for class management Atmosphere was relaxed and friendly, teacher had a good sense of humour which she shared with the children and to which they responded well. Children worked on tasks, teacher never raised voice although they had been quite 'high' in the playground. Regular routine, so children know what to do when come in from break. Books ready for them, so no time wasted. Expectation that children will work on tasks independently. I liked the way she let the children have their milk during the first guided reading session – this added informality and did not seem to detract from the learning focus in any way. Children smiled when praised for working well at end. Behaved well on carpet, although not much room for some of the children. I was not asked to work with a specific group and felt this was a waste of an extra adult, but it did allow me to move around the different groups and continue my observation.
Learning Targets Use NLS to find out how this lesson links with strategy. Find teachers' notes for Words and Pictures.

Chapter 2

Children's learning

Learning objectives
- To know some of the factors which influence children as learners.
- To recognise that educational psychology can provide insights into ways in which children learn.
- To identify ways in which these insights can be used in small-group teaching.

Challenges of small-group teaching

After student teachers have been into school on a couple of occasions, they sometimes feel that the small-group work to which they have been assigned is in some way inferior to the whole-class work which the teacher is undertaking. It is in fact probably the one time in most class teacher's careers where they have the opportunity to sit down, observe children's learning and learn how children learn. If we can develop some understandings about how children learn, this gives guidance to planning for effective teaching to improve learning. Both knowledge and skills in this area are enhanced through a careful combination of theory and practice. Educational psychology informs practice, but it needs mediating, as there is no simple formula for enhancing children's learning. Small-group teaching develops skills which can later be translated to planning, teaching and assessing work for the whole class.

The definition of learning

One definition of learning is that it is a process that goes on inside a person. Teaching then becomes an attempt to effect change in someone from the outside. Clearly the processes of teaching and learning are distinct but interrelated, although the relationship between learning and teaching is rarely straightforward. Sometimes the following things can happen:

1 **Learning arises without direct teaching** – for example, children making sense of their world.
2 **Learning arises as a result of teaching** – for example, when paints are mixed to produce different colours during an art lesson.
3 **Learning arises in spite of teaching, either positively or negatively** – for example, when children learn that they must go to the back of the teacher's queue, not to the front and can continue to do this through the course of a lesson, they learn to do nothing and just change queue position.
4 **Learning is different from that intended by the teacher** – this could be due to an inadequate, confused or incorrect explanation.

 Next time you are with a small group of children, either inside or outside school, find and record examples of each type of learning.

You may be quite amazed by what children learn without direct teaching (1) and 'get a buzz' from the knowledge that the children are learning from the activities you plan and teach (2). Different emotions arise from the learning taking place in 3 and 4. This can cause frustration and annoyance, but it can also be amusing and puzzling. It helps to imagine what it is like to be a learner in your group.

A philosophy of learning

When you are applying for teaching posts, you will find that many schools, LEA employment panels and supply agencies will ask you to write a couple of sentences about your personal educational philosophy. This recognises that what teachers bring with them from their personal school experiences, parental experiences and academic study will influence their philosophy. As teacher trainers we expect trainee teachers to be influenced by teaching and reflecting, observation, further reading and discussions with peers and teachers. We expect views to change. Teaching is an attempt to effect this change. Teachers' personal philosophy includes:

- Their knowledge about the learning process. This includes the knowledge about how children learn, as well as child development.
- Their beliefs about the child's role in learning. There are fundamental differences in belief about this. At one extreme, children are seen as blank slates onto which commercial curriculum packages can be written; at the other end of the spectrum, children are seen as creating their own learning environment which is personal to themselves, and all teaching must be centred towards the learning needs of the child, rather than of society. The pendulum swings backwards and forwards between the two extremes, and most teachers adopt a pragmatic approach which leans towards their own particular philosophy.
- Their views about the purpose of learning. School learning can be viewed as functional, aimed at equipping the workforce with the skills it needs, or it can be seen as developing the whole child.
- Their views on what children should learn. A look at the history of education shows very different views over time. The Victorian Sunday Schools limited education to reading the Bible, which was later extended by the Board Schools to basic literacy and numeracy. By the 1950s and 1960s there was a wider view of what was important. The National Curriculum formalised this into subject areas at the end of the 1980s. By the mid-1990s, it was narrowed again as the percentage of time spent on literacy and numeracy increased.
- Their personal experience of education. Our own experience of education is an important factor in creating an education philosophy.

Setting small-group tasks

One of the main learning advantages of being assigned to a small group or even working one-to-one with individual children is that the class-management aspects of teaching can be delegated to someone else, i.e. the class teacher. It then becomes possible to set individual and small-group tasks and watch as children tackle them. At first many of these tasks will be set by the class teacher, which frees the student teacher from the planning aspect of teaching so that he or she can observe, analyse and assess the learning taking place. Several of the teaching standards require an in-depth knowledge about children's learning, which can only be gained through working with individual children and in small groups – in particular, the standards related to paying careful attention to children's errors and misconceptions and helping them remedy these. This requires both watching and listening carefully to children, analysing their responses and responding constructively in order to take their learning forward. Good assessment is heavily dependent on being able to gauge how successfully the learning objectives have been achieved and using this to improve specific aspects of teaching. Small-group work is also a good opportunity to evaluate the effectiveness of different teaching strategies to improve children's learning. It soon becomes clear that children's learning styles vary and teaching strategies must be differentiated to support this. Some children may have ineffective learning styles and therefore need to be given strategies to encourage them to use more appropriate methods of learning.

What teachers bring to learning

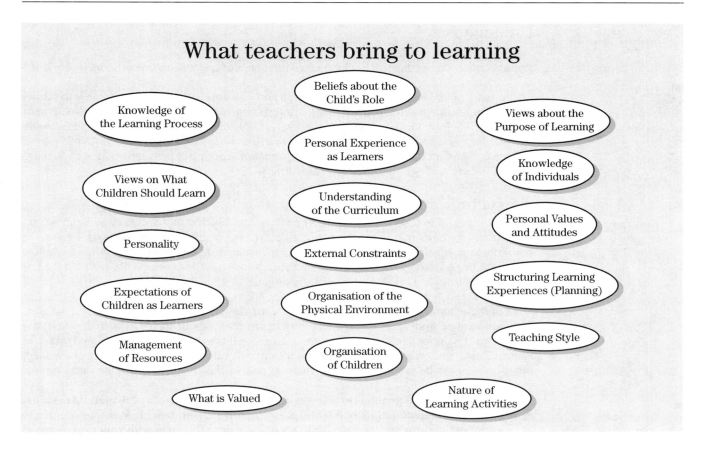

Knowledge of the Learning Process

Beliefs about the Child's Role

Views about the Purpose of Learning

Views on What Children Should Learn

Personal Experience as Learners

Knowledge of Individuals

Personality

Understanding of the Curriculum

Personal Values and Attitudes

External Constraints

Expectations of Children as Learners

Structuring Learning Experiences (Planning)

Organisation of the Physical Environment

Management of Resources

Organisation of Children

Teaching Style

What is Valued

Nature of Learning Activities

What children bring to learning

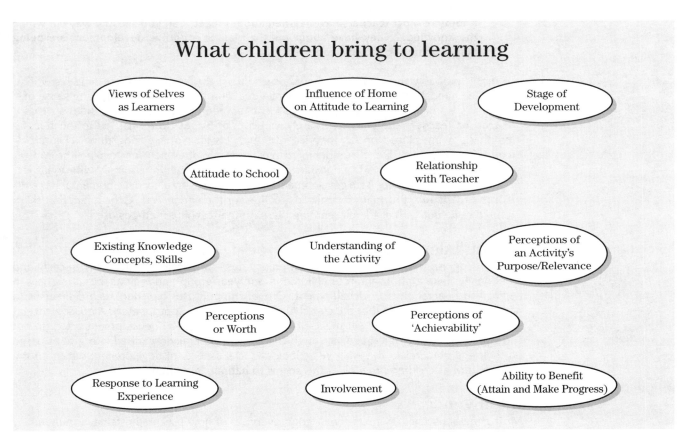

Views of Selves as Learners

Influence of Home on Attitude to Learning

Stage of Development

Attitude to School

Relationship with Teacher

Existing Knowledge Concepts, Skills

Understanding of the Activity

Perceptions of an Activity's Purpose/Relevance

Perceptions or Worth

Perceptions of 'Achievability'

Response to Learning Experience

Involvement

Ability to Benefit (Attain and Make Progress)

Uniqueness

There is nothing more unequal than the equal treatment of unequal people. (Thomas Jefferson)

Children are all unique, both as human beings and as learners. Our children come into school with different out-of-school experiences, interests, learning styles and levels of development and ability. Their maturation and age levels vary; they come in different sizes, shapes, colours and genders. The opportunity to work with individuals and small groups for a sustained period of time is a perfect opportunity to gather information about this uniqueness as well as more generic understandings about children as learners.

A psychology of learning

There are several excellent texts for teachers (see the Bibliography and Further Reading) on the psychology of learning, and it is useful to purchase one of these general texts if you have not studied psychology before. Ideas about how children learn change all the time and it is important to make sure that the general text you choose has either been written within the last couple of years or is a revised edition of the original.

Most of these books provide information about work carried out by key psychologists in the area. They record their findings and some of the criticisms made about them. As with any text, the printed word is up for discussion. When you read about Bruner, Erikson, Eysenck, Freud, Maslow, Piaget, Skinner and Vygotsky, remember that their findings and theories have all been questioned, but their work can be extremely useful in making sense of children's learning in the classroom.

 Use one of the general texts to find out more about the work of Piaget. Make a list of the different stages he identifies in cognitive development. Make a note of the approximate ages associated with each. How does this fit in with your experience of children (i) in school (ii) outside school? What implications does it have when you are teaching a specific age group? What sort of criticisms have been made about his findings? Most teachers have learned about Piaget. Can you see any ways in which the knowledge they have about his theories of cognitive development are being demonstrated in the classroom?

Piaget is probably the most well-known psychologist for teachers. At one time his work was seen almost as a gospel among general education texts in terms of making sense of children's learning. Student teachers were encouraged to buy books with titles such as *Piaget for Teachers* and plan accordingly. Criticism of Piaget's work has led to much less emphasis being placed on his theories, although his idea of breaking down children's cognitive processes into a number of stages certainly does help us to plan the most developmentally appropriate education for children. Not everyone agrees with what is appropriate education for each developmental stage, particularly early developmental stages. Some experts reject formal academic instruction for the under-fives. Others feel that the problems lie not with academic learning but with the teaching methods used.

Age and development levels

We all recognise that children grow at different rates – physically, intellectually, socially and emotionally. Take a photograph of children in one year group and look at the differences in height and general physical development. One of the purposes of school record sheets is to note these differences, so that the curriculum can be planned appropriately. A quick glance at any individual assessment sheet makes it quite clear that rates of development often do not correspond to chronological age, although children are generally organised into groups based on their age. Records in the early years look at social aspects of development which inform learning, but as children grow older this seems to happen less often.

Intelligence

Most general psychology texts give a good overview of how psychologists have traditionally identified intelligence, attempted to measure it, questioned whether it is inherited or not and looked at reasons for differences in intelligence and ways in which it may be improved.

In practice, in today's schools reading ability is often used as a primary indicator of intelligence, and some classrooms create and maintain a whole status order based on reading abilities. Recent concern about children's skills in numeracy may alter this, but essentially this leaves us with a very traditional working concept of intelligence which focuses on reading.

 What other forms of intelligence can you see in the class? Use a psychology text to identify what other different 'intelligences' have been identified.

Howard Gardner, in *Multiple Intelligences: The Theory in Practice*, suggests seven different intelligences: logical-mathematical; verbal-linguistic; musical-rhythmic; visual-spatial; bodily-kinaesthetic; interpersonal-social and intrapersonal-introspective. He points out that we have moved on from the idea that intelligence is a single entity – in other words, that we either are or are not intelligent. When you profile children in the class, it is important to make sure that you collect data on attainment in a variety of different areas. This will involve watching children at leisure as well as when they undertake tasks across the whole curriculum. It involves seeing how they create visual-spatial representations of the world and use their bodies. Gardner's theory has major implications for curriculum planning, because it requires curriculum design to cover all these intelligences. The QTS standards reflect this view of multiple intelligences through their requirement for student teachers to set high expectations for all children – notwithstanding individual differences including gender, and cultural and linguistic backgrounds – and exploiting opportunities to contribute to the quality of children's wider educational development, including their personal, spiritual, moral, social and cultural development. McGrath and Noble (see Further Reading) provide some practical strategies to develop these multiple intelligences.

Contexts for learning

Learning takes place inside and outside school and individual learning styles may be influenced by diverse individual preferences. You may be reading this text surrounded by your family and drinking a cup of tea, whereas the author might have written it in a quiet, well-lit, warm room, with fairly regular breaks! Others may be reading it in front of the television, in bed, or while moving around.

Individual preferences include those of temperature, sound levels, seating, lighting, group size, and eating and/or drinking while concentrating. It is difficult to establish and maintain a purposeful working atmosphere in a classroom which caters for such different preferences.

No one learning style is better than another; it is just different, although some children's styles may be more appropriate for effective learning. For example, a child who likes to wander around the room can distract others and avoid completing learning tasks. They need strategies to settle down, since a mobile learning style in a room of 30 children is difficult to accommodate and becomes a management problem. Sometimes the strategies exist outside the child; for example, the teacher plans for less passive learning, so that the 'movers' get the opportunity they need to move around.

One of the major advantages of having enough room to provide different types of learning centres in a class is that these areas can provide different types of activity, lighting, seating and sound. They can include reading, interactive science and role-play areas. It is also useful to remember that children, like adults, vary their preferences for different areas of learning, at different times of day, at different periods of their life and for different types of learning activity.

 What learning styles are supported through the teaching and classroom organisation and management in your class? Are some children having difficulties with this? Could additional teaching strategies be developed to accommodate a greater variety of learning styles?

Working with individuals and small groups can significantly alter the organisation and management of children's learning. You may find that some children prefer the small-group situation and closer adult support. Their behaviour improves, they maintain concentration and become more effective learners. Some children may be disconcerted by the close adult to child ratio and transfer it to their experiences outside school. They may ask personal questions and wish to move from the more formal relationship of child and teacher to child and older sibling. The advice to most student teachers is to avoid this. Keep your role as teacher and encourage the child to develop a small-group learning style which can use the adult to better effect. It is also worth noting that if a child reacts to you like this in a small-group situation, other adults working with small groups may need help to avoid the same scenario.

Learning differences related to culture, gender and special needs

Culture

Culture relates directly to the individual's learning style. Too often, we not only fail to understand people who are different from us, but also view them negatively. Genuinely valuing cultural diversity means that we can establish and maintain a purposeful learning environment which acknowledges cultural differences and plans for them.

Examples of cultural differences which may influence learning are:
- the extent to which children are encouraged to 'speak up'
- the use of gestures, eye contact and non-verbal cues when a child communicates with an adult
- the importance of time
- oral communication, rather than written
- a community language spoken at home.

Gender

Boys and girls often exhibit different behaviour and learning styles, but are entitled to the same chance to participate and learn. Gender research (Hughes 1991) shows that it is easy to discriminate unknowingly through the type of praise given, the tasks assigned, the questions asked and the time given for a response. Boys, for example, tend to be given more direct instruction, approval, disapproval and attention. Girls tend to get more teaching attention during reading instruction and boys during maths.

Special needs

The overriding ideology today is that children with learning difficulties have average or above average intelligence, and many are gifted. Learning disabilities are neurobiological disorders that interfere with the ability to store, process and retrieve information. This mostly affects reading and language skills, but can also influence computation and social skills.

The term 'special needs' is less commonly used in the UK to describe very able or gifted children. Definitions, particularly of gifted children, vary considerably, although it is generally agreed that special needs result from both genetic inheritance and environmental opportunities.

Teaching programmes for children with special needs vary considerably. (Giftedness covers the multiple intelligences mentioned above, so teaching strategies would need to include physical, musical, intellectual and social challenges.)

 Find out who monitors special needs in your school and ask them about the major types of learning disabilities which are recorded. Find out more about one learning disability which affects a child's learning in your class and identify the strategies used by the teacher to help this learner. Are these strategies recorded on an individual education plan (IEP) for that child?

There are a number of different learning disabilities and most Local Education Authorities (LEAs) provide good support in terms of identification. Broadly speaking, identification tends to be based on difficulties in more than one of these areas – language, memory, attention, fine motor skill and other functions, such as poor learning strategies and grasp of abstract concepts. Financial restrictions often limit the amount of practical support that can be given, but OFSTED inspection reports indicate huge disparity between different schools within the same area. Some of the major learning difficulties are dyslexia, dyspraxia, visual perception, auditory discrimination, dysgraphia and attention-deficit disorder. These categories are in themselves controversial, as the discussions in the media about dyslexia demonstrate. Educational consultants such as Jean Robb and Hilary Letts (Robb and Letts 1997) are concerned that this type of analysis leads to labelling children, who then respond to low expectations of their learning abilities. They also point out that a whole industry has been created out of special needs provision, while the number of children identified as having difficulties grows, rather than decreases.

Whether we agree or not with Robb and Letts, it is worth looking at their practical learning strategies. They tend to be good tips for teaching all children, such as:
• applying what has been learnt, discussing what they are doing and what has been learnt, recording through pictures, role play and construction
• breaking down stages of learning into small steps, including the purpose of the exercise, clear, precise directions and instructions for task completion
• ensuring that teaching and class management demonstrate clear structure and routines
• providing practical experiences to support the learning of abstract concepts
• paying careful attention to children's errors/misconceptions and helping to remedy them
• recognising what is achieved successfully and rewarding it, so that children with learning disabilities gain in confidence.

Children in crisis

Children's learning can also be influenced by factors such as poverty, death, the absence of a loved carer, emotional and/or physical abuse, racial prejudice, homelessness, alcohol and drug abuse. This type of stress often leads to behavioural and learning difficulties, but many children in crisis do manage to overcome these. The teacher can be the focal person for such children: he or she may be the one reliable adult in that child's life and, through their care and trust, can give the support the child needs in order to learn successfully.

There is an increasing recognition of the need to get extra, specialist help for children when the crisis is too difficult for them to handle. Michael Farrell's *Special Education Handbook* provides a comprehensive guide to this help within the UK (see Further Reading). Warning signs include unusual aggressiveness, withdrawal, depression, fearlessness, fearfulness, poor concentration and repetitive and disturbing behaviour such as headbanging.

Increasing children's learning and attainment

It is easy to feel overwhelmed by all this information about what characteristics directly affect children's learning. This is why the initial opportunities for small-group work should be seized upon and used to the maximum. We return to the area of learning needs in Section 3, where the most important thing is to have high expectations for all children and to resist labelling.

Three major characteristics of effective teachers are:
1 They have high expectations for children's behaviour and learning.
2 They are extremely good class managers.
3 They know how to design lessons and activities which help children to learn.

Learning how children learn is the first step in this process, because effective teaching and learning are led by good planning and assessment of individual children. *If a child cannot demonstrate learning or achievement, we have failed the child; the child has not failed us.*

Chapter 3

Classroom organisation and management: the effective teacher

Learning objectives
- To identify ways in which a purposeful working atmosphere can be created through the physical layout of the classroom, pupil grouping, routines and learning areas.
- To examine organisational and management strategies to ensure effective teaching of whole classes, of groups and individuals within the whole-class setting, so that teaching objectives are met and the best use is made of available teaching time.

One of the aspects we examined in the previous chapter was different learning preferences. In this chapter, we look at how the organisation and management of a classroom can support these different learning styles. In essence, this involves looking at particular aspects of teaching and examining how they reflect different teaching styles. You may be in a classroom where you are very comfortable with the teaching style, or you may be in one which challenges your views. In either case, you need to observe and record carefully so that you can analyse and develop your own individual teaching style. Specific aspects are involved in classroom organisation and management. As a student teacher, it may be possible to alter some of these, but not others. Return to this section when you are in your first teaching post and can make positive decisions about elements you have been unable to change as a student teacher.

We need to look at some of the most obvious aspects of classroom organisation and management – the physical environment, grouping, routines and regulations, and learning areas. Ann Proctor (1995) and her colleagues have a good chapter in their book *Learning to Teach in the Primary Classroom (see* Bibliography*)*. In this they look at physical, psychological and social contexts. The effective teacher affects lives: teaching is a helping and caring profession which enhances the quality of people's lives, and that includes their working/classroom environment.

The physical environment

 Draw a diagram of the physical layout of your classroom. Now ask yourself what teaching style this reflects. Particular features to look for are ways in which the teacher arranges the space; organises the placing of desks and chairs; caters for individual children's environmental preferences such as temperature, lighting and noise; the type of displays and whether they have been created by the children or adults; specific learning areas and storage arrangements. Teachers often change seating arrangements and may move furniture to enable different types of activity to take place – art and drama, for example.

Several books on teaching recommend different methods of organisation. As a student you are not expected to reorganise an established teacher's classroom. Some teachers are very willing for students to experiment – and learn from their mistakes! However, always ask first if you wish to move furniture.

Risk management: some safety tips

Effective teaching has to take place within a safe environment. Establishing this seems commonplace and UK schools carry out a regular risk assessment to ensure that they follow the latest safety guidance. It is teachers' common-law duty to ensure that children are healthy and safe on school premises and when they are involved in school-related activities elsewhere, such as educational visits, school outings or field trips. LEAs generally have a policy on health and safety which they send out to schools and update as the law changes. Policies may cover, among other things:

- named persons as health and safety contacts
- procedures for the safe supervision of children
- accident reporting procedures
- first-aid procedures
- fire precautions
- bomb alert procedures
- telephone threat report procedures
- hazard reporting procedures
- electrical safety
- hygiene and health
- contracts
- medicines
- training on health and safety
- good working practices
- visits: short educational, residential outdoor education, swimming
- environment and traffic
- school access.

Classroom Safety Checklist

- Fasten down carpets, rugs and tiles to prevent tripping.
- Make sure windows and doors are unobstructed – lay inspectors on OFSTED teams frequently record fire exits obscured by chairs, tables and general clutter once the class starts working.
- Make sure the children are always visible.
- Make sure anything breakable, sharp or toxic is carefully displayed or stored and labelled in a safe place.
- Avoid congestion in high traffic areas, such as those giving access to reference materials, pencil sharpeners, rubbers, etc.
- Create individual space so children can store their belongings safely.
- Make sure that any electrical plugs are checked, wires are not left trailing and electrical appliances (including those owned by staff) are checked regularly.
- Make sure instructional support, such as cards, clipboards, whiteboards or shared reading stands can be seen by everyone.
- Your name, the class and room number should be displayed on the classroom door, so that carers and children can find you and your class easily.
- Children also need to feel personally safe and secure. Most schools have policy statements which outline strategies on child protection, equal opportunities and bullying policies. Make yourself familiar with these.

Environmental preferences

- Provide opportunities for children to move around.
- Establish informal as well as formal seating arrangements – many children do not learn best when sitting up straight in a hard chair. Learning areas can provide different forms of seating arrangements, e.g. soft cushions and beanbags in a book corner.
- Provide different types of lighting, so that some areas are very well lit and others more relaxing – too much light can make some children hyperactive; too little can make other children passive.

- Encourage children to modify their clothing, depending on the temperature. A surprising number of children keep jumpers and sweatshirts on when it is very hot.
- Keep the room well ventilated. Classrooms can become quite smelly if the air is not moved around and changed.

Grouping

School grouping

Schools generally group their children into classes, usually classes where children are all the same age. There are exceptions to this, where children are grouped across age ranges. This is sometimes by choice, but it may also be for a number of other reasons, such as

- vertically grouped classes, sometimes known as family grouping. This occurs when schools believe that children work best in a mixed-age environment. Older children support younger ones and reinforce their own learning. Family grouping is often found where the school places particular emphasis on its children's social development. It is less popular in the UK now than it was twenty years ago
- mixed-age classes exist in some schools, where it is impossible to fill one class with children of one age group
- towards the end of Key Stage 2 some schools prefer to mix Year 5 and Year 6 children, finding that they work and behave better.

 Find out how the school organises its classes and whether all teaching takes place in that one class grouping for all the children in the class.

You need first to record the number of children in the school and the number of classes. This information can be found in the prospectus, but you will have to ask your class teacher about the school groupings. A single-form entry is the simplest method of organisation, but not all schools can or choose to organise like this. If the school has more than one form of entry, find out how children are sorted into classes. Many schools put older reception children into one class and younger ones into the other. This can have important implications for overall attainment at the end of the Key Stage if children remain within this grouping. Other schools mix the children up; sometimes alphabetically, often at random. Sometimes, children carry on in the same class grouping through the whole of their primary school career; sometimes they are moved around. Mixed-age classes occur for a variety of reasons, and individuals within those classes may have had different class groupings from other children. In recent years, there has been a return to teaching children English and maths in cross-class ability groups. This is more likely to happen in Key Stage 2, particularly in Years 5 and 6. If new children come into the school in the course of the year, find out how they are accommodated. Look also at how children with special educational needs are grouped in any one class. Do they always sit together? Do they always remain in the same year grouping, or do they work with children in other year groups? How are children who speak English as an additional language grouped? Are children withdrawn from class? What do they miss when this happens?

Class grouping

Once inside the classroom, children are grouped even further. Some teaching and learning takes place in whole-class settings. Sometimes it is divided into smaller, working groups. Such a grouping is often an instructional strategy, as in the case of grouping for collaborative learning or ability grouping in maths and English (e.g. Guided Reading). It may also be an organisational strategy designed to establish and maintain a purposeful working atmosphere. In some classrooms these groups are fixed, particularly if they are organised according to reading ability. Flexible grouping occurs when children work in differently mixed groups, depending on the task in hand.

Flexible-grouping strategies may be random, cooperative, by ability, by interest, by task, by knowledge of a specific subject, by skill and by friendship.

3 **How are the children grouped in your class? Is there an academic, racial, behaviour and gender balance?**

In some schools boys form the bulk of those children identified as having special educational needs. They may spend all day sitting in the same group, assimilating patterns of learning behaviour from each other, or sitting alone. The key features of these groups tend to be poor reading ability and an inability to sustain concentration. In some areas a disproportionate number of black boys are excluded from school. If these imbalances occur in your school, what attempts are being made to analyse them and provide strategies to ensure that these children become effective learners? There is no research correlation between success and family background, race, national origin, financial status, or even educational accomplishments. There is only one correlation with success and that is attitude. Knowing what you can and cannot achieve is called expectation, and the classic research on expectations producing success in classrooms was carried out in the 1960s by Rosenthal (*see* Rosenthal 1968). Some grouping arrangements produce children who use up a lot of energy – their own, their peers' and their teacher's – achieving negative results. The same amount of energy could be directed towards achieving positive results.

Routines

Routines can be seen as the three Rs – rules, routines and regulations – all of which have to be in operation before effective teaching can take place. Routines are the backbone of daily classroom life. Regular procedures known to the class make it easier for children to learn, enable them to make progress and achieve more. Of course, routines make it easier to teach, although naturally they differ from teacher to teacher and class to class. Recording these differences enables student teachers to improve their own practice. They eliminate many potential disruptions and help to establish a safe environment which supports learning.

It is often difficult to see these well-established routines, particularly when they work well. The routines for getting attention and signalling for help are likely to vary from class to class. Effective teachers model the behaviour they want and practise it with the whole class, giving the children time to demonstrate that they know and understand it. These routines can be reinforced through photographs, lists of class rules (often made with the children themselves) and written support.

Below are two suggestions for establishing routines for seeking help. The first one is designed as a poster to which children can refer. The second is a procedure which needs to be practised and understood before it will work.

Example

How do I spell a new word?
Use a 'Have-a-go' card

- Think about meaning. Does it give any clues to spelling patterns?
- Say the word slowly. Listen carefully.
- Write the word syllable by syllable.
- Make sure you have represented each sound with a letter or letters.
- Look carefully to see if the pattern looks right. If not:
  – try different patterns that might be right
  – see if you know another word which is similar.
(example given in *Writing Resource Book: First Steps Programme, 1997*)

Example

Signalling for Help

One example of a successful routine for signalling for help is given in a book given to all NQTs in Tucson, Arizona. The authors suggest that each child is given an index card folded and taped into a three-sided pyramid. One side is blank, one side reads 'Please help me' and the third side reads 'Please keep working'. The blank side normally faces the child. But when the child needs help, he or she signs by turning the 'Please help me' side towards the teacher. This in turn, puts the 'Please keep working' side towards the child as a reminder to continue quietly until the teacher comes. This is a silent procedure which secures the necessary help without disrupting the whole class. It also avoids the very public admission of difficulty involved in raising a hand for help.

 What sort of routines are in operation in your classroom? Try and place them into different categories and add to them as you observe more teachers in action. You might find it useful to make them into a checklist.

Categories could include:
- start of the day – registration, dinner money collection, children arriving late, walk-in work routines
- work routines – naming and/or heading paper and books, use of pencil/pen, presentation, incomplete work, number of pages completed
- instructional activities – signals by teacher/child for attention, talking during seated tasks, getting work marked, activities when work completed, movement round class, expected behaviour, number of children in learning/activity area
- ending the session – putting materials away, tidying up, leaving the room
- interruptions – rules, talking to other children, handing in work, monitoring
- other procedures – lunches, getting changed for PE, assembly, moving from one place in the school to another, milk/snack time, adult helpers
- room/school areas – teacher's desk, books, computer, toilets, pencil sharpener, rubber, learning areas, playground, movement round the classroom
- checking work – working collaboratively/independently; giving in homework
- academic and personal feedback – rewards and incentives, communication with parents, written comments on work, self-recording requirements.

Characteristics of a well managed classroom

1 Class management refers to all of the things that a teacher does to organise pupils, space, time and materials so that teaching and learning can take place. Effective class management can be seen when pupils are on task, deeply involved with their academic work and rarely misbehave. Remember, the teacher is responsible for organising a well-managed classroom, so that pupils can learn in a good working environment. Observation of existing good practice provides the first step to learning the craft of class management which results in:

- A high level of pupil involvement with their work.
- Pupils who have clear and accurate expectations of what is required of them. They know the purposes/objectives of the tasks set for them as individuals. They need to know the purposes of both written and non-written tasks such as when they are involved in speaking and listening activities. Many teachers record their lesson objectives on the board, so that they and the pupils are reminded of them.
- Relatively little wasted time, confusion or disruption.
- Pleasant, relaxed and work-orientated atmosphere.

2 Maximising children's learning and minimising disruption involves:
- High levels of preparation – the lesson content, the furniture, the floor space, work areas, wall spaces, bookcases, teacher area, teaching materials, yourself. Observe carefully how the physical environment of the classroom contributes to good management.

- Identifying strategic locations for pupils who cause behavioural problems. Behavioural problems will occur from time to time. The extract below is taken from a handbook issued to newly qualified teachers. The author compares disruptive behaviour in class with infractions in hockey. When the infraction occurs in hockey, there is an area, or strategic location set aside for the offender. He argues that the same needs to occur in teaching.

Some pupils who cause behavioural problems

The Aggressive - the hyperactive, agitated, unruly child
The Resistant - the child who won't work
The Distractible - the child who can't concentrate
The Dependent - the child who wants help all the time

Strategic Locations
Separate - the pupil must be separated from the class or at least from other problem students. Appropriate for aggressive and resistant pupils.
Close by - must be placed close to teacher. Appropriate for distractible, dependent and occasionally resistant pupils.

3 Becoming a well-organised teacher
Remember the first day is the most critical. Even when you are in a classroom as an observer, pupils (and teachers) will be observing you. They, and the parents, will expect you to perform effectively.

- **Have positive expectations for the children you are teaching and for yourself as their teacher.**

Expectations are different from standards. Standards are levels of achievement. Positive expectations help produce high standards. Say to yourself 'This is an exciting class. This is going to be the most memorable professional experience I have ever had. As a result we will all do well.'
The most successful schools have expectations that everyone will succeed.

- **Time management.**

Teaching takes time; learning how to teach takes even longer. Time management is likely to be one of the biggest challenges in classroom management. You need to be able to manage your own time well so that you can manage both yours and the children's. Time management is a thread that runs through good class management – organising the day, organising the classroom, organising the day-to-day and weekly timetables, recording pupils' progress and keeping disruptions to a minimum. Below are some suggestions.

1 Set goals – professional and personal – and review them regularly. Don't attempt to do too much. Target the possible.
2 Make a daily list of the things that need doing.
3 If possible do the hardest task as early in the day as possible, so you get it out of the way and don't have to spend time and energy worrying about doing it.
4 Identify your personal working habits. Do you work best first thing in the morning? If you arrived at school half an hour earlier you would accomplish more than by staying two hours after school.
5 Learn to say no to activities for which you do not have time. Student teachers need to have a social life, but kick boxing followed by a few drinks may not be the most effective way of spending the evening preparing for the next day's lessons.
6 Delegate – family responsibilities may need to be shared and delegated.
7 Learn to concentrate and stick to tasks.
8 Avoid perfectionism – an additional two hours on a worksheet may just not be worth it.
9 Set time limits for tasks and set deadlines for yourself and your class – work expands to fill time.
10 Operate a one touch policy for mail, including e-mail. Put it into the wastebin (or delete on the screen) or attend to it immediately.
11 Have an answerphone so you can monitor phone calls.
12 Make time your ally, rather than your enemy.

- **Create a good initial impression – you do not get a second chance to make a first impression.**

1 Arrive early. The time of arrival depends on school practice. In some schools, teachers arrive as early as 7 a.m., in others the majority may arrive about 8.30. In many schools there is a short staff meeting before the day begins. You should ask to attend this so that you can learn how the school is organised. Many schools encourage students to attend staff meetings and professional development sessions which occur after school and at weekends. Again, you should make the most of these opportunities and, if not asked directly, politely enquire if you can attend.

2 Remember you are treated as you are dressed. In an ideal world, we would be accepted for ourselves, not our appearance. In the real world, appearance is under constant scrutiny. Dress for respect, credibility, acceptance and authority.

3 Welcome pupils with a smile. Most teachers prepare their children for visitors. Make sure that the children know your name and that you are given an opportunity to get to know them. Whenever you work with a small group, make sure that they know who you are and if possible conduct some form of 'getting acquainted' game.

4 Show you are interested in the children. You may find it useful to spend time with children out of the classroom, for example during playtime, having a school dinner and in after-school clubs. Consult with the class teacher. Remember that if you agree to take on additional responsibilities, such as going on a school trip, you must do it. Nothing is worse than a volunteer who back tracks at the last minute.

5 Don't spend time on clerical tasks in the classroom. Observation schedules, evaluations, etc. can be done when the children are not around.

6 Encourage invitational learning – whatever task you are doing, make sure that you create a welcoming and invitational atmosphere.

Learning areas

Look back to your original plan for the classroom. Can you identify any part of the classroom where the teacher has planned for independent learning activities? Record this on your original plan if you have not done so already. What are the children learning and how is this learning being evaluated?

Planning and designing effective learning areas is one of the hardest tasks for the teacher because it is so dependent on ensuring children's self-sustained concentration. Direct teaching, provided class management is satisfactory, is much easier. The teacher remains in control. Once children are working by themselves in a learning area, control is subcontracted. When planning for these areas is well done, it helps children not only to learn efficiently, but also to develop self-control and independence. Judging by OFSTED inspection reports, this is often planned better in nurseries and infant classes than at Key Stage 2. Clear learning objectives are required for any learning area such as a role-play section, science discovery corner, maths display, listening centre or class library. These learning objectives will change over time as pupils achieve their learning outcomes. Learning areas are the real test of whether teaching methods are sustaining the momentum of pupils' work and keeping them engaged through stimulating curiosity and communicating enthusiasm. Sometimes adult helpers are assigned to working with children in specific learning areas. These adults, whether employed by the school or acting as volunteer help, need to be well briefed. They should have a clear idea about the purpose of the activity and their role within it. Sometimes their task may simply be observation, which can be recorded and later assessed and analysed with the teacher. This informs them both about future planning for the area and the best use of continued adult support. Well-trained nursery nurses and classroom assistants can provide excellent support for children's learning, but several OFSTED reports record poor use of this valuable personnel resource.

Planning

Planning is the most important aspect of organisation and management. It is linked closely to assessment, because unless you assess what has been learnt you cannot move on to the next planning stage. Planning includes arranging the physical environment of the class, deciding rules and regulations, collecting materials and organising the other adults working in the classroom. The other side of planning is that for teaching the academic content of the curriculum. This is dealt with in greater detail in the next chapter and includes long-, medium- and short-term planning. Student teachers rarely become involved in more than short-term planning, although they need to understand both medium- and long-term planning. Good planning takes practice, but much can be learnt from looking at the way in which the placement school plans. Perhaps the most important thing to remember is that planning cannot be limited to content. It is far more professional than that. A good teacher can look to an inexperienced observer as if he or she is teaching 'off the top of their head'. In today's primary schools, no one can do this. Substantial documentation exists to inform planning, teaching, class management, assessment, reporting and recording. The skill for the student teacher is learning how to understand these plans and use them most effectively to support his or her own teaching.

Efficient and effective teachers know what they are doing and do the right things consistently. The effective student teacher gains skills and knowledge about the ways in which the class is taught and managed by their regular teacher. They can then develop this knowledge and use it in their planning for their own teaching, adapting and changing as well as replicating existing practice. Once routines are changed, children need to be informed and encouraged to practise new procedures.

Chapter 4

Curriculum issues for the beginner

Learning objectives
- To gain knowledge about ways in which teachers plan the curriculum.
- To identify different types of curriculum.
- To differentiate between long-, medium- and short-term planning.
- To recognise the need to set clear targets for children's learning, building on their prior attainment.
- To ensure that children are aware of the substance and purpose of what they are asked to do.
- To evaluate learning objectives in terms of lesson planning.
- To write a lesson/activity plan to a specific format.

Planning the curriculum
This section looks at ways in which several of the planning standards can be realised, starting with lesson/activity plans. As the learning objectives indicate, effective planning has to involve assessment as well as knowledge about ways in which to plan. Good planning must be informed by what children have already learnt, both inside and outside school. It also needs to be informed by knowledge and understanding of:
- the overall aims and objectives of the school
- the purpose, scope, structure and balance of the National Curriculum and religious education
- subject knowledge
- research evidence about teaching children of different ages and abilities in the subject and how to use this knowledge to inform and improve teaching
- how new technologies can be used to enhance learning
- common misconceptions and mistakes in different subject areas
- subject-specific health and safety requirements.

Although no one expects the newly qualified teacher to know all this the first time they enter the school, it is true that the beginning teacher has the same tasks and responsibilities as the most experienced member of staff. Children will expect you to perform as a teacher at the same time as you are learning to become one.

The curriculum
Pollard and Tann (1994) distinguish between the official or formal curriculum, the hidden or latent curriculum, the observed curriculum and the curriculum as experienced. The hidden, observed and experienced curricula are particularly relevant to the overall aims of the school, especially children's personal, spiritual, moral, social and cultural development. The formal curriculum has to plan for these, but they are demonstrated through the other curriculum. We can teach children that they should play well together, but it is only through observing them informally over a period of time, both inside and outside the classroom, that we know whether the teaching has been effective. Even then we cannot be sure that it was as a direct result of what has been taught.

The official curriculum

The majority of standards refer to this. The law states quite clearly what children should learn, and in England there are now schemes of work (SOWs) which set out not only what children should learn, but when and how they should learn it. This 'planned course of study' is also known as the official or formal curriculum. It makes planning much easier because the content is already defined. In recent years central government has tightened its hold on what goes on in schools as part of its commitment to raising attainment for all children. One of the advantages of being familiar with the history of education is to understand that there is nothing new in this central control. Schools which have logbooks dating back to the last century have some wonderful descriptions of standards and the role of the central government inspector who visited and tested children to see if they had reached the required level. Then as now, the emphasis was on literacy and numeracy.

The hidden curriculum

This curriculum is 'picked up' rather than learnt. The previous chapters of this guide have identified several aspects of the hidden curriculum. These include messages about the role of the teacher; the role of the learner, in particular the role of the individual child as a successful learner; attitudes towards learning; ways adults expect different groups to behave and contrasts between this and peer expectations. Many schools have good personal and social education (PSE) programmes which acknowledge the pervasiveness of the hidden curriculum and its influence on children's progress and attainment. These programmes deal directly with the type of learning which takes place in the hidden curriculum. The chart below shows how gender issues may be fitted into a strong PSE programme. It is taken from Hughes, P. (1991) *Gender Issues in the Primary Classroom*.

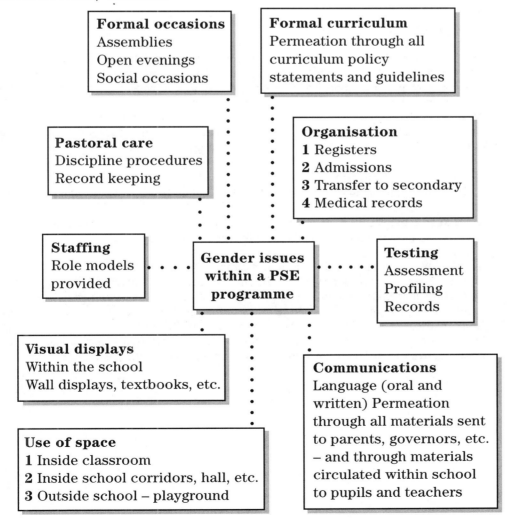

Formal occasions
Assemblies
Open evenings
Social occasions

Formal curriculum
Permeation through all curriculum policy statements and guidelines

Pastoral care
Discipline procedures
Record keeping

Organisation
1 Registers
2 Admissions
3 Transfer to secondary
4 Medical records

Staffing
Role models provided

Gender issues within a PSE programme

Testing
Assessment
Profiling
Records

Visual displays
Within the school
Wall displays, textbooks, etc.

Communications
Language (oral and written) Permeation through all materials sent to parents, governors, etc. – and through materials circulated within school to pupils and teachers

Use of space
1 Inside classroom
2 Inside school corridors, hall, etc.
3 Outside school – playground

Peter Lang (1988) suggests that the outcomes of a good PSE programme, which tackles the hidden curriculum, result in:

- mutual trust between child and child, child and teacher, teacher and teacher, teacher and parents
- children regarding themselves and others as persons of value, whatever their sex, colour, creed or appearance
- children confident in their relations with staff, parents, visitors and adults
- children more interested in and better at learning as a result of being regarded as persons rather than vessels for learning
- children more able to cope with conflict, crises and transitions, success and failure, pain and joy
- children having responsible attitudes to themselves and others and to their learning in and out of school
- children understanding and relating to the groups of which they are part and becoming aware of the communities and societies of which these groups are part.

This does not just happen, but has to be planned for. There may be a specific time for it on the timetable, but it has to permeate the whole life of a school to be effective. Planning any lesson involves planning for children's personal, spiritual, moral, social and cultural development, although the learning objectives may never appear on the lesson plan. Teachers have a moral obligation to help children grow into completely rounded and successful people.

The QCA have issued initial guidance for primary schools on personal, social and health education and citizenship. This can be viewed on the QCA website www.qca.org.uk

The observed curriculum

The observed curriculum is what is actually taking place in the classroom: the lessons and activities you see. This may be different from the intended official curriculum, for a variety of reasons, and one of the skills in lesson observation is to note and evaluate the differences. The beginning teacher is much more likely to display differences between the planned and observed curriculum; but many excellent primary teachers make changes between planning and teaching. Indeed, you will observe lessons where teaching changes during the course of the session as the teacher responds to children. The effective teacher has a sound educational reason for this, and the process indicates the subtle skills involved in good teaching.

The experienced curriculum

This is the curriculum as seen by the children. This is what they take away from the lesson.

 Read a general text on the history of curriculum changes over the past 150 years. Most generic education texts provide a good summary.

Any text you read records the controversy about changes in the curriculum. Texts and journal articles only record the views of the writers. Support your reading by asking teachers what curriculum changes they have observed in the past five years and what they feel is likely to change in the next five. Note also whether the text concerns itself only with the formal curriculum or looks at other forms of curriculum. One of the most fascinating things about the history of education is to see how history repeats itself: what appears to be a new initiative can generally be found to have some parallel in the past.

Whole-school planning

Schools vary considerably in how they plan. Nearly all have documents covering long-, medium- and short-term planning. This is covered in more detail in the next chapter on curriculum planning.

Long-term planning generally covers one academic year and may be limited to content headings under different subjects. Some schools, particularly those with mixed-age classes, have a two- or even three-year rolling programme.

Medium-term planning may be termly or half-termly, and provides much greater detail. Student teachers generally use these medium-term plans as their starting point.

Short-term planning may be weekly or daily, and will vary from teacher to teacher. As a student teacher you must have detailed daily planning for everything you do: you need to write a lesson/activity plan for everything. The better the structure of the lesson and the more precise the directions on what is to be accomplished, the higher the achievement rate. The bottom line is child achievement, because success is what matters in the real world – it is measured by such things as goals in football, sales figures in retailing, and media coverage in public relations. Individual lesson/activity plans must be evaluated in terms of both your own learning and that of the children. If you are given a group of children to monitor, make sure that you record the purpose of the activity before you start working with them.

 Ask to see the long-, medium- and short-term planning for your class. What information can you gather from this about how English and maths will be taught over the next week? Many schools will be using the National Literacy Strategy and the Numeracy Framework for their long- and medium-term planning.

Planning Checklist

	Period of time covered	Subjects covered	Additional comments
Long-term plans			
Medium-term plans			
Short-term plans			
English			
Maths			

Planning objectives

For the children

The first involvement student teachers have in planning is generally writing lesson or activity plans, which are developed from the school's medium- and short-term planning. Writing learning objectives for these is one of the hardest aspects of curriculum planning. You will learn by looking at objectives written by teachers, fellow students, practice, and through using particular words as starting points. Teachers' manuals for commercial schemes of work often include lesson objectives and should always be consulted before using any programme. You will also learn by evaluating and reflecting on what progress children have made in the lesson and what you have learnt yourself.

Ineffective teaching is about coverage: 'doing volume/alliteration/sound', for example. Effective teaching involves children being kept aware of instructional objectives and receiving feedback on their progress towards these objectives. Although it sounds obvious, if children know what they are to learn you increase the chances that they will learn it. This is easy to test in a small-group teaching situation, when you discuss with children the purpose of the activity. If children think the purpose of the session is 'to have fun', they may enjoy it, but they may not be learning.

For yourself

Learning objectives are targeted at children, but, as a student teacher, you will have learning objectives for yourself. These should not be written down in the lesson/activity plan, although it is useful to think through and record your specific learning objectives before you go into school each day and then evaluate them at the end of the day and week. The teaching standards provide some of these objectives, but many of them need to be broken down. For example, 'establishing and maintaining a purposeful working atmosphere' involves a series of strategies, each with its own objective. The short exemplification in Appendix 1 provides an initial guide to this. Often you will find that you have learnt more than the children. Even highly experienced teachers occasionally find that in a lesson they learn more than the children, and teachers are learning in every lesson. 'Why is Sabba having difficulties with halves and quarters?' 'How can I increase John's spelling knowledge?' They, too, can be surprised at how children react to specific activities and lessons.

Identifying prior knowledge

Children often know more than we expect and have hidden skills. A simple brainstorming, skywalking session at the start of an activity can reveal what knowledge and understanding children already have. When you first start working with a small group, informal discussions at playtime and lunchtime can reveal a great deal about what children have already covered. Your own learning objective for one day might be to find out more about the children's knowledge of authors, for example. A walk around the playground and having a school dinner are two very good ways of getting to know this as well as getting to know the children. Which children notice the big display on Janet and Allan Ahlberg, which children have any of their books, who uses the public library? If at lunchtime you sit with children from a class above or below your own, you can discuss their knowledge of authors and from this begin to make some informal assessments about progression in children's learning. When identifying your own learning objectives, children's needs must take priority, and this is shown in planning documentation in the vast majority of schools.

The language of lesson objectives for children

Some of the documentation provided by the school, LEA and central government gives guidance on lesson objectives in particular subjects and phases of learning, but it can offer no more than guidance. In the previous paragraph, we looked at the individual nature of children's learning. However good a government or commercial scheme of work is, it has to be personalised for particular children in a particular school at a particular time. Such schemes provide the current discourse, or language, for learning, but date rapidly. This is why most schools have a rolling programme for updating schemes of work. Section 2 looks at this in more detail.

Much has been written about writing learning objectives, and most general texts on learning to teach will contain some examples and rationales for their chosen method. In this chapter we are using some ideas based on the work of Benjamin Bloom. Much of the advice given to students – and teachers – is based on this, although it may not be clear to the adviser where it came from originally. Schools, training manuals and institutions vary in the advice they give to students. Lesson- and activity-planning sheets contain different headings. Some require extensive documentation; others are much more open-ended. Sometimes lesson objectives can be written as bullet points; sometimes they have to be full sentences. Practices can vary even within the same school or training institution. These differences should be viewed positively as it enables the beginning teacher to look at what suits them best. There are three aspects of learning objectives which are universal:

1 Objectives must be written down before the lesson or activity begins because they tell the teacher what is to be taught, why it is to be taught and, often, how it is to be taught.
2 Objectives should be shared with children, so that they know what they are responsible for: this is usually done orally, although it may be written down.
3 Objectives should be shared with adults working with a group of children so that they know what the purpose of the activity is and their role in it.

Content and targets

When objectives are written as bullet points, as they are in this study guide, they begin with verbs. These tell the learner what is to be achieved and tell the teacher what to look for in order to see if the child has accomplished it. This sounds very mechanistic, but it is just a starting point for planning. Ideally, particularly when working with small groups, teachers and children plan targets together. For example, at the end of a session sorting plastic shapes by colour, the teacher may encourage the children to see if there are any other ways of sorting, and identify this as the next learning target. This is not child-driven – the teacher has a framework of objectives – but the content and targets can be set with the children. For example, in a lesson on the Vikings, children could identify what they already know and then what they would like to know. The teacher could then ask them how they would find the information they need, how they would record it and how they would present it.

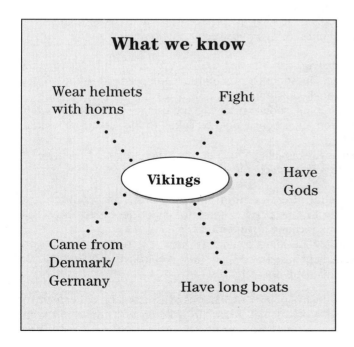

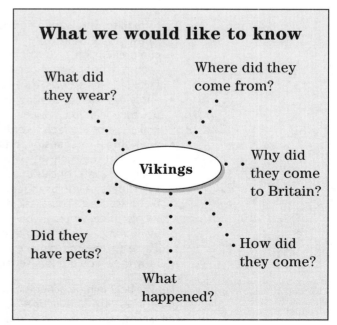

You could make a display of books and a CD-ROM on the Vikings available before the lesson, to give the children an opportunity to gain prior knowledge, even if this were limited to the covers of the books and software on display. Of course, the teacher has to be clear whether the key objectives are English- or history-based, and these may influence both the content and teaching strategies used.

'Child-centred' education is always rather a misnomer when it is used to suggest that children determine what they are going to learn. In the example given above, it is the teacher who is guiding the children's statements about learning objectives. The very detailed coverage of some of the most recent schemes of work seem to allow fewer opportunities for teachers to do this with their children, but the skilful teacher can still continue to 'sell' the idea of choice, so that children do feel as if they 'own' their own learning. As adults, we know how much better we feel when we can make choices about learning. Reading a distance-learning study guide is a choice about learning strategies, even if the content may be very similar to listening to a lecture!

Writing objectives

When you first start to write objectives it might be useful to think of them as requiring the learner to engage in different levels of thinking. Bloom divided verbs into six related categories, starting with knowledge and moving towards evaluation:

1 knowledge
2 comprehension
3 application
4 analysis
5 synthesis
6 evaluation.

This is not a linear progression. Five-year-olds should be involved in evaluation, synthesis and application just as much as eleven-year-olds. Reviewing objectives alerts you to making sure they do not all fit into one category, e.g. knowledge.

Remember, thinking skills are involved in:
- **knowledge** – defining, filling in, identifying, labelling and recalling information. Children are asked to remember material by recalling facts, terms, basic concepts and answers. Questions to monitor this learning are literal ones, using words such as 'who', 'what', 'why', 'when', 'show', 'spell' and 'list'.
- **comprehension** – describing, retelling, summarising and paraphrasing in order to show comprehension and understanding. Questions to monitor this learning would include 'What facts or ideas show ...?' 'How would you summarise ... ?'
- **applying** – demonstrating, investigating, showing, solving and using. These ask children to use their learning in a new situation. Questions would be linked to this, asking children to make use of the facts in order to....
- **analysing** – categorising, classifying, examining and deducing. These require the learner to show that they can see parts and relationships. Questions would require children to make inferences and conclusions.
- **synthesis** – verbs such as changing, combining, planning, pretending, and reconstructing. These ask children to take parts of the information to create an original whole. Tasks would involve adapting, changing and modifying.
- **evaluating** – words such as choosing, deciding, evaluating, justifying, ranking and valuing. These ask children to make a judgement based on criteria. Tasks would involve asking children how they would prioritise facts and justify their choices.

For the beginning teacher the most effective objectives, in terms of assessing his or her learning outcomes, are knowledge- and skills-based, i.e. what the children will know and what intellectual/social/physical and communication skills will be developed. Start off with these and limit the number per lesson or activity to three or four. Make them subject-specific.

Attitudes – you may wish to include 'developing specific attitudes' as one of your learning objectives, but positive learning attributes such as curiosity, confidence, perseverance, responsibility and interest are generic. They form part of the overall philosophy of teaching and learning. Many schools have policies on teaching and learning and these subsume all lesson objectives. If you want to focus on a specific attitude, then include it in your lesson objectives. The content needs to show how the attitude will be developed, and the lesson evaluation needs to provide evidence of how it has been developed.

Concepts – intended learning involves understanding concepts. Conceptual development has a huge research base (see the Bibliography for some suggested reading). At this stage in your career, think of concepts as subject-specific vocabulary, and target which concepts you wish to develop in any one session. Generally, technical vocabulary can be found in the scheme of work. For example, in the QCA scheme of work for Year 4 IT, the unit on 'Modelling effects on screen' identifies words such as 'procedure', 'repeat', 'penup', 'pendown' and 'clear'. Learning objectives for the scheme then move into key ideas and techniques, but a specific lesson based on an understanding of the word 'procedure' would need to look at the word and ensure that children understood it in this context. Some words cover a huge number of concepts. For example, think of how many subject-specific meanings a word like 'change' can have. The QCA schemes of work are helpful in writing lesson plans but they need to be contextualised. Sometimes learning objectives need more focus for individual lessons.

 Look at one of the lesson plans below, which were written by two PGCE students during their first block experience. Decide into which category most of the verbs fit for lesson objectives/intended learning.

Lesson 1. Plan for maths, 2 December

Age and number of children: 17 children aged 5
Duration of the lesson: 40 minutes

Intended learning
1 Develop awareness of 'more than 3' by introducing the number 4.
2 Begin to count 4 objects accurately.

National Curriculum
Recognising and using numbers to 10. Through practical activities the children are beginning to understand and record numbers.

Child difficulties
Some children will undoubtedly have difficulty counting 4 objects correctly. This first lesson on the number 4 will establish which children will need substantial revision. I intend that the green group and possibly one member of the blue group shall spend this lesson on purely practical work, such as threading beads in fours.

Subject knowledge
Nuffield Primary Maths.

Resources
Beads and threads, pegboards, multi-link, pencils, crayons, worksheet, straws.

Organisation
It is intended that for a large part of this lesson, the children will work on the carpet. They will move to their groups for 10 minutes' group work after going to the toilet at 11.30.

Teacher input
Mental maths estimating to 10 for blues and reds. Estimating to 5 for the greens and A... who struggles with numeracy.

Development
I will use multi-link to develop the idea that 4 is one more than 3. I will also get the children to count me out four straws to establish who can count up to 4 accurately. I will use the magnetic wedge to show the children how to form the number 4.

Group activities
Red group: This group will be working on a worksheet, adding one more to a group of objects to make four. They will then be practising formation of the number 4.

Blue group: This group will be working with the pegboards, making patterns with 4.

Green group: This group will be working with threading beads, following patterns to thread 4 objects.

Differentiation is by task and as far as mental maths is concerned, by asking the children questions which are based on lower numbers.

Supplementary activities
Puzzles, number games, number jigsaws, finding numbers in the room.

Lesson 2. Plan for maths KS2: AT2 – Number 2b, 4a

Theme:	Multiplication of normal quantities and decimal quantities
Date:	Friday, 19th June
Time:	10.55
Duration:	1 hour
Number of children:	7 (lower ability)
Age:	Yr 6

Intended learning
By the end of the lesson I hope the children will:
*   understand how to perform multiplication
*   understand how to perform multiplication of decimals with up to 2 decimal points against one figure
*   know how to set out a multiplication in order to find the correct answer easily
*   have improved their skills of setting out calculations systematically and neatly
*   have developed and sustained a willingness to participate in activity during the introduction to lessons and individual work
*   have responded positively to the lessons, i.e. taking part in the lesson and activity with enthusiasm

Resources
Chalkboard and chalk
Worksheet 3 – Multiplication
Maths books
Pencils
Cambridge Maths, Module 7, set 1, page 4.

Organisation
I will introduce and teach the lesson.
The children shall sit at their table whilst I teach the lesson.
For the activity/worksheet, the children will stay sitting at their table.

Introduction

I will ask the children:
- Can anyone tell me how we do multiplication?
- Which column do we start off with?
- If the number we have generated from multiplying the end column is more than 9, what do we do?

Anticipated development

I will ask the children:
- If I gave you a multiplication question to complete, do you think you would have any problems with it whatsoever?

I will:
- ask for a volunteer to do a question for me that is written on the chalkboard

  35 x 6

  24 x 9

  32 x 7
- ask for everyone's attention whilst the person does this question
- ask the volunteer to talk their way through the question all the way to the answer.

This should be repeated until I am satisfied that the children have remembered how to do this properly.

I will ask the children:
- If I gave you a <u>decimal</u> multiplication question to complete, do you think you would have any problem with it whatsoever?

I will:
- ask for a volunteer to try to complete a question for me

  12.5 x 4

  25.5 x 6

  32.4 x 5

  ask for everyone's attention whilst the person does this question (John, especially, should pay attention)
- ask the volunteer to talk their way through the question all the way to the answer.

This should be repeated until I am satisfied that the children have remembered how to do this properly.

Activity

The children will now do a worksheet which consists of:
1) multiplication without decimals
2) multiplication of decimals
3) multiplication problems.

Supplementary activities

If the children finish ahead of schedule, they should do the following:
- Cambridge Maths, Module 7, set 1, page 4.

Conclusion

To conclude I will ask the group to help me complete some decimal multiplication questions on the chalkboard which are perhaps a little more difficult than the ones that they have been doing to make sure they understand how to do multiplication.

65.3 x 5

77.3 x 5

79.7 x 5

Look at one of your earliest lesson/activity plans. Comment on the objectives. Some words are unhelpful to use as lesson objectives because they make it difficult, often impossible, to determine what the children have to do; for example, verbs like 'appreciate', 'be happy', 'celebrate', 'enjoy', 'like', 'love' and 'understand'. Student teachers often ask a class 'Did you enjoy that story?' and then happily record that as an achieved objective. Yet how do we measure enjoyment, love and understanding? Questions like this are potentially quite dangerous to the novice teacher. What happens when 30 bored children shout 'No' at you? Evaluating a book, video or piece of work involves more than a one-word answer and children should be encouraged to justify their opinions. Small-group teaching can provide a starting point for this – most of us need some structure before we can discuss anything purposefully. Chambers (1993) provides excellent starting points for some more imaginative types of discussion.

Objectives need to be so clear that another teacher walking into the room can understand the activity.

In some schools weekly short-term planning is displayed so that parents can see what and why their children are undertaking specific activities. Nurseries and reception classes have often led the way here, with photographs of children 'playing' and the purpose (objectives) of this play. This involves writing objectives very succinctly and ensuring that they are written to demonstrate children's achievements, not coverage. And yes, the writer of the study guide has used one of the unhelpful words – 'understand'.

Lesson/activity planning

This is one recommended format for lesson/activity planning.

THEME/LESSON TITLE:
DATE:
AGE AND NUMBER OF CHILDREN:
INTENDED LEARNING (OBJECTIVES):
CHILDREN'S DIFFICULTIES/MISCONCEPTIONS:
RESOURCES AND MATERIAL REQUIRED:
POSSIBLE SAFETY IMPLICATIONS:
ORGANISATION:
TEACHER INPUT:
INTRODUCTION:
DEVELOPMENT:
CHILDREN'S ACTIVITIES:
SUPPLEMENTARY ACTIVITIES:
CONCLUSION:
REFLECTION AND EVALUATION:

Planning for individual literacy and numeracy lessons needs to be carried out independently from the weekly planning sheet. Experienced teachers do not need the support of headings such as 'resources'. Student teachers do. An alternative lesson format follows for the Literacy Hour, created by an LEA literacy consultant.

This format provides a guide for you to see how small-group activities within the Literacy Hour format fit into the whole lesson. No-one expects a student teacher to take over the whole hour as soon as they start teaching. However, students who work in schools which work to the NLS format, should find this format more helpful in their planning than the more generic format supplied above.

Literacy Hour Lesson Plan Format

Learning Objectives

Remember that the NLS learning objectives are medium-term objectives, designed to be evaluated over a term or half-term. You will need to have more focused learning objectives, linked closely to the whole-class or group activity. If the literacy hour is separated into four sections, each will need its own specific learning objective. The structure of the literacy hour identifies three whole-class inputs – the shared text work at the start of the lesson; the focused word work (KS1) or the word and sentence work (KS2); and the plenary. Each whole-class section should have a specific learning objective.

Each group and independent work activity also needs a learning objective. This helps to avoid setting children a time-filling activity which has no learning outcome.

Of course, it is obvious that many of these planned activities have more than one learning objective, but at the start of planning any literacy activity for the literacy hour it is more helpful to look at identifying the key learning objective, rather than create a minefield of objectives.

Organisation and Resources
* How will the children be arranged at the start of the lesson, then afterwards?
* What resources will be needed, e.g. books, artefacts, newspapers, glue, felt tips.

Teacher Input

Shared Reading or Writing at Text Level ... lesson introduction

How will you 'set the scene'? What stimulus will you use to tune the children into the text you are using?

Sentence or Word Level ... lesson development

Try to link the sentence or word level work you are focusing on with the book you have been using to help children to contextualise the new concepts/vocabulary/spelling you are presenting. List one or two of the questions you will be asking.

Children's Self-Supporting Activities to include Guided Reading or Writing (refer to task activity planning board, if there is one)

Green Group
Blue Group
Yellow Group
Red Group
Purple Group

state clearly and concisely what each group of children will be doing after the shared teacher input. Show examples of diagrams or activity cards, etc. These activities can rotate around the groups or children but ensure that you differentiate for the differing levels of ability. State which group will be working with you for guided reading or writing work.

Plenary Session ... lesson conclusion

How will you draw the lesson to a close? Maybe focus on one group each day and get them to share their work (consider simple role play and drama here). Sometimes you may want to use this time to 'pull the threads together' in relation to the new concept in grammar or word level work you have been working on.

Evaluation

Were the objectives achieved in each section? It is important to evaluate each section of the literacy hour, so that you can see whether teaching is more effective when working with the whole class than with a small group. The following headings can prove useful for evaluating each section.

1 Had the intended learning been achieved? If not why not?
  As discussed earlier, good teachers often adapt and change their learning objectives in response to children's learning needs.
2 What evidence can you use to support your conclusion?
  Evidence may be written work, but it can also include responses to questions, use of resources and attitudes to the task set. In literacy we hope to inspire children to read and write, how do we gather evidence of inspirational teaching?
3 Was the provision relevant to all children's needs?
4 Did anything in the children's responses surprise you?
5 Appraisal of your own teaching performance – communication, organisation, control.
6 The management of other adults.

The lesson evaluation should point the way forward to the next lesson and should indicate what you need to work on and who you will need to work with.

Always plan

Any activity carried out with children must be planned for. A lesson and/or activity plan is embedded within the school's short-, medium- and long-term planning. It has to provide a clear structure for the lesson and, usually, a sequence of lessons. These have to maintain pace, motivation and challenge for children. They will use assessment information on children's attainment and progress, so that future curriculum planning takes account of what children have already achieved, i.e. the next lesson plan will build on what has already been achieved, identify misconceptions and errors, and look at how content, teaching strategies and resourcing can be adapted to support progression in children's learning.

As you become more proficient in lesson planning, you can start to identify and plan for children who have special educational needs, as well as those who are very able and those who are not yet fluent in English. The purpose of the activity must be clear, both to you and the children. This is true whether you are working with 30 children, or just one.

When you first start working in a primary school, you may be asked to carry out an activity with a small group which forms part of the teacher's planning. Make sure that you understand the purpose of the activity, otherwise it tends to become merely childminding, and the educational purposes of the session are lost. Children are quick to sense this and it prevents the establishment of a purposeful working environment. This is also true for reading a story at the end of the day. It is not a time-filler; it has a purpose, and this purpose needs to be recorded in terms of learning objectives. If you ask another adult to work with you, they should have a copy of your lesson plan or a special plan for their activity. This needs to cover the purpose of the activity, i.e. the learning objectives, what the adult is required to do, what the children are required to do and the technical vocabulary to be used. Small-group activities are ideal for assessing children's learning, and nursery nurses and trained learning support assistants can be extremely insightful and provide good observation and assessment notes for you.

Assessing lesson objectives: First steps

For children's learning

You will find out if the children have learned what you intended them to learn through:
• observing them
• listening and talking to them
• marking their work – Section 3 looks at marking in more detail, and you may find it useful to refer to this as well as to look at the school's marking policy.

Children's learning must be recorded. The most manageable way of doing this is through:
• an evaluation of each lesson/activity plan
• keeping daily records of children's progress
• daily discussion on child progress and attainment during the course of the lesson/activity with the class teacher and anyone else who has seen the lesson.

For teaching skills

You will find out if you have learned what you intended through:

- identifying whether your teaching-skill focus was achieved and what evidence you have for this. If it was not achieved, why not? How will you structure your next session to achieve it?
- assessing what you did during the lesson
- assessing what you learnt.

Reflection and evaluation

A critical analysis of the activity/lesson is vital in order to identify the implications for future planning in terms of progression in learning for the children. It is also important in terms of progression in learning of teaching skills. There are a wide variety of different aide-mémoires for this, of which two are given below. Many schools are developing their own.

> **Example**
>
> **Aide-mémoire 1:**
>
> When reflecting and evaluating, you should consider the following aspects. This should always be done on the day of the lesson.
>
> 1 Has the intended learning been achieved?
> 2 What evidence can you use to support your conclusions?
> 3 Was the provision relevant to all the children's needs?
> 4 Did anything in the children's response surprise you?
> 5 Appraisal of your own teaching performance: communication, organisation and control.
> 6 The management of yourself and, where appropriate, other adults.
> 7 How can you use your assessment to inform future planning?

Aide-mémoire 2:

Individual sheet used in a school

NAME OF SCHOOL

TEACHING PRACTICE – LESSON ANALYSIS SHEETS

Name: Class: Appraiser:

Lesson: Date: Time:

Pre-lesson thoughts:
Introduction:
Control:
Exposition:
Development and pace:
Preparation:
Work with children:
Appropriateness:
Conclusion:
Positives:
Possible improvements:
Post-lesson thoughts:

Using OFSTED criteria

Another method of evaluating lessons is by using the same criteria as those used in OFSTED inspections. Clearly, it needs to be adapted because it is a summative assessment and not intended to be used to plan for the next lesson or sequence of lessons. This is an adapted form supplied by an independent contractor.

Example

OBSERVATION FORM

Context of the observation – i.e. a description of lesson content

Teaching
Knowledge and understanding
Methods and organisation
Expectations
Planning
Management of children
Use of time and resources
Use of assessment
Homework
SEN/EO

Response
Attitudes
Behaviour
Personal development
Relationships
SEN/EO

Attainment
Children BA, AV, AA
Know
Understand
Can do
Indicate National Curriculum level or national experience

Progress
Gains made by children of different abilities
Prior attainment
Understanding
Skills
Consolidation/reinforcement

Other significant evidence
SEN/EO
SMSC
Parent support in class
Non-teaching support
Accommodation
Resources
Efficiency
ICT

Chapter 5

Curriculum planning

Learning objectives
- To look at ways in which schools translate their aims into curriculum plans.
- To examine planning formats for the short, medium and long term.
- To analyse different forms of medium- and long-term planning.
- To explore ways in which curriculum planning can provide opportunities for children's personal, spiritual, moral, social and cultural development.
- To identify ways in which assessment information can be used to plan future lessons and sequences of lessons.

Whole-school planning
School aims into curriculum planning
The diagram below, slightly simplified from its original, marks the starting point for curriculum planning in one school. The school had a new head and deputy and the time seemed right for reassessment of its previous planning model. The starting point was a weekend away to agree school values. The terminology varies from school to school: some have aims and objectives, some just have aims. The values/aims and/or objectives are usually displayed prominently around the school, and will almost certainly appear in the school prospectus. Some schools also have mission statements. Although this sounds like a religious term, many county schools now have mission statements.

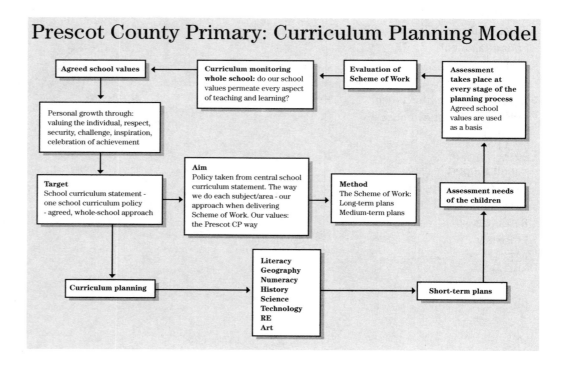

Prescot County Primary: Curriculum Planning Model

- **Agreed school values**
- **Curriculum monitoring whole school:** do our school values permeate every aspect of teaching and learning?
- **Evaluation of Scheme of Work**
- **Assessment takes place at every stage of the planning process** Agreed school values are used as a basis
- **Personal growth through:** valuing the individual, respect, security, challenge, inspiration, celebration of achievement
- **Aim** Policy taken from central school curriculum statement. The way we do each subject/area - our approach when delivering Scheme of Work. Our values: the Prescot CP way
- **Method** The Scheme of Work: Long-term plans Medium-term plans
- **Target** School curriculum statement - one school curriculum policy - agreed, whole-school approach
- **Assessment needs of the children**
- **Curriculum planning**
- Literacy Geography Numeracy History Science Technology RE Art
- **Short-term plans**

Find the aims and/or objectives for a school you know. Ask about the processes which went into deciding what they should be. What implications do they have for curriculum planning? Most local libraries contain school prospectuses. You might find it useful to make comparisons.

Here are the aims and objectives for one school (not the one whose planning we are going to look at).

Aim
All children should be given opportunities to develop their potential in ways which will lead them to become positive and contributing members of society, with a caring and tolerant attitude to others.

Objectives
Children should learn to:
- acquire knowledge, skills and concepts relevant to today's society
- communicate clearly and confidently
- develop self-esteem and independence
- develop lively and enquiring minds
- appreciate the value of knowledge, skills and understanding for their own sake
- appreciate the natural world
- experience a range of leisure activities
- become aware of the multicultural nature of society and encourage equality of race, sex and creed.

There is little with which anyone could disagree here, and this is true for most aims and objectives. The key question is how the school plans to ensure these objectives are achieved and how to evaluate this. As with a lesson plan, they are the objectives around which the content is planned. These objectives must be monitored and assessed. Most of them are generic, although some, e.g. 'communicate clearly and confidently', can also be linked very specifically to particular subjects. These particular aims and objectives are somewhat vague and make it difficult to track through curriculum planning. The school's OFSTED report made this a key issue for the governing body.

School curriculum statement
Some schools have a curriculum statement which looks at how the school's aims and objectives will be worked through the curriculum. This is marked by the curriculum planning stage, where objectives are taken from the central school curriculum statement. As each curriculum area has distinctive aims, these have to be worked through alongside the more generic school aims.

Long-term planning
Long-term planning is generally carried out as a one- or two-year rolling programme. Look at the long-term planning sheet from one school, shown on pages 41–48. The nursery, reception and Years 1 and 2 take the form of a one-year plan because they have single-age groups. Years 3/4 and Years 5/6 are in mixed-age groups and therefore have a two-year plan.

Medium-term planning: termly or half-termly
At one time schools had to devise their own medium-term plans, based on the school's scheme of work for each subject area. Today, most schools use the termly planning sheets provided by central government. The National Literacy Strategy (NLS) provides the main framework for the English scheme of work and appears as a very distinctive medium-term planning sheet. (This is also available on computer disk.) Most schools extend this so that the scheme of work for English exceeds the contents of the NLS. The NNS is more inclusive, although some schools do extend its content.

Example

Method of work: three levels of curriculum planning

THE THREE LEVELS OF CURRICULUM PLANNING

Planning Level	Participants	Purposes	Outcomes
Long-term: the whole Key Stage/pre-Key Stage 1	Headteacher, all staff and governors	To ensure: • coverage of the 9 subject orders/areas of learning and RE across the whole Key Stage/ pre-Key Stage 1 • progression in each subject across the whole Key Stage/ pre-Key Stage 1 • balance within and across subjects in each year of the Key Stage/ pre-Key Stage 1 • appropriate allocations of time • appropriate links between subjects • continuity between Key Stages	A broad framework for each year of the Key Stage/pre-Key Stage 1 which reflects the school's overall curricular aims and objectives, and • specifies the content to be taught in each subject • organises content in manageable and coherent units of work • allocates time to each unit of work • sequences work • identifies links between aspects of different subjects
Medium-term: each school term or half-term	Class teachers supported by subject coordinators	To develop the Key Stage/pre-Key Stage 1 plan for a particular year into a detailed sequence of subject-specific and linked units of work. This should make use of nationally agreed documents such as NLS, NNF and QCA schemes of work. (www.gca.org.uk)	A detailed specification for each unit of work to be taught within the term, setting out specific learning objectives; emphasis, priorities and depth of treatment; resource requirements: links and references to other units of work; the nature of child tasks and activities; suggested teaching strategies and child groupings; strategies for differentiating work; assessment opportunities
Short-term: each week or day	Class teacher	To ensure • a balance of different types of activity throughout a week • differentiation • appropriate pace • constructive feedback • time for teacher assessment • monitoring, evaluation • any modification required	Detailed daily or weekly lesson plans and associated records to ensure effective day-to-day teaching and inform future planning

Example

Long-term planning – Nursery

	Term 1	Term 2	Term 3
Personal Social	New children: encouraged to leave parent easily. Older children: playing with and helping new ones. Personal hygiene.	Social skills: please, thank you, etc. Dressing/undressing.	Taking turns, sharing toys, equipment, etc.
Language/ literature Speaking/ listening Reading Writing	Encourage speaking clearly. Listen to register and stories. Access to class library. Recollect own name. Experiment with various tools.	Learn simple songs and rhymes. Terminology of books: front, back, page, picture, etc. Handle pencil and crayons correctly.	Role-play situations (may be adult-initiated). Introduce Letterland characters. Trace pictures, own name. Copy name.
Maths	Colours: names matching/sorting. Positional language.	Patterns: single and alternative colours.	Number rhymes. Shape: 2-D shape recognition.
Knowledge Understanding	Explore nursery environment. Ask questions.	Experiment with tools and materials.	Correct use of computer. Simple programs.
Physical development	Stop and start on signal. Basic skills. Use of scissors. Threading large shapes.	Find a space, stretch and curl. Practice with scissors. Threading smaller shapes.	Use of small equipment. Independent use of scissors: cutting lines.
Creativity	Sing simple songs. Introduce art tools and correct usage.	Experiment with musical instruments. Variety of art techniques.	Accompany songs. Continue art techniques.

Long-term planning – Reception

	Term 1	Term 2	Term 3
Personal Social	Personal hygiene. Discuss feelings. Increase independence in dressing/undressing.	Promote confidence in new situations. Hygiene in school and at home.	Promote independent social skills. Encourage sharing and taking turns.
Language/literature Speaking/listening Reading Writing	Encourage simple sentences in oral work and turn-taking. Operation of listening centre. Teach directionality of print. Introduce phonics and books from schemes. Encourage writing of own name. Participation in shared writing.	Encourage attentive listening to instruction. Promote increased vocabulary. Themed activity area. Recollect letters of alphabet by shape and sound. Retell stories using picture clues. Teach correct letter formation. Write own name from memory. Copy under captions.	Repeat songs and rhymes to a variety of listeners. Act out familiar stories. Recollect complete name and familiar words. Begin to distinguish between upper- and lower-case letters. Encourage independent writing.
Maths	Sorting for variety of criteria. Matching 1to1, more or less. Copying and continuing patterns. Measurement: ourselves.	Counting to 10. Recognise and value to 5. Positional language. Ordering by size. Recreating patterns. Shape: basic 2-D and 3-D.	Ordering to 10. Recognise and value to 10. Introduce simple addition.
Knowledge Understanding	Teach body parts. Discuss families, past and present life. Simple techniques, e.g. glueing, folding. Introduce computer.	Encourage children to use experience to ask and answer questions. Experiment with primary colours. Learn own address. Discuss local environment. Use of mouse and arrow keys.	Encourage children to make predictions, e.g. when cooking. Choose relevant tools and materials for task. Encourage independent use of computer.
Physical development	Spatial awareness. Teach basic skills: stop, start, run, jump, skip, hop, tiptoe. Manipulation of small beads, shapes, etc. Use of scissors.	Use of skills in short sequence. Basic skills with small apparatus. Use of scissors to cut variety of paper/thin card.	Use of skills on large apparatus. Develop control and work in pairs with small apparatus. Extend cutting skills.
Creativity	Join in school singing practice. Extend and develop use of art equipment and techniques. Printing: random, using hands, feet, sponges, leaves. String and bubble. Use of variety of paper.	Copying rhythms: clapping and percussion. Encourage expression of own ideas. Colour: properties of paint. Artist: Mondrian.	Play in time to music. Use of objects/artefacts for stimulus: observational drawing. 3-D: salt dough, clay, plasticine, materials.

Example

Long-term planning – Year 1

	Term 1	Term 2	Term 3
English	Genres of literature Personal narrative Taking turns Listening to others	Traditional stories/rhymes Collaborative writing Role play	Poetry Narrative writing Formal speaking
Maths	Shape	Graphs Fractions	Money Measure – length, time, capacity
Science	Sound	Light	Growth Life cycles
Technology	Cutting Joining	Moving joints	Design proposals, individual and pairs
History		Famous people	Family to grandparents
Geography	Weather	Journeys	Local study
Art	Colour – mixing tones, shades Application – roller, blow painting. Various artists	Landscapes – different techniques, painting oils /pastels, collage,- textured landscapes. Artists – Brueghel, Constable	3-D - paper sculpture clay, salt dough, plasticine
Music	Dynamics Tempo	Duration Timbre	Pitch Texture
PE	Gymnastics Dance	Small apparatus Team work Dance	Outdoor games Gymnastics
RE	Friends	Famous people who helped others	Family
IT	Mouse and keyboard skills Communicating information	Communicating information Handling information	Control Word processing Communicating information

Example

Long-term planning – Year 2

	Term 1	Term 2	Term 3
English	Author study/Poetry Narrative writing Phonic skills	Continue Non-narrative Continue	Research skills Information retrieval Making books
Maths	Measurement – non-standard/cms Shape Data handling	Multiplication Division Time	Tens and units Measurement – weight, capacity
Science	Materials – textiles	Moving things	Building materials
Technology	Using textiles	Junk models	3-D buildings
History	Clothes	Transport	Buildings
Geography	Our country	Locality study	Homes/buildings Settlements
Art	Textiles – collage, printing/weaving	Observational drawing Artists – Lowry, Klee	Abstract drawing Painting Clay work Photography
Music	Duration Dynamics	Timbre Texture Sound effects	Pitch Tempo
PE	Gymnastics Cooperative games	Gymnastics Dance	Outdoor games Games skills
RE	Joseph – clothes	Journeys	Special places of worship
IT	Roamer Keyboard skills Save and print	Communicating/handling information	Word processing Modelling

Example

Long-term planning – Years 3/4

	Term 1	Term 2	Term 3
English	Sentences Parts of speech Punctuation	Narrative Handwriting Shakespeare	Drama Non-narrative
Maths	Addition/subtraction Place value Topic each term – time, or...NNF	Tables Division 3–D shape, or...NNF	Algebra Measurement
Science	Materials	Living things	————————
Technology	Design/make structures and models Prepare menu Food technology	Design/make weather instruments, Environment for animal	Paper making Hieroglyphic tablets Jewellery
History	Tudors	Ancient Egypt	continue
Geography	Contrasting locality Developing country - India or Egypt	Local weather (keeping records)	World weather
Art	Drawing line and tone Observation from memory, imaginative Shadow/depth Artists (outline)	Texture – collage Weaving, sewing Paper sculpture 3-D work continue	Printing – press print, block, mono Repeating patterns using 3 colours
Music	—————— Timbre	——— Structure ——— Dynamics	—————— Pitch
PE	Ball skills – football, basketball, netball Safety on apparatus Dance ——————— swimming	Small ball skills – hockey, badminton, Gymnastics Dance 2 terms of 3 ———	Athletics – running, throwing, jumping Dance ———————
RE	Caring	———————	Rules, rights, responsibilities
IT	Word processing	Control	Graphics

Example

Long-term planning – Year 3/4

	Term 1	**Term 2**	**Term 3**
English	Reporting back Presentations Sentence structure	Story writing for an audience Poetry	Descriptive writing Author study
Maths	Addition/subtraction One topic each term Data handling or	Tables Division Problem solving or	Algebra Probability
Science	Sound	Forces	Light
Technology	Making armour	Continue Food technology	3-D models
History	Invaders (outline)	Invaders (specific)	Aztecs
Geography	Local studies	———————	Environmental study
Art	Colour mixing Colour wash Portraits Abstract – Kladinsky	Artists – Surrealism Magritte Collage, Drawing perspective	Shape and Form Papier mâché, clay Paper sculpture
Music	——————— Duration	——————— Tempo	——————— Texture
PE	Gymnastics Dance ——————— swimming	Ball skills Dance 2 terms of 3 ———	Athletics Outdoor games ———————
RE	Miracles	———————	Light
IT	Data bases	Logo	Modelling

Example

Long-term planning – Year 5/6

	Term 1	Term 2	Term 3
English Set 1	Writing styles Spelling Handwriting	Information retrieval Poetry Reading skills	Author study Drama and role play Punctuation
Set 2	Listening skills Reading skills Writing – narrative Vocabulary and Punctuation	Speaking skills Reading skills Non-narrative Grammar	Discussion Information retrieval Dialogue Author study
Set 3	Writing narrative Spelling Handwriting Grammar Listening/reading skills	Continue Vocabulary and Punctuation	Poetry Author study Non narrative
Maths All sets at own level	Place value Addition/Subtraction Negative numbers Probability Coordinates Flow charts	Multiplication Division Fractions Decimals 2-D and 3-D shape Length, Area, Angles Symmetry	Problem solving Revision – + ÷ x Investigations Mass Weight
Science	The Universe and solar system	Evolution of animals	Reproduction and sex education
Technology	3-D modelling linked to science	3-D modelling linked to history and science	Home technology Surveys/questionnaires
History	Britain 1900 –1930 First World War	Britain 1930 –1950 Second World War	Britain 1950 – Present
Geography	Basic map work	Contrasting UK locality	Rivers
Art	Observational drawing 3-D modelling	Colour Painting, e.g. Blitz, propaganda posters	Collage Modern fashion and artists
Music	——————— Creative music Timbre	—— Structure —— Dynamics	Pitch
PE	Gymnastics Games skills ————————	Gymnastics continue Six weeks of creative dance per term Folk dancing	Athletics Basketball Problem solving
RE	Creation stories	continue	Myths and legends Comparative religions
IT	Control information	Data handling Control information processing	Data handling

Long-term planning – Year 5/6

	Term 1	**Term 2**	**Term 3**
English	——————— see earlier plan, p. 47. Repeat for each set ———————		
Maths All sets at own level	Place value, Addition, Subtraction, Money, Graphs, Data handling, Patterns, Algebra	Multiplication, Division, Fractions, Decimals, Percentages, Time, Length, Scale, Ratios, Direction	Problem solving Revision + – x ÷ Investigations, Volume, Capacity
Science	Forces	Materials	Sound and Light
Technology	Strength and flexibility of materials Modelling linked to history	Joining materials – e.g. bridges Structures	Moving pictures, cameras, periscopes, Kaleidoscopes
History	Ancient Greece		Local study
Geography	Communication Settlements	Routes	
Art	Sketching 3-D modelling Printing – pattern	Observational drawing Photochromatography Collage	Painting – line, tone Printing
Music	——————— Duration	Structure ——————— Tempo	——————— Texture
PE	Gymnastics Games skills Dance	Gymnastics Games skills Dance	Athletics Basketball Badminton
RE	Messages		Feelings
IT	——————————— see earlier plan ———————————		

Medium-term planning

The central government schemes of work now cover all subject areas and are available in all primary schools and at the QCA site www.qua.org.uk Not all schools adopt them. This is a healthy situation. Look at these medium-term planning sheets from one school. One is for history and English for the spring term of a Year 1 class. The other is an extract from a five-week maths unit for a Year 5 ability group. This was completed prior to the implementation of the National Numeracy Strategy by the school

Spring Term: 1st half
Class Y1H Year Group: Y1

HISTORY
Princesses/Princes, Past and Present

Activity	Learning Objective	Organisation/ Differentiation	Resources	Assessment
	To match objects to two people from contrasting periods of time – present and past	Adult support	Worksheet	Children should give simple explanations for their choices
Looking at evidence – clues. The Happy Princess – fact. Princess story – fiction. Illustration of what the word Princess evokes	To consider evidence and make decisions about the two stories	Questioning	The Happy Princess Fictional princess story	Children should be able to tell whether or not a story or book is fact or fiction
Queens – fact or fiction Sorting activity	To look for clues which may inform us, tell us what we want to know	Giving written explanations	Worksheet	Children's ability to sort successfully
Princess Elizabeth – video – write story	To illustrate how we can find out about the past	Picture clues Oral clues	Video and worksheet	
Queen Elizabeth – questions				

English

Phonics, Spelling and Vocabulary	Grammar and Punctuation	Comprehension and Composition	Texts
Blocked work	Blocked work	Blocked work	Titles
'Pr' words – prince, princess, pretty, prickle, pram, press, pray, present	To recognise full stops and capital letters when reading and understand how they affect the way passage is read	To identify and compare basic story elements, e.g. beginnings and endings in different stories • Beginning • Concentrate on setting • Opening sentence	Princess and the Pea Guided reading
Spelling Tina – Assess Group 1 – far, car, party, park, video, much, milk, drunk. Group 2 – sun, run, fun, rub, tub, nut, ut, but, sum. Andy - two letter words			Blue -Ride-went, bent, sent. Red -When it Rains - come, comes. Green-Breakfast, happy face-opposites Yellow-What are you doing, what do you like best - Sentences completing.
Phonics - 'dr', 'pr', 'tr', dictionary work. Word endings - 'ed', 'ing', 'all'. Vocab. extension - size words. Thesaurus work - Amazed, astounded, astonished.	To expect reading to make sense and check if it does not and to read using expression applying to the grammar of text cloze.	To use their dictionaries and to understand their alphabetical organisation. To identify and discuss characters, e.g. appearance behaviour - speculate and discuss - how story develops - characters - action.	Rumpelstiltskin Guided Reading
Spelling Lizzy – care, careless, useful, useless, gentle, young, fur, nurse, purse, weak. Group 1. for, pull, full, cup, under, said, rich, six, fix. Group 2. look, book, all, call, ball, fall, wall, here, sing, king. Anne – man, can, ran, sat, hat, bat, had, sad, cap, map.			Blue - My Bike-bike hike-like Red- Hair-describing words Green-where will you sleep? 'ee' words where is my grandma? making sentences close my nest is best: 'est' 'ee' words Yellow - Grandma's letter
Plurals 'S' Rhymes - like/bike bite/white nine/mine. Phonics - 'old' 'oo' - good, wood, foot Old,told,fold,cold,bold, gold,hold,sold 'nd' - end, mend, send, bend, lend.	To predict words from preceding words in sentences and investigate the sorts of words that fit, suggesting appropriate alternatives, i.e. making sense.	To retell the story giving the main points in sequence and to notice difference between written and spoken, comparing versions. Ending - changing end of story.	The 3 Little Pigs Guided Reading
Spelling Tom – stool, lunch, cheese,goose, geese, tooth, teeth, cloth, bench. Group 1. like,bite,ride, slide,white,nine,line, mine,where,there.			

Group 2. old,told,cold, this,end,mend,send, good,wood,foot James – pet,met,let,set, fed, bed, red,pen,ten/ yes	To use the term sentence appropriately to identify sentences in text i.e. those demarcated by capital letters and full stops.	To identify and discuss range of story themes and to collect and compare: • changing theme of story • changing characters	Blue - when it rains - come - comes Red - My shadow - we,he,me,she,prep, over,under,throw, down Green - Riding - close rhyme, Baby in the trolley Yellow - Snowman - close Beep beep - 'ce' words
Vocab – said/quacked/ grunted etc. Extension Phonics - 'ill'			The Little Red Hen Guided Reading
Spelling Eve –news/ saw/paw/awful/ new/ few/drew/grew/ chew/draw - swap with next week. Group 1. them,story,ill, hill,very,because,want, was,gold. Group 2. what,and,sand, hand,thing,ring,morning play,are George-did,hid,lid,pin, win,tin,in sit,him,his,tip			Blue - Hair - describing words Red - we like - writing sentences, I like etc. Green - Running, fast,faster,fastest what's inside The Pizza Yellow - picnic in the sky
Using dictionaries: Rhymes - name,game, tame,fame,came,same, dame,by,cry,try,sky,why, my Phonics 'ee' words	To recognise full stops and capital letters when reading and understand how they affect the way a passage is read.	To use terms fiction/ non-fiction, contents/index	The Royal Dinner Food - non-fiction Guided Reading
Spelling Peter – change/changed/ break/broken/ brighter/brightest/ miner Group 1. they,story,he, name,game,came, same,by,cry,try,sky. Group 2. keep,deep, sleep,tree,see,feet,time, into,help,you. Peter – lot,got,hot,not, sport,top,shop,dog, fog, stop			Blue - My shadow Red - River Green- what are you doing - what do you like best Yellow - At the pool - Boss

Short-term planning

Short-term planning is carried out by individual teachers, but if the school has more than one form of entry it is likely that teachers will plan together. The plans shown on pages 52–54 cover a week in a Year 1 and a Year 6 class. The teachers plan ahead using the columns headed 'Learning Objectives' and 'Differentiated Activities'. The assessment and way forward column is completed at the end of each day, so it provides an ongoing assessment record. This third column provides the key for the following week's planning. It provides one way of detailing assessment information on children's attainment and progress which can then be fed into planning future lessons and sequences of lessons.

KEY STAGE 1: Short-term planning

Personal growth through: valuing the individual, respect, security, challenge, inspiration, celebration of achievement.   Year: Y1H   W/B: 25th January

	Learning Objectives	Differentiated Activities	Assessment & Way Forward
Literacy	To assemble information from own experience. To identify and compare basic story elements, e.g. beginning, middle, end. Spelling – see literacy sheet. To recognise full stops and capital letters when reading and understand how they affect the way passage is read.	**Diary** Record own news. Use sentences. Increase description. **Red and Blue** Middle Cinderella story. Constructing sentences – writing independently using workbook/bank. **Willow pattern** Look at and discuss different ideas from last week. What if they were turned into something different – fish, tiger, etc. Try recording independently. **Capital letters** Need to use adult support to assess – matching lower case to capital – name/sound.	Develop independent strategies – keyword bank, etc. Blue and Red - Need lots of adult support. Some struggling to compose thoughts. Some having difficulty presenting thoughts on paper. Need to do next week, adult support not available.
Numeracy	To continue learning number bonds. To use this knowledge and apply it during problem solving. To encourage the children to group their answers into tens to make addition easier. To count up in tens then add units to appreciate conservation of number.	Team number bonds. Extend knowledge 10+6 9+6 8+6 7+6 8+5 or 8+2+3 becomes 10+3 $\boxed{10} + \boxed{10} + \boxed{10} = 30$ 4+1 4+2 5+1 5+2 6-1 6-2 3-1 3-2	Starting to use bonds in problem solving. Monitor - girls. Especially – carpet work
Science	That different everyday objects are made from the same materials.	Make a display of wooden objects choosing attractive or unusual objects – where did material come from? Choose object and use as many words as possible to describe it – how it feels, how it looks, etc. • Use simple reference books to find out more about each material.	Assessment. Describe the object they chose, e.g., wooden egg – smooth, hard, won't break. Groups together objects made of same material and names it.
History	To look for clues which may inform us, tell us what we want to know.	Pictures of a real princess. Looking at evidence – clues. Looking at pictures/photos of princesses past and present. Stereotypes.	Skills – developing. Move on to Elizabeth 1 Encourage – looking for evidence.
Geography	To develop concept of plans. To develop concept of aerial view.	PLANS Matching aerial view to an object. Extend to a diagram of object rather than picture.	Develop next week by asking children to draw own plan. Introduce house plans.
Art	To develop an awareness of colour in artefacts and design.	Willow pattern. Looking at houses – pictures, photos – observing differences. Bird Border – experimenting with wax and chalk. Display.	Observation – detail increasing. Still needs developing.
Music	To experiment with new rhythm – patterns as an accompaniment to the tune.	Programme 4. Houses around the world. Little boxes – Pitched percussion – repeating note throughout song.	Introduce more instruments next week.
IT	Continue rolling programme.	Red Group Assess column – abs	• Need to change programme. See J. K
PE	To encourage originality. To develop contrasts.	Time to move Programme 3. The story of the dragon monster.	Need to repeat to develop clearer contrasts. • Reinforce immediate stillness when music stops.
RE	To 'wonder' at God's creation. To reflect on our duty to care for God's world.	Story of Creation continued.	Try recording thoughts next week. Ask children how we can make a difference.

KEY STAGE 2: Short-term planning

Personal growth through: valuing the individual, respect, security, challenge, inspiration, celebration of achievement.   Year 6F   W/B: 25th January

	Learning Objectives	Differentiated Activities	Assessment & Way Forward
Literacy	To look at how arguments can appeal to the known views and feelings of the audience. To understand the term 'bias'. Be able to summarise different sides of an argument and clarify strengths and weaknesses. To use different genres as models to inform their story introductions.	**Thursday – T.A group. Reading** Sheets on oil strikes – look at the newspaper articles on the same issue from two different view points. Discuss the use of the word 'bias' and what this means. Discussion about which is biased and why (both are in different ways). Look at the distortion of the truth and how the articles do this. Children to write an unbiased report on the issue of Northstar Oil. Complete for homework: **Friday – L.A group. Writing** Look at the work from last week on character description openings. Children to redraft after discussion of main errors and good points. Write a scene setting opening to the same story – 'the stranger'. Give the children On a Beach on a Cold Day.	Children have a very good understanding of 'bias' and use of opinion. The children started the report in class and will complete this for homework. Children did not complete the scene setting version, so I sent it home to be in on Thursday next week.
Numeracy	To make 2-D shapes with increasing accuracy, recognise their geometrical features and properties and use these to classify shapes. To recognise reflective symmetries of regular 2-D shapes. To understand the terms 'diameter', 'radius' and 'circumference'. To understand inverse operations. To understand and use fractions to estimate, describe and compare proportions of a whole. To understand that fractions have equivalents.	**Topic Maths – Shape.** Look at all the shapes again and their names. Complete properties of each shape. Look at how to find symmetries of shapes – mirror and folding. Cut out all shapes and find all lines of symmetry. (Practical tasks) Stick shapes into books and write how many lines of symmetry. Look at pattern: regular shapes have same number of sides as lines of symmetry. Look at circles – drawing circles – how to do this. Terms – diameter, radius, circumference. Number – continue problem solving, work from Cambridge maths. Homework – equivalent fractions by (x of the numerator).	Tom needed lots of extra support to keep him on task. Keep eye on situation. Mark absent – need to go over with him. Need to complete reflective symmetries of regular shapes. Next week onto differentiated work. (Need to complete write up on the experiment completed with Peter.) Daniel has completed all Cambridge maths, move on to fraction work in class.
Science	To learn that pitch and loudness of sounds produced by some vibrating objects can be changed. (Investigative science – see science plan)	(Pitch) Go over dynamics and common errors, e.g. saying high or low instead of loud or quiet. Children to complete corrections – conclusions to answer aim. Go over what pitch is. The children will have 2 chime bars (long and short), guitar, elastic bands (different thickness) and will experiment how to alter pitch. I will demonstrate recorder and bottles. Write up on this Mr Griffiths and experiment on sound travelling through material.	Children had a better understanding of pitch and dynamics after this lesson as it was obvious which one was which. Peter – string telephones, wooden meter rulers, fork on string...one ear + 2 ears. Better understanding for me as well as children.

	Learning Objectives	Differentiated Activities	Assessment & Way Forward
Geography	To learn about the similarities and differences between English and Italian schools.	Education – recap on the sheets. Children to complete the comparisons.	Choir children have not completed this work.
RE	To learn that Hindus believe in a God but that he takes a variety of forms.	Hindu Gods. Completion of work on this. L.A. 3 main forms: Brahma, Vishnu and Shiva M.A and T.A. 5 main forms. Write out the main points.	Move on to the Creation story next week.
PE	Be able to practise and refine symmetrical and asymmetrical movements on the floor and on the apparatus. Be able to work in pairs.	SYMMETRY & ASYMMETRY Warm up by student **a** find ways of bridging from apparatus to apparatus, mats to apparatus, etc. Try symmetrical and asymmetrical line – discuss this. **b** Go over last week's symmetrical movements in pairs. Try asymmetrical movements in pairs. **c** Think about balances and symmetrical and asymmetrical **d** Large apparatus – work in pairs. Sequence symmetrical balance, 3 symmetrical moves, 3 asymmetrical moves and an asymmetrical balance. Show off movements from a variety of pairs. Cool down – series of 5 stretches.	The children had a few problems spacing the small apparatus out. Once this was solved they had no problems. Worked well in pairs. Need to practise these movements next lesson also.
Music	To learn how to use 2 beaters on glockenspiels an xylophones. Be able to perform in small groups. Be able to play a variety of untuned percussion instruments. Be able to play musical patterns from rhythmic notation.	**Y6F** Children to think about a glockenspiel/xylophone in1/2's. CDEFG/ABCDE L.H R.H Play simple tunes using both hands so they are getting used to where the notes are in relation to each other (see IT plan for extra music). **Y5B** a quick recap on what rhythms are. Go over the untuned percussion instruments and how to use each one. Play simple rhythmic phrases from the flashcards first. Swap instruments around the table. Mix rhythmic phrases and say and play them.	Children are working well but need extra practice. Children worked really well. We worked on control of the instruments and the children listened carefully. Next week use tuned and untuned percussion instruments.
IT	Be able to select suitable information from programmes presented to them. Be able to load CDROM independently.	Encarta – children will be finding relevant information about the Baroque period – main composers, use of instruments and style. Internet with Mr Jorgensen if the disc arrives.	Due to 'a.m.' being the only time available to Y^ we have not been able to use the computer suite as we do all literacy and numeracy lessons in the morning. **nb.** No D.T/Art or extra science this week due to gallery trip next week and extra art in the last week of term for the art gallery in school.

Daily planning

Increasingly teachers, as well as student teachers, are being asked to prepare daily planning schedules. There is often an element of fear in this. OFSTED inspections have paved the way for headteachers to ask for daily lesson plans despite the fact that good short-term planning does not require experienced teachers to continue with the same sort of daily planning as student teachers. The large A3 sheets used for weekly planning in Numeracy and Literacy are thus supplemented by additional 'lesson plans' for each lesson of the day. Publishing companies have been keen to move in with expansive lesson plans for each subject, which reinforces the idea that teaching can only be effective if it is backed up by its own little rainforest. The danger is that this leaves no time or energy for other more creative activities, such as making games and researching new teaching approaches.

Good nursery planning points the way forward for a manageable system here. In the example on pages 56–57, we can see how the single A4 sheet for the short-term planning is expanded into a useful daily plan. The assessment/way forward section is completed after the lesson.

Assessment and evaluation of planning

We will look at child assessment in more detail later on, but at this stage it is essential to recognise that assessment and planning are closely related and assessment of a lesson or a sequence of lessons informs the next stage of planning. Evaluation of the scheme of work, a sequence of lessons, or just one lesson, takes place in two ways.

Informal

Teachers are constantly undertaking informal evaluation of their planning, either by themselves or in conversation with colleagues. This informal evaluation is linked to assessment of children's learning as an outcome of planning and an evaluation of their own teaching. The importance of this informal assessment and evaluation is often missed, just because it is informal. It might involve a short conversation in the corridor, a longer one at lunchtime, a statement at a school-based in-service, or even waking up in the middle of the night thinking how something could be planned better next time!

Formal

This provides a written record of how successful planning has been in achieving the desired learning outcomes for children. The planning sheets above identify assessment of children's learning in different ways. The QCA schemes of work provide objectives and expectations at the end of each unit. The QCA suggests that progress and assessment are checked by matching the expectations to achievement by the end of the year.

The medium-term plans shown on pages 49–51 are similar to the QCA exemplar schemes. They have an assessment column which records what children are expected to learn at the end of the unit. This is all done prior to teaching the scheme.

In the weekly planning sheets (pages 52–54), assessment and ways forward are identified in the third column. This column is filled in at the end of the week and informs the planning for the following week. Daily lesson or activity plans which students must complete are evaluated at the end of each day.

Teachers assess children's learning formally on these sheets. The comments made here are generic, so individual assessment records are kept elsewhere, although sometimes children's names do appear. Most schools have workable assessment records for each child in the core subjects, but foundation subjects are more likely to be assessed through content completion. Children's learning is assessed in terms of the progress they make through the scheme or unit of work and the attainment levels they reach. One school abandoned its commercial maths scheme when it realised that it did not move children through fast enough. Children were unable to reach Level 4 by the end of Key Stage 2 because they were working almost a year behind.

Nursery Short-Term Plan

Date Spring 2 Week 3	Welcome Circle	Timetabled Activities	Small-Group Time	Final Circle
Monday	**Shared reading** 'Don't Do That' Looking at sentence structure/features of a book (cover, page, etc.)	**Hall 1 Dance** 9.15–10.10 and 1.00–1.30. Complete a range of circle dances, e.g. Ring a Roses, Windy Weather, Frosty weather, There was a Princess Long Ago, Farmer's Den, Sally Goes Round the Sun. 'Running About with Rhyme' p.58 Beginning to Write	**Name recognition** – look at initial phoneme on own names. Play 'Kim's Game' using a range of different travel objects	**Maths** Numbertime video. The number 6 – make a table of things of '6'. Sing the no. line
Tuesday	**Rhyme Structures** A Farmer Went Trotting. Looking at rhymes at the end of sentences (A2 format)	**Art Room** 9.15–10.10 and 1.00–1.45. Not in use this week	Drop money into cup, children close eyes, can they tell how many went in? Look at name cards	**Number Rhymes** Ants Go marching p.5 Mathsph. Grand Old Duke p.11 Mathsph. Old King Cole p.15 Mathsph
Wednesday	**Speaking and Listening** Show and tell opportunites for children to discuss their own events of the week. Oxford Reading Tree 'The Street Fair'	**Music** 10.15–10.45 and 2.15–2.45. Bobby Shafto. Make Your Sound Like Mine p.26. Tap Your Name p.35. Stick Tapping p.34. Drummer in the Ring p.23. Musical Box p.22	**Reaffirm the sound R** Can children find items in a feely bag. Name cards	**PSE** Read the story of Dogger, discuss feelings of Bella and Dave
Thursday	**Alphabet Recognition** Use Longman Reading Project Tape to introduce alphabet, pointing to A2 size poster, ask children to match sound cards to poster. Give children a range of different objects to hold, what letter do they begin with and can they find it on the alphabet board?	**Library** 10.15–10.45 and 1.00–1.30. Children to find books about ways to travel, find books about moving, and choose a favourite to read	**Knowledge and Understanding** Using set rings sort a set of animals by range of animals by range of different criteria, i.e. stripes, legs, tails, etc. Name cards	**Knowledge and Understanding** Discuss things which move both in and out of the nursery, what makes them move? Talk about forces, pushes and pulls
Friday	**Shared story** Tell the story of the Three Billy Goats Gruff	**TV** 11.00–11.30 and 2.45–3.15. 'Not Like That Like This'. Rat-a-tat, Red Unit p.8–9	**Speaking and Listening** Play a variety of action rhymes. Name cards	**Video Story** Rat-A-Tat-Tat, 'Not Like That Like This'

Nursery Daily Planner
Date: Spring 2 Week 3 Day 1

Intended Learning Outcomes	Pupil Activity	Organisaton/Differentiation/ Resources	Assessment & Way Forward
Language/Literacy To be able to obstarnd sentence structures and begin to understand the way books operate, i.e. front/back/page, etc To have the opportunity to identify initial phonemes	Children will sit in a position which enables them to see the text, we will discuss the various elements of the story and encourage them to predict and reflect 1. Children will use their name cards to identify phonemes, we will place the cards on the Moscari board, can they locate their name? 2. Children will play Kim's game	**WCT** On carpet, whole class, story 'Don't Do That' **SGT** On carpet in differentiated groups, name cards, squares, find own name, triangles give initial phoneme Range of transport vehicles	
Mathematics To practise ordering and rote counting numbers to 10 To become aware of the physical representation of associated time	1. Children will watch the Numbertime video no. 3, look at the number line, find the no., discuss nos which come before/after. Miss out numbers when saying them, do children spot the mistake? 2. Children will discuss the passing of time, how we tell the time, look at a range of watches and clocks, look inside one at the cogs then make a pictorial representation using fluorescent paint on black paper	**FCT** On carpet, whole class, Numbertime video, number line, squares will place nos. in order Brenda 4 children Art Area, black paper, paint, cardboard to make cogs. Klixi. **Hall** 9.15–9.45 and 1.00–1.30 See schemes of work in resources for detailed information	
Physical To have the opportunity to understand how their bodies work, how they can move in different ways, at different heights and speeds	1. Children will complete a range of circle games, i.e. The Farmer's Den, Sally Go Round The Sun, Ring a Roses, Windy Weather, There was a Princess Long Ago, etc. 2. Children will listen to rhymes, they will be cats or dogs and have to move onto a carpeted area when the rhyme is called, i.e. logs, frogs, hogs, or mats, fats, rats, hats, etc.		
Creative To create a visual representation allowing them to observe patterns created when objects are moved through paint	Children will use cardboard combs, splotch paint onto card, run combs through, observe patterns	**Suzanne: Nursery Area** 4 children, card, paint, paper, sketch books	

The QCA schemes are non-statutory because there is no legal requirement to use them. As was pointed out earlier in this chapter, this is a healthy situation because it enables schools to contextualise the curriculum for their own children. For example, if you live in Chester, your approach to teaching about the Romans in history is likely to differ markedly from how you might approach it if you live anywhere else. Nearly all schools had already drawn up comprehensive schemes of work for all curriculum areas, but several are now using all, or part of, these QCA exemplar schemes. The QCA sees the schemes as a resource for primary teachers 'to use as they see fit'. They have been drawn up with the help of practising teachers and subject associations.

National Literacy Strategy and Numeracy Framework

The NLS File and Numeracy Framework are used by many schools as the basis for their English and mathematics schemes of work. Most schools using them have already adapted them significantly in line with their experience. You may find that the changes made by the school include:

- a more comprehensive scheme, e.g. extended writing sessions in English; cross-curricular activities in mathematics, with design and technology linked closely to shape work
- additional support for children with special educational needs, including withdrawal from mainstream lessons
- additional support for children with English as an additional language
- additional support for children with behavioural difficulties, who find sitting listening for significant periods of time difficult
- mixed-aged groups to enable children to work at levels appropriate to their learning needs
- revisions in light of central government changes
- revisions in light of local authority recommendations.

Commercial and website schemes of work, including lesson plans

There are many commercial schemes of work available for use. Most major publishing companies have a primary publishing division and catalogues displaying their wares are generally free. There are a number of regional educational exhibitions during the year and these are well worth visiting as they provide a good update on new publications and resources.

Many companies are moving into advertising on educational websites (e.g. www.learnfree.co.uk). They often offer sample pages from their texts, which provide a flavour of what is available. Company websites sometimes do this as well and there is likely to be a tremendous growth in the use of websites to promote sales in educational publishing as teachers become more visible internet users.

Companies such as Scholastic, and the *Times Education Supplement,* also produce monthly magazines which contain advertisements and reviews of new publications. Scholastic, for example, produce *Child Education* (under-fives and KS1), *Junior Education* (KS2), *Infant Projects* and *Junior Focus*. They also give student discounts!

You need to be cautious about using commercial plans, either from the Internet or from published schemes. Anyone can put a scheme of work and/or lesson plans on the Internet. Some of them are very poor quality, written by people with very limited experience in school. Commercial schemes are generally better because they have been reviewed and need to be of a better quality in order to sell.

This chapter has been kept at a very practical level in order to try and help student teachers make sense of what they see in school. There is a long history to the development of a national curriculum and what children should learn and be taught in school. Educational philosophy and sociology look at the nature of knowledge, areas of experience and curricular subjects for schools. General texts in educational sociology give a strong background to the political as well as the social implications of curriculum change.

Chapter 6

Monitoring, assessment, recording, reporting and accountability

Learning objectives

- To recognise the link between assessment and raising achievement in primary schools.
- To examine the close relationship between planning, assessment and target setting.
- To know about different types of assessment and be able to identify and evaluate these in school.
- To know how to mark and monitor pupils' assigned classwork and homework.
- To become familiar with statutory assessment and reporting requirements and know how to prepare and present informative reports to parents.

Raising achievement

Stringer and Powell's book *Raising Achievement in the Primary School* is an essential read in connection with this chapter. The authors identify twelve characteristics for the successful school.

1   A supportive atmosphere where all members of the school community are valued, enthusiastic and happy.
2   A can-do culture of learning in which children are aware of their progress and can see improvements in their performance day to day.
3   Children's learning is steadily improving – identifiable in both teacher assessments and external monitoring.
4   A strong sense of community; a culture of caring for each other that leads to responsible self-discipline and the absence of conflict and bullying.
5   Teachers have high expectations of children. Children have high expectations of themselves; they are growing in confidence and independence, and actively participate in stimulating and varied lessons.
6   Work is regularly and constructively marked and the outcomes are shared with children in a way that involves them in their own learning; assessment informs future teaching.
7   Achievement is celebrated individually and corporately, and displays of work are prominent.
8   Expectations about behaviour are clearly defined and pupils' growing responsibility is backed up by a consistent set of rewards and standards.
9   Thriving extracurricular activities exist, with high teacher and child involvement.
10 The involvement of parents in the school as partners in their children's learning; clear communication with parents that unites them with the school in achieving successful learning outcomes for their children.
11 An active governing body that is involved and responsive and gives clear guidance and support to the school.
12 The school is fully integrated with the community through links of all kinds.

We take up many of the criteria of a successful school elsewhere, but there are three criteria which are obviously assessment linked (2, 3 and 6). Assessment permeates many of the others (e.g. 7, 8 and 10). In the literature about assessment and in our use of it, it is salutary to remember that it is about achievement, not ticks on a page, record books or tick lists.

Monitoring lessons: the starting point

Learning how to monitor pupils' learning is essential to developing a strong assessment base. Small-group work provides a good starting point for practical experience because monitoring the learning of four or six children is easier than starting with thirty. It is best to start with one child and then move on to systematic assessment of more than one. The child profile included in Appendix 2 (pp 165/6) gives a focus for a more holistic view of the child.

Monitoring starts with clearly defined learning objectives and then involves:

- monitoring how well individual children achieve these objectives
- identifying the difference between unsatisfactory learning and unsatisfactory learning objectives
- identifying children for whom the learning objectives are inappropriate - too frustrating /insufficiently challenging – and devising more appropriate learning outcomes
- identifying individual learning patterns, evaluating their effectiveness and adopting teaching strategies to improve them - for some children, this may involve monitoring behaviour in the first place
- listening carefully to children, analysing their responses and responding constructively in order to take learning forward
- understanding pupils' misconceptions and helping to remedy them
- recording observations systematically and linking them with learning targets
- establishing a firm database to report on children's progress to themselves, their carers, other teachers, governing bodies, LEAs and government departments
- maintaining a flexible approach to children's learning so that children continue to be treated as individuals and are not pigeon-holed into learning categories to make monitoring easier.

Marking is the most visual method of monitoring pupils' work during the course of a lesson and when work is sent home. It provides feedback to both the children and parents. Ideally marking should take place alongside the child, so that it becomes a teaching tool, rather than a summative assessment (see below for the difference between formative and summative assessments). Marking is generally the first experience student teachers have of formally assessing children's work. Most schools have a marking policy to help new members of staff, including student teachers, and to ensure compatibility between classes. Sometimes this is very simple, like the one below.

POLICY DOCUMENT FOR MARKING

The aims of this marking policy are to encourage the children to achieve the highest possible standards of presentation and to take a pride in all their work.
'To be aware of what can be termed excellence in whatever field and curricular area and strive to achieve it.'

School Aims and Objectives
- To help teachers to assess and evaluate the children's work and to provide a framework within which all teachers can work.
- All work in books should be dated.
- Work should be marked before further work is undertaken in any one book.
- Written or pictorial comments should be added to children's work where appropriate.
- If study skills are being undertaken in areas other than English, then spellings and grammatical errors should be corrected where appropriate.
- Corrections should be made at the discretion of the teacher and according to the child's ability.
- In order to encourage the highest possible standards of presentation:
  - both sides of the page should be used
  - dates and titles should be underlined at the appropriate stage
  - where appropriate, there should be a margin
  - at Key Stage 2 children who write neatly should be rewarded by being allowed to use a pen.

This policy will be evaluated within the next twelve months.

Sometimes the policies are much more detailed, as the following example shows.

 Example

PROOF-READING AND EDITING GUIDE

This is to be used by both teacher and children when engaging in a writing conference, to remind the writer/author of possible changes to be made to a piece of writing.

Symbol	Explanation
ᴍ	Does this word need a capital, or is it wrongly capitalised?
0	What punctuation is missing here? (comma, full stop, question mark, exclamation, speech marks, apostrophe)
⟨speek⟩	Would you please check this spelling?
A	Is a word or phrase missing?
<u>Then</u>	Can you find a better beginning for the sentence?
[said?]	Can you find a word that is more expressive?
//	Could this be a good place to start a new paragraph?
*	Does this make sense?
△	Would you please see me.

Effective marking policies

- Marking assessment criteria should be clear to children, parents and teachers.
- Assessment criteria should not be a secret, and it is useful to discuss with children their understanding of the marking system.
- Marking should show children that someone is taking an interest in their work.
- Marking shows parents that their child's work is being monitored.
- Marking celebrates children's achievements.
- Marking identifies areas for improvement.

Marking for the trainee teacher is made much easier when a marking policy is in place, but there are also other factors to take into account, such as:

- ensuring that children know what sort of standards are expected
- helping children to understand that both effort and attainment are rewarded and making it clear which is which
- telling children what they need to do to improve
- making sure that marking is not just being done for the sake of it – because the words look better corrected than not corrected.

Trainee teachers should also note, by looking at how their class teacher marks work:

- when and how the teacher marks in different subject areas
- the style of handwriting used to mark work
- the use made of different coloured pens
- the use made of marking in terms of individual achievement, i.e. is it recorded anywhere else?

Different forms of assessment

Assessment is carried out informally and formally. Both are an integral part of teaching. (The National Numeracy Framework has a useful overview of assessment. It looks at short-, medium- and long-term assessments and passing on information about pupils' attainment and progress. This is closely linked to its advice on planning for mathematics.)

- **Informal assessment** takes place all the time and is linked closely with monitoring. It involves looking at what children are doing, assessing what they need and responding to this. Informal assessment can involve non-verbal communication such as a nod, smile, frown or movement of the head. It also involves explanations, questions, and words of praise or admonishment. It is carried out 'on the hoof' and forms the basis of the interaction between the teacher and

the class and the teacher and individual child. Approximately 1,000 of these interactions take place in any one day. All of them require a decision from the teacher.
- **Formal assessment** is planned for in advance and is an integral part of monitoring both learning and teaching. Below we look at different types of formal assessment known as 'instruments of assessment'.

Purposes of assessment

Conventional views about assessment identify four main purposes:

1 **formative**: identifying positive achievements in children's learning in order to move it forward. This area of assessment touches the beginning teacher as soon as he or she enters the classroom.

2 **summative**: this measures what has been learnt over a period of time. Traditionally, end-of-year tests did this. The SATs and Teacher Assessments, at the end of both Key Stages, can be seen as summative assessments of children's learning at a specific point in time.

3 **diagnostic**: these are used to identify specific learning difficulties for which there are known strategies to improve learning. Miscue analysis for reading is one diagnostic test, which provides a detailed analysis of the type of problems which children may have. Diagnostic testing is closely linked to specific teaching strategies to improve performance. The Reading Recovery Programme is an example of this process in action.

4 **evaluative**: these evaluate learning outcomes in terms of overall success. Schools are encouraged to evaluate new initiatives such as the National Literacy Strategy in terms of its overall success in raising standards over a period of years.

The distinctions between these four different assessment purposes are less clear cut in practice. Practice SATs papers, for example, are used diagnostically to identify areas for improvement as well as provide practice for children.

Instruments of assessment

This sounds rather like some form of torture, but is just a useful term to differentiate between different types of assessment. Most schools use a variety of different ways of assessing learning, child progress and achievement. This is because no single assessment form is sufficient. Below are some examples of assessment instruments you may find in school.

Records of achievement/personal portfolio assessments

Records of achievement (ROA) or personal portfolio assessments contain pieces of work, certificates and reports collected over a period of time to demonstrate progress and attainment for each individual child. Good portfolios can include audiotapes, photographs and evaluations of the content by the teacher and child, e.g. 'I chose this piece of work because...'. There are three different types of ROA:
- 'show' ROA, which include only the best
- descriptive ROA, which demonstrate what the child can do without evaluating it
- evaluative ROA, which assess and measure the quality of work, usually against levels in the National Curriculum, i.e. annotated pieces of work.

Standardised tests

Standardised achievement tests are potentially powerful tools for teaching. They are the most objective and scientific measures we have. But they make many people feel uncomfortable. In the days of the eleven-plus they were associated with denied opportunities, unfair tracking policies, negative labelling of eleven-plus failures, intellectual and cultural bias and political machinations. However, standardised tests of many different types are a fact of life, and teachers cannot ignore them if they wish to do the best for their children. They take a variety of different forms, but the most well known are the **Standardised Assessment Tasks (SATs)**, originally taken at the end of Key Stages 1 and 2 and now available for intermediate years. When first introduced the SATs were intended to assess attainment in all curriculum subjects. Today, they cover only English, maths and science. The SATs at the end of both Key Stages are part of statutory assessment and their results have to be reported to parents. This reporting covers both individual and cohort results. Cohort results must be reported alongside national results.

There is a huge commercial market for standardised tests. You can see this by looking at educational publishers' catalogues. A few cover personal and social development features, but the vast majority cover different aspects of English and maths, e.g. reading, spelling and number. Some of these tests provide teachers with a 'spelling' or 'reading age' for children. You may find some of these 'reading ages' in teachers' record books. Some standardised tests are more valid than others. Test manuals should report validity and reliability factors and should always be consulted before using the test. You also need to use your knowledge about tests and the research process as such tests can be extremely biased. Culture and gender are the most common biases, but tests also date quickly. The 1987 Task Group on Assessment and Testing (TGAT) contains two useful appendices, one by Harvey Goldstein, looking at validity of such tests, and the other from the Equal Opportunities Commission, raising issues related to gender bias. Educational researchers also often supply subject-specific tests, which they base on the work they have done in their subject area.

A growing number of standardised tests are available on CD-ROM and aimed at the domestic as well as the school market. It is also likely that commercial websites will move into this area. Test the child, identify a learning need and then move into the hard sell to parents?

Children need to know how to take standardised tests, and it is not 'teaching to the test' to provide practice for them in understanding instructions (oral and written), learning to use time efficiently, guessing wisely (e.g. eliminating answers in multiple-choice questions) and applying special strategies.

Assessment through Learning Continuums

Programmes such as the Australian-based First Steps Language Programme provide Learning Continuums in different areas – reading, writing, spelling and oracy. The Continuums are based on learning indicators shown by children at different stages. Children are assessed by watching their learning behaviour and then placing them on the relevant point on the Continuum. One of the most powerful aspects of this form of assessment is that it provides teaching emphases to move children from one stage to another. For example, Phase 2 of the First Steps Reading Continuum is called 'Experimental Reading'. Key indicators include:

- realising that print contains a constant message, i.e. the words of a written story remain the same, but the words of an oral story may change
- focusing more on expressing the meaning of the story than on reading words accurately
- using prior knowledge of context and personal experience to make meaning, e.g. uses memory of a text to match spoken with written words.

Major teaching emphases for this phase include:

- share with children times when you challenge or disagree with the text
- before, during and after reading, promote discussion that goes beyond the literal level.

Baseline assessment

Since 1998 it has been a legal requirement that schools conduct an approved baseline assessment procedure to measure children's attainment on entry. There are now about 90 such approved schemes, making it difficult to make comparisons between schools. Most schools already had some form of baseline assessment in place and find that it

- provides useful assessments of all children entering the school, which can then be used for planning a meaningful early years curriculum relevant for individual children's learning needs
- identifies those with special educational needs
- provides data to support value-added claims for school improvement.

Individual education plans

Individual education plans (IEPs) are teaching and learning plans for children identified as having special educational needs (see Chapter 9). An IEP is drawn up by the school's Special Educational Needs Coordinator (SENCO) working with the child's teacher. Others may be involved in drawing up the plan, such as a Learning Support Assistant (LSA) who works with the child, the child's carers, advisory teachers and an educational psychologist. Ideally the child should be involved, but this is less likely. The IEP is based on guidelines set out by the *Code of Practice on the Identification and Assessment of Special Educational Needs.* Most LEAs supply guidance plans for children on different stages of the Code. There is a legal obligation under the Code to implement and keep records on IEPs for children at stage 2 of the Code and above.

Observation checklists
Teachers often devise observation checklists so that they can target and assess particular learning performances such as working collaboratively, problem solving and finding information from non-fiction texts. Some of the most common commercial checklists are related to personal and social behaviour and to early reading strategies, e.g. holding a book correctly.

Observation comment slips
Post-it notes, clipboards and notepads can be used systematically to record children's learning during the course of a day. These can then be used to assess children's progress and attainment and target setting for individual children.

Record books
Teachers can keep a variety of different record books and sheets which involve child assessment.

The medium-term planning sheets in the previous chapter involve identifying assessment opportunities, and short-term planning involves assessing children after teaching has taken place and documenting ways in which this assessment could be used for future planning. Teachers also keep subject record books to cover particular areas of the curriculum and records on the progress and attainment of individual children in specific subject areas. In subjects such as English and maths several different aspects of children's learning may be recorded. These may be linked to different Attainment Targets set out in the National Curriculum documents. Schools devise common recording devices to identify different stages in the learning process; for example

☐   no assessed learning
/   partial learning
X   understood

Records for many foundation subjects tend to be limited to curriculum coverage in order to keep assessment manageable.

Performance assessments
Many schools have experimented to find other methods of assessing children's learning, and both the literacy and numeracy strategies include sessions where children can 'perform their assessment'. Observation checklists and comment slips are used to record them. Performance assessments include:
- **written products of various kinds** – journals, letters, discussion papers, diaries
- **kinaesthetic products** – games, puzzles, sculpture
- **visual products** – charts, graphs, murals, video presentation, photographs, flow charts, timelines
- **verbal products** – role-play, drama, debates, oral reports.

These 'performance products' can show that learning has taken place and also serve as part of the learning process. It can be argued that they are more authentic than traditional assessment measures because the monitoring of learning and its assessment then become a learning experience in themselves. Children have to relate their learning to real-life situations and the teacher's role is to observe, rather than to instruct and/or assist. Performance assessments encourage teaching and learning for performance, rather than measurement.

One example of this can be seen in the oral mental arithmetic sessions recommended in the Numeracy Strategy. These:
- teach children to perform their knowledge

- establish clear performance targets, which move beyond simply covering curriculum content and working towards performances of understanding
- publicise criteria and performance standards
- provide models of excellence
- teach strategies explicitly
- enable ongoing assessments for feedback and forward curriculum planning
- celebrate performance.

Assessment and recording

Nearly all these instruments of assessment have built-in recording methods. One of the most comprehensive commercial record schemes was developed by a group of teachers based at the Centre for Language in Primary Education in London. This became known as the Primary Language Record (PLR), and many of its assessment and recording strategies were adopted, wholly or in part, by other LEAs. It involved observation diaries, samples of work, and records of discussions with parents and children. The PLR was completed throughout the year, so it provided an ongoing record of children's progress and achievement. The handbook for teachers still provides an excellent guide to the type of assessment comments which can be most usefully recorded and used for target setting (ILEA 1987). It is particularly strong on looking at the language strengths of children who have English as an Additional Language (EAL).

 Identify different instruments of assessment used in your school. Write down those in use in your class and evaluate them in terms of use and manageability. Discuss your findings with your mentor.

Some instruments of assessment, such as Individual Education Plans (IEPs), include some form of target setting and review. This is particularly important because one of OFSTED's most frequent complaints concerns the limited influence of assessment on curriculum planning. Schools are encouraged to remedy such deficiencies by developing an assessment policy that focuses on using formative assessments to enhance pupils' learning. In fact, many of the existing assessment procedures can be used for target setting. McNamara and Moreton (1997) provide a cautionary note about target setting in their book *Understanding Differentiation*. Their evidence, collected over many years, shows that working to a target set by someone else is very difficult. Our own life experiences tell us this. How many of us fail to keep to the targets we have been set, for losing weight, cutting down on alcohol or giving up smoking? One of the reasons Weight Watchers are successful is that targets are reached through rewards and peer support, rather than someone else setting them for us. Assessment may also be used to assess teacher performance. There is no simple connection between child achievement and the quality of teaching, although there is often a link between pupils' progress and teaching performance.

Planning, assessment and target setting

Chapter 5 on curriculum planning shows very clearly the close relationship between planning and assessing. Your own lesson planning gives an even closer insight into the need to link planning closely with previously assessed learning. Evaluations of lessons and activities should always include some form of target setting, so that curriculum plans can be informed by what children already know and can do. Student teachers also need to assess and evaluate their own performance and link this with targets for improvement.

One school found that weekly planning sheets for the Numeracy Framework did not enable them to adjust and adapt their planning quickly enough to make teaching effective. They felt that assessing children's learning after a full week could result in some children making unsatisfactory progress. They therefore adapted planning sheets so that teachers planned for the first three days of the week. An example of this is shown here. The original is A3 size.

The plenary on Wednesday was linked closely to assessment of progress so far. The additional row between Wednesday and Thursday is then used to assess and target learning for the Thursday and Friday of that week.

Weekly Planning Sheet for Mathematics

Year 2 **Class 2** **Week 6**

	Key Vocabulary	Mental/Oral Objectives		Main Activity Objectives		Plenary	Resources
	Fives hundreds, zero. Full, halves, quarter turns, Right angles, clockwise/anti-clockwise	Count on in 5s from back to zero or any small number. Count in 100s to 1,000 from and back to zero.		Use mathematical vocabulary to describe position, direction, movement. Recognise whole, half and quarter turns to L/R, clockwise. Know a right angle is a measure of a quarter turn – recognise the right angle in ☐ and ☐ Give instructions for route with straight lines and quarter turns			
		Activities		**Activities**	**Differentiation**		**Resources**
Mon		Count on in 5s from and back to zero–up to 100 5 times table		Revise turns. Follow a route–straight lines and quarter turns to L/R Routes around classroom –children to give instruction	Give directions – to follow a route – cars on mat – straight lines a nd quarter L/R turns Plan a route around classroom. Work in 2 small groups – record on copymaster 20 Support. Straight ahead, L/R quarter turns. Use Nelson enlarge maze	Revise turns	Nelson Copymaster 20 Cars, street map, large batteries for robot, maze, pen, extension Nelson books
Tues		(ditto)		Right angles – as a measure of quarter turn – L/R. Identify in squares and rectangles. Make L by folding paper twice	L in capital letters Draw carefully and mark with x	Right angles. Look at capital letters	Paper to fold
Wed		(ditto) 5s from small number and back to zero. 5 times table		(Use robot – instructions) Directions around classroom	Support – work through Nelson routes. Directions activity – Nelson Nelson routes. Support – Nelson directions activity Give each other directions around classroom. Cars directions – swap	Assessment Plenary	
		Key Questions		**Formative Assessment**			
Thu				Number revision			
Fri							
	Children not reaching objectives:			Children exceeding objectives:		Notes:	

Target setting

Target setting is seen as an important element in raising achievement in schools. Central government have required LEAs to target set and school governors are involved in target setting for individual schools. Each school must agree its targets with the LEA. Schools are also required to publish pupil performance targets annually in the core subjects of the National Curriculum. National performance data are published annually.

Target setting and school improvement

Over the next few years, this is likely to result in much more individual target setting than has been done in the past. It is likely to concentrate on English and maths and criteria used will be drawn from the Literacy and Numeracy Strategies. The QCA has linked target setting with their exemplification materials in a pack produced for the NLS. Central government sees target setting as essential for school improvement in their guidance to schools (DfEE 1998). They recommend a five-stage cycle of improvement focusing on child performance. Target setting is implicit in this.

The school:

Stage 1   analyses its current performance
Stage 2   compares its results with those of similar schools
Stage 3   sets itself clear and measurable targets
Stage 4   revises its development plan to highlight action to achieve the targets
Stage 5   takes action, reviews success, and starts the cycle again.

Target setting and the class teacher

The class teacher's role in this is clear, **whatever the age of the children**. They need to be able to set challenging and realistic targets to feed into the school targets. Standardised tests are frequently used to provide a range of information about child performance and target setting based on this. The class teacher then forecasts on his or her knowledge of the child, on evidence of past achievements and on the pupil's self-appraisal. Forecasts can be for one or two years. This gives a sensible time-scale for working with children to achieve or exceed the forecast.

SMART targets

Good targets are

S   specific
M   measurable
A   achievable
R   realistic
T   time-related

Examples given by the DfEE (1998) include:
'to increase the percentage of children attaining Level 2 in reading by five percentage points' (for an infant school).
   and
'all pupils perform at Level 4 or above by the end of Key Stage 2, as measured by national tests in 1999' (for a primary school).

Many schools are in practice identifying much more specific targets than this in order to be able to achieve the more generic ones. Below is an example of different ways in which target setting was initially established in two schools. Both schools have refined the process since then and it will be further refined by the time you read this. It gives an idea of how schools started to target set in response to central government directives.

Example

A CASE STUDY:
USING KEY STAGE 2 SATS FOR TARGET CRITERIA

Two years ago, two deputy headteachers in two schools were both made responsible for assessment across the school. Both were concerned that a significant number of children were underachieving. Their initial concerns were the English SATs at the end of Key Stage 2. They used the marking criteria from the writing SATs to identify English writing targets for each level and then monitored a piece of work from each child using the criteria as a continuum. Here is an example for Level 3.

NAME ....

ENGLISH WRITING TARGETS

PURPOSE AND ORGANISATION
• **Beginning, middle and ending**
• **Imaginative – NOT things that people do in everyday life**
• **DESCRIPTIONS OF CHARACTERS – How they look, their feelings and their actions**
• **SETTING – Where it takes place**

GRAMMAR AND PUNCTUATION
• **Full stops**
• **Capital letters**
• **Accurate use of question marks**
• **DIRECT SPEECH – NOT everyday language (something interesting)**

GRAMMAR AND STYLE
• **USE OTHER WORDS TO CONNECT SENTENCES INSTEAD OF 'AND' – TRY WORDS LIKE:**
  then, but, when, so, because
• **USE ADVERBS, e.g. The sly fox slowly crept across the barn**
• **WIDER USE OF NOUN PHRASES, e.g.**   NO – monster
                                          YES – the large green monster
                                          NO – the pony
                                          YES – the little grey pony

And, yes, the scores did go up significantly. Perhaps an even better measure of raised achievement was the comment made to me by a child in one of the schools: 'We're getting much cleverer now than we used to be'.

IEPs and target setting
Many SENCOs have a long experience of setting learning and behavioural targets for their children. The IEPs identify these targets and record them on specific forms. Most LEAs provide examples of appropriate target setting for children identified with special educational needs and provide forms for this to be recorded. Forms vary from authority to authority, but generally cover a description of needs, targets, criteria for success and a time-scale. Provision is made for regular reviewing. Initially teachers do the target setting, but as McNamara and Moreton (1997) point out, this has limited effectiveness, and they recommend a gradual movement towards peer targeting. They suggest children are taught to help each other to target set by:
• helping to identify the problem
• setting a broad target
• setting a specific target
• identifying a time-scale and a reward
• choosing a method of teaching and learning which suits the learner

- devoting time (in a one to one situation supporting learning that is most helpful)
- assessing progress in a way chosen by the learner
- rewarding success
- reviewing to identify the problem and work towards changes in the method.

The quality of target setting via IEPs varies considerably between schools and it is useful to see IEPs from more than one school. At one time there was a tendency for IEPs to concentrate on basic phonic skills linked with behavioural targets such as 'sitting still for more than five minutes'. As SENCOs in mainstream schooling have become more skilled, the IEPs have improved in their focus, target setting and effectiveness.

Look at some of the comments you have made - orally or written to children. What sort of targets are you setting in your daily practice? How will the targets be recorded? Who will monitor pupils' progress?

The process of target setting is not new. Teachers have always made oral and written statements which make targets explicit, e.g. 'Next time, see if you can ...' and 'Try to remember ...'. Targets need to be precise: 'Improve your writing' is too general – presentation? length? quality of content? Targets based on National Curriculum levels used to be set as checklists and several publishers produced empty booklets of checklists for each curriculum area. Stringer and Powell (1998) suggest a rubber-stamp approach, where the stamp identifies content, effort and presentation, each of which are given a separate mark. You need to know how your school sees target setting and discuss with the assessment coordinator how targets are recorded and monitored.

Reporting

It is a legal requirement that teachers report upon the achievements of their children each year. Surprisingly, it was not until 1991 that reports had to be made to parents about the progress of their own children. This takes the form of a written report, and must provide results of any National Curriculum assessments and examination results, and brief particulars of achievements in National Curriculum foundation subjects and other subjects and activities in the school curriculum. Schools must provide information about pupils' general progress and arrangements for discussing the report with teachers. At the moment schools have their own format for reports and some are very attractively presented.

Trainee teachers are rarely involved in report writing, but when they become newly qualified teachers they find the task particularly difficult. Schools generally adopt a school writing style so that parents get some idea of continuity in terms of reported progress and achievement. The schools also keep copies of reports, so that it is possible to look back over how pupil progress has been recorded for any one child. The best way of finding out how to write reports is to examine reports from more than one school. Some schools prepare reports twice a year.

 Ask your mentor if you can see examples of reports from each school year. As well as looking at the comments written and developing your own word bank, imagine how you would feel if you were the parent/child reading the report. How informative are the reports? How much guidance do they give the parents in terms of future target setting for their child? When you have looked through a number of reports, try writing one for one of the children you have profiled. Appendix 2 provides a useful format for a child profile – see pp. 165/6.

Effective report writing is a technique. The work on the misuse of praise looked at in the next chapter is also relevant here. There is sometimes a delicate balance between the brutal truth and a bland statement. Comments in the reports need to match the records of individual children, to be understandable, to set future learning targets and to match legal requirements.

Reeves in *Reporting to Parents* (see Further Reading) provides some useful advice on writing reports.

1 Keep notes during the year – these should be systematic and useful. They need to include details of judgements you've made, information about specific achievements or difficulties, records of activities undertaken and particular discussions with parents.

2 Don't spring surprises – written reports should not stand alone, but should be used alongside other ways of communicating with parents.

3 Pay attention to language and style – this is much easier to do now that reports can be word processed. Handwritten reports involve writing neatly, checking spelling, looking at sentence construction. Tools can be used to check this on word-processed reports.

4 Pay attention to details – spelling the child's name, using the correct name (e.g. a nickname may be used in school, which is hated by the parents).

5 Be concise – don't waffle and ensure that you are not using meaningless phrases.

6 Make what you write useful to the parents – this involves being specific in what the child can and cannot do, and where parental support would be most useful.

7 Avoid jargon.

8 Set the context. It is easy to write a very positive report about a slow learner, without disclosing that the child is having learning difficulties. Parents need to know how their child's progress compares with other children's. Teaching is a caring profession, and we don't like hurting or upsetting people. Parents need to know if something is wrong. This also needs to be linked with 2 'don't spring surprises'. Parents of able children are often disappointed by the low levels expected of their child. Challenges for these children are also important.

9 Be positive – remember Gardner's multiple intelligences. Try to ensure that you can report on areas where the child is successful as well as areas where there are problems.

There are many software packages available for teachers which provide word banks to help with report writing. Schools may purchase them, or individual teachers may feel frustrated enough to buy them for themselves. Remember that they need to:

• be easy to use
• produce personal, detailed reports
• have banks of sentences which relate to curriculum areas as well as general comments
• have the facility to adapt or to join to sentences, so that you can insert your own wordings
• be able to link with the school report format
• be responsive to any legal requirements, e.g. the Data Protection Act, and their updates.

The sharing of information

Of course written reports are not the only way in which information is shared between parents and teachers. Parents give information to the school about contact numbers in case of emergency, medical details, particular abilities and weaknesses, social and behavioural facts. Other less formal communications may include parents evenings, surgeries, open days, workshops, information meetings, casual conversations, contact books (often reading), celebratory events such as school plays, assemblies, etc.

As e-mail becomes more accessible within homes and schools, parents communicating with teachers by e-mail is likely to become a key area for development.

Chapter 7

Working for good pupil behaviour and discipline

Learning objectives

- To evaluate ways in which teachers can set a good example to the children they teach, through their presentation and their personal and professional conduct.
- To examine research and developments on pedagogy in relation to effective teacher behaviours for good child behaviour and discipline.
- To recognise that children have specific needs.
- To develop skills and strategies for maintaining a purposeful working atmosphere.

Starting with ourselves

 Spend five minutes writing down what concerns you most about class management in relation to child behaviour.

These are some of the written responses I received last year from one group of students: fighting and shouting out; children becoming violent towards either myself or other children; repercussions from parents after a child has been spoken to about his or her behaviour; bullying; aggressive and defiant children who will not settle and cause/egg on other children to cause disruption during whole-class exposition; a too-frequent focus on one disruptive child; children who constantly move about during the introduction to a lesson or during a story; being ignored after correcting bad behaviour; being made a fool of – losing the respect of the children; how to deal with a child without physically handling him or her; losing control by reacting badly and therefore coming off worse; not listening to me or laughing at me and not taking me seriously.

These can be sorted into different categories. Several relate to self-worth, and how child misbehaviour challenges this. Another category touches on legal aspects, e.g. a handling policy for violent or disruptive children. The final category is really the search for strategies with which to cope. Only one student mentioned parents, but this is an important aspect for teachers and is dealt with in greater detail in Chapter 10 on home–school–community links. Can you put your concerns into any particular category?

Caring teachers

This might seem a rather strange title for a section on child behaviour, but teaching is not private practice. It is not about making money, although it does pay an income. It is a helping and caring profession assisting people to enhance the quality of their lives. As the author Pearl Buck once wrote, 'Only the brave should teach. Only those who love the young should teach. Teaching is a vocation.' Teachers have to care and show that they care. To do this they need to follow certain guidelines.

Dress appropriately

We never get a second chance at a first impression. Whether we like it or not, we judge others by their dress and they judge us too. It may not be right or fair, but in the real world we are not accepted for ourselves but for our appearance. Clothes 'do not make the man', but they can be a contributing factor in unmaking a person. You need to dress appropriately for four main reasons:

1 respect
2 credibility
3 acceptance
4 authority.

In teaching there is a fifth reason. You are acting as a role model for children, so you need to look professional, proud, dedicated, responsible and appreciated. The world outside expects us to prepare our children for it, and this includes the way people dress. Children quickly comment on clothes, sometimes directly, e.g. 'I like your tie, sir'. Even when they don't say anything they will be comparing you with other professionals they know – their parents, doctors, police, nurses. When you dress, you are making a statement about yourself to the world.

Value yourself

Teachers influence children's lives. Valuing children and valuing education are essential for success. Unfortunately teachers – and teacher trainers! – often get a bad press. Such a blame culture helps no one except the journalist who writes the story and the politician who creates the soundbite. Staying positive can be difficult. Look at some of the techniques we describe later which can help to improve children's self-esteem and adapt them to your own situation. In some respects, valuing yourself relates to the above section on dress. Primary teachers may never be really wealthy, but they do have a reasonable and reliable income. If you value yourself, invest in yourself – a new suit, a good PC, study texts. You're already investing in yourself by buying this book.

Share yourself

You need to be prepared to share something of yourself – this is a good way to demonstrate that you respect children as fellow human beings. Children sometimes ask trainee teachers intimate questions, e.g. 'Who's your girlfriend?' 'Do you like Mr...?' Make it clear that these are inappropriate. Sharing yourself with children in your role as a teacher does not involve acting the part of an older sibling. A surprising number of children do not realise this, particularly when you work with them in a small group. Part of your role as a teacher is to help them develop appropriate behaviour in situations which may be new to them. Some questions may be directly racist and/or sexist. Valerie Walkerdine, in *Democracy in the Kitchen*, showed how two boys in a nursery class were able to use their gender to challenge their female teacher. No trainee/teacher or child should be subjected to sexist or racist harassment, and if the class teacher and school cannot help, contact your college tutor. Most schools do have procedures for this, but it is important to deal with the matter immediately.

Keep a sense of humour

Laugh and enjoy. Laughter does not have to be disruptive. Admit you do not know everything. Being honest is more credible, and certainly teaches children that there is not an infinite amount of knowledge which is contained within the teacher's head, ready to be poured into their brain. As the (slightly adapted) advertisement says: 'I don't know, but I know someone who does'.

Remember you're a learner, too

Teachers and learners are no different. We are all learners, and children can teach us a great deal. Learning is a lifelong process and children need to see this from the models they have in school. This may be hard to do when you are a student teacher. I remember going into one school where the student teachers were given an identity badge to wear which said 'Student Teacher'. They said it made them feel idiots. In many ways this is a sad reflection on how children view learning, but we did change it. The badges now say 'Visiting Teacher'. Over the years I have visited hundreds of classrooms as a teacher trainer observing students, and more recently as an OFSTED inspector collecting data on teaching performance. I have learnt more about teaching and children's learning doing this than I ever did when I was teaching and managing a whole class as a primary teacher. It is a wonderful luxury, sitting with a small group of children. You are part of the 'experienced' curriculum and you record the 'observed' curriculum. We need to be humble about our own learning; for unless we are continuous learners we cannot be teachers. And I always tell the children that I am in the room to look at them and see how hard they work. As with lesson plans, observation objectives are about how effectively children learn, progress and achieve.

Be tough

Learning is important. Children are important. They are our future. School is a small part of children's lives, but it can change them. Later in this chapter we look at behaviour management in detail, but this starts with the belief that what children do in school matters. If you believe it, the children will as well.

Reward effort

There is a lovely saying: 'Nothing improves a child's hearing more than praise'. This also applies to us as teachers, which is why the blame culture of the media is so destructive. Children (and adults) need to know that education is a journey, not a destination. The process is important. Learning to read is not about 'barking at print in unison' but understanding, enjoying the reading and interpreting the text at an individual as well as at a group level.

See the invisible children

About fifteen years ago, I walked into the house after a difficult day at school and found my daughter crying at the top of the stairs. 'Mrs ... treats me like a mouse, as if I'm not there.' Her friends today would be amazed that she ever felt like a mouse, but that was her 'experienced curriculum'. And yes, I did go to the school the next day and saw the teacher, without Rachel knowing.

After this, I looked at invisible children in my class. They, too, needed identifying and spending time with. Jean Robb and Hilary Letts suggest several strategies in their books to identify these (1995, 1997, see Further Reading) This might seem unnecessary – after all, they are not causing any trouble; but are they being monitored in the same way as more vocal children? Is their learning effective? Are they as unhappy in my class as my daughter was in hers? Only when we come to write their reports at the end of the year do we realise that we have spent from September to June in the same room as a child and we know nothing much about them.

One of Robb's and Letts's strategies to identify these children is to make sure that when any child offers suggestions in class you note their names on the board. For example, if you are brainstorming for information on a topic, you write the suggestion and the child's name. Over a period of time, this identifies the invisible children because their names are not recorded. Robb and Letts also point out that this gives children who may be slightly deaf, or those with poor memories, a visible means of recording the progress of a lesson. It also provides a record for individual assessment purposes, particularly if carried out on a large sheet of paper which can be examined in more detail later.

Another way is to monitor two children's behaviour over a day.

 Every twenty minutes, write down what the children are doing. You could use a chart like the one below. If the children are out of sight, e.g. having lunch, record this and do not be over-concerned about the timing. At the end of the day evaluate the record and discuss it with the class teacher.

This exercise only takes a couple of seconds, but the results are fascinating. I can remember doing this as a primary teacher and being mortified because, according to my record chart, Karen, who seemed to work hard, but underachieved, never spoke to a single child during the course of the day. She worked steadily at the tasks set, but never discussed them with anyone or chatted. I then looked at her in the playground, while I was on playground duty, and found she was a much more lively character. Meanwhile Tony, whom I'd labelled as being continually 'off task', turned out to be 'on task' at each of his twenty-minute records.

Example

TIMED ACTIVITY SHEET

Time	Child A	Child B
9.00		
9.20		
9.40		
10.00		
10.20		
10.40		
11.00		
11.20		
11.40		
12.00		
12.20		
12.40		
1.00		
1.20		
1.40		
2.00		
2.20		
2.40		
3.00		
3.20		

Reflections
Child A:

Child B:

Monitor the sub-teachers

Another group of children whose learning is often not monitored very effectively are those bright, able children who work steadily through the tasks set and then help others to complete theirs – the 'sub-teachers'. Even if they are not acting as sub-teachers they are often extremely effective at time-managing their work rate, so that their pace keeps up with the average and they are not drawn on to extension activities which just repeat what they have already done. Again, the twenty-minute check can pick this up. This is not to deny the effectiveness of learning through teaching another child, just to evaluate it for the sub-teacher.

Have high expectations for all children

As we recorded earlier, there is no research correlation between success and family background, race, national origin or financial status. The correlation with success is attitude. Research has also shown that low achievers are:

- less likely to be asked by the teacher to contribute; teachers are most likely to ask children who they think are the most likely to answer the question, and give them more time to respond
- less likely to receive praise from, and have eye contact and general interaction with, the teacher
- more likely to have their conduct emphasised, rather than their academic achievement
- more likely to be at the receiving end of rudeness, lack of interest and inattentiveness from the teacher
- more likely to be physically separated from the rest of the class.

Raise expectations

Raise expectations by:

- offering praise which is sincere and specific
- calling equally on all the children
- giving children at least five seconds to answer
- making eye contact when children speak, and listening to what they have to say
- grouping children in different ways for other activities, if they are already ability-grouped for English and maths
- showing an interest in the children's lives
- modelling the respect and courtesy you expect
- encouraging children to set goals for learning.

Value diversity

Schools provide the perfect forum for learning about diversity, and educational publishing companies are very much better than in the past at conveying the richness of our cultures in their books, resources and posters. The curriculum has to be culturally responsive if it is to grow: we have always borrowed good ideas and adaptability is a key factor to survival. The culturally responsive teacher needs to show that the cultural diverse curriculum:

- is integrated, not simply an add-on
- is authentic and connected to children's real lives
- has clear learning objectives
- recognises multiple intelligences
- is part of a coordinated whole-school strategy, with good staff support and resources.

It needs to avoid:

- the 'super-hero' syndrome
- stereotyping
- concentrating on particular features, e.g. faith.

Research on becoming an effective, caring teacher

Personal qualities

At the very beginning of this guide we looked at teachers in our own lives. When we interview students we look for personal qualities during the course of the interview because we feel that they help influence behaviour and performance in positive ways. Qualities include warmth, patience, tolerance, curiosity, humour and liveliness.

Other qualities are less obvious in an interview and, indeed, can only been identified once you start teaching. Fortunately many of the qualities required by effective teachers can be taught if the initial qualities are there. Much research has been done in this field, and you will find it useful to compare research findings with your own performance and with expert teachers with whom you work.

Kounin (1970), researching into effective personal teaching qualities, found that expert teachers shared three important behavioural qualities which enabled them to 'nip problems in the bud'. These were:

1 **'with-it-ness'**– teachers let children know that they are aware of what is happening all the time. They regularly scan and monitor the classroom and position themselves where they can see all the children. Student teachers often find this skill very difficult, particularly after they have spent time working with small groups. The skill can be developed and starts when working with the small group. Make sure that you are aware of what else is going on in the room. If a child from outside your group is misbehaving, make sure that you take action if the teacher has not seen what is going on. If you ignore it, they will mis-learn.

2 **overlapping** – good class managers can do more than one thing at the same time without disrupting the class. They can work with individuals or a small group and still deal with other children who have questions. This involves giving children routines for seeking help and teaching them to discern which questions warrant your immediate attention.

3 **pacing** – Kounin also found that effective teachers pace their teaching–learning sessions well. They keep attention on instruction and not on misbehaving children. This is done by avoiding extended reprimands or overreactions and ignoring minor inattentions. Serious misbehaviour is promptly attended to in non-disruptive ways, e.g. eye contact, a brief comment, a question directed at the miscreant. This lesson momentum or pace is only possible when you are well prepared.

Kounin also found that effective teachers were no different from ineffective teachers in responding to or dealing with misbehaviour after it had occurred. The significant difference was teacher behaviour prior to the child's misbehaviour. 'With-it-ness', overlap activities and maintaining the momentum not only prevented misbehaviour, but also helped to deal with it if/when it occurred.

Brophy and Evertson (1976), in an extensive review of classroom research into effective teaching, found other important teacher qualities associated with good child behaviour and discipline. These include:

• **self-confidence** – this enables teachers to hear complaints without becoming authoritarian or defensive. For the student teacher this is particularly difficult as it is coupled with a lack of information about children. Children test student teachers – 'We've done this before'; 'This is boring'. You need self-confidence in order to evaluate the value of the comments and react accordingly. The important thing to remember is that you are not alone. The class teacher, mentor and college tutor can give support, but only if you have enough confidence to ask for it in the first place. You then need to decide which strategies to adopt.

• **positive attitudes** – this sounds too obvious to mention, but researchers in classrooms have found over and over again that children respond well to teachers who show that they like and respect them. This involves getting to know children. Running an after-school or lunchtime club is an ideal way to do this as it involves sharing an interest and establishing a good rapport. Spending time with children in the playground is useful, but take care that they are not always the same children, to avoid them being labelled as teacher's pets.

• **high expectations** – if you expect children to be able and responsible, they tend to act that way.

• **authoritative leadership** – Brophy and Evertson found that effective teachers seek feedback and consensus on decisions and make sure that children understand their decisions. Much commercial research has been done on effective leadership in business and the conclusions are the same for business as for schools. Authoritative leadership is more effective than either authoritarian rule or non-directed, laissez-faire leadership.

Prevention is better than cure

One of the teaching standards requires trainee teachers to 'monitor and intervene when teaching to ensure sound learning and discipline'. In effect, it starts before this, because there are many things that teachers can do to create appropriate learning behaviours. These include good class-management strategies, effective instructional strategies and an awareness of children's emotional needs.

Class management

Research shows that effective teachers spend very little time dealing with misbehaviour. They do not just ignore the behaviour; they establish strategies to prevent children's misconduct. We looked at several of these good class-management strategies in Section 1, and you will have recorded several during your time in school. They include:

- routines
- consistent enforcement of negotiated rules
- careful lesson planning
- smooth transitions between lessons and activities.

Effective instructional strategies

Effective instructional strategies can also help to reduce children's misconduct, and we looked at some of these in Chapter 2 on children's learning:

- giving children structured choices
- addressing different intelligences and learning styles
- keeping children motivated and engaged.

Children's emotional needs

Good teachers address children's emotional needs by:

- fostering their self-esteem
- teaching them to be responsible and fair
- showing them how to resolve conflicts
- encouraging cooperation and collaboration
- helping them to value individual differences and talents.

Theoretical approaches to child management

Ayers and Gray, in *Classroom Management*, provide an easy guide to theoretical approaches to classroom management (1998, see Bibliography). It gives a good framework for understanding the philosophy behind the many different and varied ways in which children are managed in schools. It also provides an insight into your own strategies and suggests ways in which these may need to be extended, refined or even rethought. They identify seven major approaches:

1 *The counselling approach* – major proponents Carl Rogers, H. Ginott, T. Gordon and Bill Rogers. Teachers with this approach concern themselves with promoting effective communication between themselves and their children. It acknowledges that people see and interpret the world differently and that teachers need to facilitate learning by making it meaningful for children. Children need to be respected and valued and teachers use helping and preventive skills. Many classroom discipline plans are based on this type of approach.

2 *The democractic approach* – major proponent R. Dreikus. The democratic teacher helps and redirects children to develop self-discipline and self-motivation. This contrasts with the autocratic teacher, who dominates children and inflicts punitive consequences for rule-breaking.

3 *The behavioural approach* – major proponents I. Pavlov and B. Skinner. This provides a simple, practical and effective approach which can be a powerful agent of change. It has had a bad press in the past, but is now a popular approach because it is easy to learn, straightforward to apply and embodies a systematic approach to assessment and target setting. It is based on a theory of learning which assumes that behaviour is primarily a response to observable events; that behaviour is determined by its consequence, and because it is learnt it can be unlearnt. The practical aspect of this theory is that it provides a systematic methodology for behaviour assessment because it provides for a baseline to be established, which can later be examined after behaviour has been modified.

4 *Research-based empirical approach* – major proponent J. Kounin. This work is based on looking at what goes on in classrooms. It is not based on any particular psychological or educational theory, and details of Kounin's practical findings are given earlier in this chapter.

5 *Cognitive approach* – main proponents A. Beck, A. Ellis and A. Bandura. This looks at the ways in which our cognitive processes influence the ways in which we learn and influence the behaviour of both teachers and children. 'Cognitions' are defined as including beliefs about learning and behaviour, self-image, self-esteem, attitudes and imaginings. There is a recognition that these cognitions need not be based on fact. Practical outcomes include

teaching self-motivation, identifying and clarifying beliefs, counteracting distorted beliefs and modelling good behaviours.

6 *Ecological and ecosystemic approach* – main proponents A. Molnar and B. Lindquist. This theory rests in the belief that problems in classroom management arise out of a negative environment. In Section 3 we will look at invitational learning, and in Section 1 we looked at managing a classroom environment to promote learning. Both of these strategies are based on Systems Theory. Practical applications of this theory involve environmental change and whole-school policies.

7 *Assertive discipline approach* – main proponents L. and M. Canter. This is based on the theory that both teachers and children have rights and duties. Children need and respond to limits set by teachers. Teachers therefore have to set those limits and establish them with support from parents and school management. A classroom discipline plan includes rules, positive recognition and consequences. It aims to achieve a safe classroom environment, enables teachers to teach effectively and facilitates pupils' learning. Assertive discipline has been very effectively marketed in both the UK and the USA, but as with behavioural approaches, there have been many criticisms of its long-term effectiveness.

Teaching for order and control

There are chapters on teaching for order and control in all general books on teaching, and those which take a psychological perspective will take you through research that has been carried out over many years on this area of classroom and school life. There are also several books devoted solely to this area. Jim Docking's *Managing Behaviour in the Primary School* (1996) is a recent example. It covers prevention and cure, bullying and playground behaviour. Chris Kyriacou's *Essential Teaching Skills* (1997) is another classic. Ted Wragg's *Class Management* (1993) provides a complete unit to work through, either alone or with a group. The photographs in the last book make particularly good discussion points and it is interesting to note the different responses they draw from people. The books all cover much the same ground, but the most recent texts will provide you with the type of supporting structures you can find in school today. All schools have some sort of behaviour policy statement, often linked to an anti-bullying policy, and two of these are included in Appendix 3 to this guide (pp. 167-176).

 Find the policy statement for behaviour or bullying in your school. Compare this statement with the two statements in Appendix 3. What do all the statements have in common? Where do the statements differ? Can you think of any reasons why your school has made mention of particular aspects which are not mentioned in either of the statements in Appendix 3?

The purpose of a behaviour policy is to support the aims of the school. The staff in the two schools featured in Appendix 3 drew up the policy statement together and, like all policy statements, they are reviewed through an ongoing programme of policy renewal to take account of new circumstances and any changes in the law. Neither contains a statement on holding policy. Any policy must go through the governing body, and schools often have the name and signature of the chair of governors on all their policy statements. Schools also monitor and evaluate behaviour policies as part of this ongoing cycle of change and review. Clarke and Murray (1996) give a very practical overview of developing and implementing a whole-school behaviour policy.

Discipline

The goal of any behaviour policy is to teach self-discipline so that children can make progress with their learning. In order to teach this we need to be quite sure that we understand what it means, and also acknowledge that there are cultural differences which may influence how we approach this with particular children. Good discipline strategies are those that prevent problems. These include:

- **instruction** – actively teaching children to be responsible for their behaviour. This involves providing them with strategies for governing their own actions, e.g. 'count to ten before taking an action which might hurt you or someone else', and the value of following reasonable rules. As we saw earlier, it is important to practise these strategies with children.

- **management** – working with children to create and enforce classroom rules and routines.
- **positive reinforcement** – of good behaviour as well as negative consequences for misbehaviour.

Behaviour problems

Behaviour problems are those which interfere with your teaching and children's learning. They interfere with classroom life and destroy a purposeful working environment. As with effective teaching qualities, a great deal of research has gone into this area and, again, the general psychology texts and more specific individual behaviour management manuals give more details. Briefly, findings show that many children with behaviour problems share one characteristic: poor self-image. This manifests itself in pervasive problems which influence the whole of the child's life:

- uncertainty about feeling good about themselves
- physical and/or verbal fighting
- insensitivity
- lack of self-discipline
- inattentiveness, poor listening skills, lack of sustained concentration
- disregard for their own, other children's or the school's property
- stealing
- failure to put things away and clean up after themselves
- doing only what they want to do
- constant socialising
- depression, withdrawal, boredom, apathy
- constant demands for their rights.

 Identify a child in your class who displays at least four of the above characteristics. What strategies are you adopting to help the child?

> Observe the strategies adopted by the class teacher and other adults working with the child. If the child has an individual educational programme, what strategies and targets are given on this?

Strategies for managing

There are many texts which suggest different strategies for handling children with behaviour problems, and the skill comes in evaluating these for any particular child. Here are some more generic pieces of advice:

- Keep calm. This is much easier to write than to do. Once you become frustrated and agitated it becomes contagious. It helps not to take the child's behaviour personally.
- Set a positive tone and model an appropriate response. Robb and Letts (*Creating Kids Who Can*), using their experience with many troubled children, suggest using the 'I-messages'. This involves discussing problem behaviours with the child, and lets you tell the child how their behaviour makes you feel. An effective statement would include describing the behaviour, stating the effects of the behaviour, and stating how it made you feel. It may tell the child what to do to correct it, or it may be more open-ended, inviting the child to find a solution. Circle time and role-play can also be used to raise these issues in a more public forum. This gives the child the opportunity to respond positively.
- Make sure children understand it is their behaviour you dislike, not them. Many children with poor self-image need to be told this directly: 'I like you, David, but I find your behaviour unacceptable'.
- Do not blame, or use sarcasm or ridicule.
- Avoid win/lose situations and emphasise problem solving, rather than punishment. Jenny Mosley's 'circle time' materials, outlined in *Quality Circle Time in the Primary Classroom*, are particularly useful here. A good personal and social education programme encourages children to talk about their feelings and concerns. Circle time strategies often provide them with the language they need to describe their feelings.
- Insist children take responsibility for their behaviour and model the behaviour you expect. If you want consideration, then you must model it.

- Ensure children understand their misbehaviour. Sometimes it will need to be described and very young children may need it acted out. Children need to be clear what is wrong before they can understand the consequences of their actions.
- Be aware of cultural differences: a child looking at the floor when being told off would be regarded as defiant in some cultures and respectful in others.
- Encourage cooperative behaviour and offer cooperative activities. Build up a positive group identity.
- Actively teach personal and social skills. Children's literature, both fiction and non-fiction, can be useful here.

Five persistent problems

Bill Rogers has worked on behaviour management all over the world. In *The Language of Discipline* (1990) he identifies five distinct 'tricky personalities' and the strategies teachers can use to handle them. Do you recognise children in your class? Do you recognise adults you know?

1 The chatterbox
- Give a positive direction, e.g. 'Face this way Jane', followed by 'thanks'. He finds that using 'thanks' rather than 'please' communicates the expectation that the child will comply.
- Give a strategic pause after identifying the child – this communicates the expectation that the child will look towards you and listen. This can just be a slight pause after using a pupil's name.
- Don't get drawn into secondary issues – singled-out children may sulk or argue; acknowledge their feelings but return the focus back to the primary issue. If the child says 'We were talking about work' the response needs to acknowledge this, but you should redirect the focus, e.g. 'Maybe you were, but I want you to face the front and listen, thanks'.

2 The clinger
- Start tactically ignoring, keep the focus on the lesson and reward non-clinging behaviour.
- Establish alternative routines – the card system described earlier, where children have an index card folded and taped into a pyramid; the 'ask three' strategy, where the child must ask three children before asking the teacher.

3 The boycotter
- Offer a choice, or apparent choice, with consequences attached: 'If you choose not to work now, you will need to do it during your free time'. This lets children know that they have control over their own behaviour. It is their responsibility.
- Give time – if you turn away and respond to another child, the boycotter has the chance to comply without losing face.
- Re-establish the relationship with the child as soon as possible. This can be done after the child has complied with a smile or comment.

4 The debater
- As with the chatterbox, focus on the primary behaviour and do not get drawn into the debate.
- Avoid overreacting, which will only extend the conflict.
- Avoid power struggles.

5 The sulker
- Again, focus on primary behaviour, not secondary. A private discussion after the lesson can help the child understand that the behaviour is not acceptable. The earlier in the year, or practice, that this can be done, the better. Time the invitation carefully so that it comes just before the discussion. This avoids a prolonged discussion/sulk on 'What have I done?'.
- Be positive and explain how such behaviour affects working relationships. Be pleasant so that the relationship can be repaired.

Tips from teachers

Ask teachers you know what tips they can give you for disciplinary action.

Schools have their own procedures and you need to know and follow these.

- time out in another class, in another part of the room (not for too long, or they will forget what they have done)
- make sure the child knows what they have done wrong
- don't humiliate children
- don't use schoolwork as a disciplinary measure
- don't punish when you are angry
- don't punish the whole class for one individual
- have a group of lightweight punishments as a first step
- last in the queue for lunch
- removal of an in-school privilege, e.g. lunchtime club
- removal of a home privilege – needs to be done with parents.

Positive and assertive discipline

Behaviour management is now big business and several consultancy companies provide advice on improving discipline within schools. The better ones relate their strategies to educational theories linked with effective practices (as mentioned above). Two distinct strategies advocated are positive discipline and assertive discipline.

Positive discipline

This means rewarding appropriate behaviours and 'disarming' misbehaviour by refusing to give it status, e.g. if a child starts demanding attention, the teacher ignores him or her, looks elsewhere and only rewards the child with attention when he or she continues with the task. This, of course, is easier in theory than in practice, and for this reason the following steps may be useful:

- **Define a goal** – what do you want children to know and value?
- **Recognise positive steps** – practise recognising and rewarding the attitudes, actions and skills that help children, e.g. Do they concentrate on their work? Can they appreciate another viewpoint?
- **Reinforce positives** – help children to notice their own accomplishments and recognise small steps forward.
- **Be positive** and appreciate progress, remembering the starting point.

Assertive discipline

This is a strategy designed by Lee Canter and set out in *Assertive Discipline* (1992) and one which is particularly popular with educational psychologists, but concerns many teachers because it appears to focus on negative, rather than positive, behaviour. Initially Canter suggested that children who misbehaved should have their names placed on the board. Later he withdrew this recommendation because it appeared to reward negative behaviour. Today he suggests a three-point strategy:

- teach specific behaviours – don't assume children know what you want; describe, discuss, model and practise the behaviour you want.
- use positive repetition – if children perform an activity as you want, comment on it, e.g. 'Thank you Susan, you have worked hard today'.
- use negative consequences – children need to know what will happen if their behaviour falls out of line.

Several LEAs have invested in the assertive discipline approach and certainly, as a whole-school approach, it has had some very positive results. Good in-service on assertive discipline involves the staff meeting over a period of time with an experienced trainer. The school draws up a whole-school approach and makes considered plans for reviewing and evaluating it. The trainer may come in later to provide additional support and overall evaluation. The major problem with assertive discipline is that once the initial training is over it can degenerate quickly, and trainee teachers pick up bits without having oversight of the overall philosophy.

Children's needs

Children have wide-ranging and complex needs. Traditionally, Maslow's 'Hierarchy of Human Needs' (1954) has been used as a framework for trainee teachers to help them understand that some needs will be of greater immediacy for children than others.

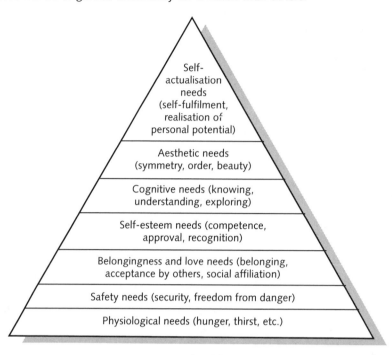

Self-actualisation needs (self-fulfilment, realisation of personal potential)

Aesthetic needs (symmetry, order, beauty)

Cognitive needs (knowing, understanding, exploring)

Self-esteem needs (competence, approval, recognition)

Belongingness and love needs (belonging, acceptance by others, social affiliation)

Safety needs (security, freedom from danger)

Physiological needs (hunger, thirst, etc.)

6 Can you think of any child in your class at the moment who may be at the base of this pyramid, i.e. does not have the very basic requirement for food, sleep and adequate shelter? What sort of strategies do schools adopt to help children for whom these basic needs are not being met?

Sadly, children lacking these very basic necessities are far more common in our classrooms than we might expect. When children's basic needs are not being met, their ability to settle down and learn will be severely restricted. Some schools have recognised this and offer a simple breakfast when children arrive in the morning. If you look carefully in the media, schools have often supported families who have been made homeless or have had their refugee status taken from them and been threatened with expulsion. Of course, it is not the 'school' which does this, it is individuals within schools who take a stand on potentially very difficult and controversial issues. Looking at children's needs in this way raises issues about the need for schools to have a much more holistic approach than they are at present being encouraged to take. A holistic programme would cover 'the whole child' – social, emotional, physical, academic, intellectual, psychological and ethical. This chapter has touched on safety needs and the need for love, affection and belonging. Good class management is about helping children to feel safe and wanted in school. Children should feel that school is a place where someone will look after them and others will not be allowed to bully or intimidate them. For some children school may be the only place where this happens. School may also be the only place where they are accepted and have a feeling of belonging. When we look at children's needs in this way, it is clear that teachers have a huge responsibility. It is one shared with colleagues and the mission statements of many schools, and the working through of the mission statement, are testaments to the professionalism of the vast majority of teachers.

The need for self-esteem

Everyone needs to feel good about themselves. Both the policy statements contained in Appendix 3 are clear that strengths should be acknowledged and children's self-esteem should be integrated into any learning programme. The focus is on the positive.

Twelve ways to help children like themselves

1 Show that you care.
2 Give children responsibility.
3 Use words and phrases that build up self-esteem and avoid those that hurt it.
4 Define limits and rules clearly.
5 Reward clearly, but do not over reward. Emphasise the positive.
6 Help children develop tolerance towards those with different values, background and ideas.
7 Discuss problem behaviour in terms of the behaviour, not the child.
8 Take children's emotions, feelings and ideas seriously.
9 Be a good role model.
10 Have high, but reasonable, expectations for children.
11 Be available.
12 Show children that what they do is important to you.

 Now see if you can write another twelve ways. Several books and other resources are available which give direct teaching strategies.

> The Bibliography and Further Reading cover all the books mentioned in this chapter, but with the growing emphasis on citizenship it is likely that other books and resources will be coming out over the next few years. So keep watching, as many of the good books in the field have been out for some time and date back to the late 1980s, to when the curriculum in primary schools was much more open and more curriculum time could be spent on aspects of personal and social education, such as raising children's self-esteem.

Self-actualisation

Self-actualisation is at the summit of Maslow's hierarchy and can be defined as the ability to reach our potential, to feel that we can be successful and have control over our own destiny. Schools have the potential to really help children achieve this by involving them in their own learning process. Teaching a child does not necessarily mean that something has been learnt. Learning is helped when children are involved on an affective level, both in terms of a high interest factor and feelings of success. The section on multiple intelligences (Chapter 2) indicates that success can be defined on many levels. This is one of many reasons why schools award certificates for a variety of different activities, acknowledging that success can be achieved in many areas.

A cautionary look at praise

Trainee teachers tend to overuse praise. This sounds like a contradiction of everything that we have just written. But we know from our own experience that if we are praised for something we are able to do easily it becomes valueless. Praise can also hide negative messages. It can be given to encourage a stumbling class reader, who then feels humiliated because he or she recognises they have a reading problem. It can be given to different groups in different ways. Walkerdine's work in maths, when she followed a cohort from primary to secondary school, showed that boys were praised for the academic substance of their work and girls for its presentation. Praise is used appropriately when it is:

• sincere and spontaneous
• delivered privately
• directed to noteworthy accomplishments
• specific
• focused on individual improvement and not comparisons with other pupils.

Chapter 8

Improving primary teaching skills

Learning objectives
- To explore teaching strategies involved in planning and teaching challenging tasks.
- To identify different types of questioning to improve teaching skills.
- To identify different types of explanation to improve teaching skills.
- To examine ways in which children can be encouraged to work together in groups to enhance learning and raise attainment levels.

The title of this chapter is taken from Ted Wragg's book *Primary Teaching Skills* (1993) and at first sight it may seem odd that you have had to wait until Section 3 before looking at this in more detail. Ted Wragg's book is based on research carried out over three years in primary classrooms at the Leverhulme Primary Project and intended for a much wider audience than student teachers. Two other books which came out of this research make ideal learning texts, particularly if students meet to discuss some of the issues. The texts are *Questioning* (Brown and Wragg 1993) and *Explaining* (Wragg and Brown 1993). Like *Class Management* (1993), in the same series, these books use photographs and illustrations to sharpen thinking and reflection.

'Planning tasks, including homework, to challenge and motivate children' is an advanced teaching skill. It follows on after other skills such as maintaining a purposeful working atmosphere and setting clear targets for children's learning. The idea of advanced level teaching skills is not a new one. In the USA, Advanced Skills Teachers have been rewarded for some years. This type of reward for good teaching is still a fairly novel idea in the UK, although good teachers are aware that their teaching skills and subject knowledge change and improve over time.

Before reading this chapter, look back at what you have already covered in Sections 1 and 2 – in particular, the sections on children's learning, classroom organisation and management, assessment and child behaviour and discipline.

 Look at the notes you have made in your own readings in these areas and reflect on any different views you hold now.

Now that you have more experience of being in school and have read more, you should be modifying some of the views you may have held at the start of your course. You are being unsuccessful as a teacher if you still think exactly the same way as you did at the start. You might find it useful to discuss with fellow students those areas of your thinking that have changed most. The relationship between research findings in psychology, children's learning and planning is a key area. Look at how often the learning theories discuss the importance of language for cognitive development. Children working in lonely isolation each day is not considered a good learning strategy. Children learn much from working together on a structured group task.

Nine of the standards for the award of qualified teacher status are concerned with the assessment, recording and reporting of children's achievements, but evidence shows that one in four students is unclear about what criteria they should adopt when grading children's assignments. The reason for this is that students tend to concentrate on planning and control. Indeed, these are vital, but by this stage you need to be moving on and looking at ways in which children can be challenged, so that their learning progresses and they achieve more than they would have done if they had stayed at home!

Planning challenge

You need to:
- have positive expectations
- invite children to learn and be challenged
- create a task-orientated environment
- invest time in teaching discipline, procedures and routines
- observe and challenge children's use of time
- set targets
- question
- explain
- use group learning so children can challenge each other.

Have positive expectations

Your expectations of the children will greatly influence their achievement in class. Expectations are different from standards. Standards are levels of achievement.

Teachers (and parents) who have positive expectations will help children reach high standards. Children tend to learn as little or as much as their teachers expect, so teachers who are positive and set high expectations will help children to attain greater academic performance than classes whose teachers are more negative and have lower expectations.

The work that some schools have done on raising attainment levels in the end of Key Stage SATs is evidence of this. Teachers in such schools have said 'our children can do better' and have then analysed the results to look at ways in which children's learning can be supported and extended. It is a delicate balance between instructional planning and planning which frustrates the learner. Negative expectations produce teaching plans which give children tasks they could do before they entered the classroom. The overuse of the photocopiable sheet as a time-filler is a good example of planning driven by negative expectations. 'The children will behave badly if left by themselves to work; if they have some colouring in to do, they will get on quietly.'

Invitational learning

Invitational learning (Purkey and Schmidt 1990) is based on three assumptions, all of which have been covered in the chapters you have already read:
- all of us have untapped potential in all areas of human development
- everyone is able, valuable and responsible and should be treated accordingly
- people, policies, procedures and teaching programmes should all invite people to reach their fullest potential.

Most of us can relate this quite easily to our own educational and working experiences. Invitational learning is about 'inviting' people (adults and children) to fulfil these propositions. Invitational learning makes these further assumptions:

- learning opportunities are everywhere, but little happens until the invitations are sent out, received and a positive response made. Your plans need to make the most of the learning opportunities inside and outside school
- a positive self-concept is the product of an invitation made. The successfully challenged child grows through success
- human potential is always there, waiting to be discovered
- the effective teacher is constantly inviting children to realise their potential
- all children are important.

Planning, teaching and class management must all be invitational if they are to convince children that you know they can do it. This requires having an invitational classroom and manner, for example:

Inviting verbal comments
'Congratulations!'
'Thank you so much.'
'You've worked really hard.'
'You can do much better than this; let me show you how.'
'Please tell me about it.'

Uninviting verbal comments
'It won't work.'
'OK, you can go now.'
'This needs tidying up.'
'You never finish.'
'What do you expect from these children?'

Inviting personal behaviours
Smiling
Listening
Being on time or early

Uninviting personal behaviours
Having a glazed or 'vacant' expression
Getting up and getting ready to move on
Arriving late and unprepared

Inviting physical environment
Attractive displays
Clean classroom, corridors and school
Living plants
Fresh air

Uninviting physical environment
Tired, worn displays
Dirty, untidy and uncared-for classroom
Dead plants, or none at all
Stuffy atmosphere

Inviting thoughts (yours!)
I could learn to do that.

Uninviting thoughts (not yours!)
I could never do that.

Think of the young children you know. Are they exciting, curious, enthusiastic and attentive? As teachers we want to invite them to stay that way.

Creating a task-orientated environment

A degree does not make you a teacher. You need to know about how children learn; different forms of planning and assessment; discipline plans; procedures and routines; motivation theory; identification of special needs; higher-order thinking skills, and much more. The task-orientated classroom which challenges learning is one in which the teacher has already learnt:

- to plan so that children are involved with their work, either when they work independently or when it is teacher- or peer-led
- to ensure children know what is expected and are generally successful
- to waste little time, through poor organisation, confusion or disruption
- to create a purposeful working atmosphere, which is work-orientated, but relaxed and pleasant
- that the textbook is not the curriculum
- to encourage independence – children enter the classroom knowing what they are going to do, e.g. self-registration, going to their seats or the learning centre, getting out materials, starting a set task

- to decide what you need to record – most schools make this decision for you, but you may want to extend this, particularly on teaching practice, to attendance, homework, class work, tests, the skills mastered, class participation, behaviour, progress over a period of time, etc.

Investing time in teaching discipline, procedures and routines

At the very beginning of your teaching practice, and also when you first start teaching, do invest time in making sure the children know that you understand the school behaviour policy/discipline plan, the procedures and the routines in the class. This minimises classroom disturbance and maximises learning. Sometimes trainee teachers find it useful to make clear to the children what they expect from them – behavioural expectations can be translated into rules. As we saw earlier, these can be general or specific. General rules cover a range of behaviours, e.g. respecting the property of others and being polite. Specific rules cover things like keeping your hands, feet and objects to yourself, and listening to instructions the first time around.

Trainee teachers are more likely to need specific rules for their classes. These need to be limited to about four or five, for example:
- follow directions the first time they are given
- raise your hand and wait for permission to speak
- keep your eyes on the teacher when he or she is talking
- keep your hands, feet and other objects to yourself
- don't bully or tease the other children.

Discipline is about positive expectations of behaviour, and rules should be limited to this rather than academic behaviour. Dangerous messages are given if the two are mixed, e.g. 'You will miss PE if you don't finish this maths'. The consequences of breaking rules can be positive or negative, i.e. you can give rewards and penalties.

Procedures are another essential part of maintaining a purposeful working environment. These – some already discussed in Chapter 7 – include procedures for dismissal, for quietening a class, for the start of the day, for children seeking help and for moving around the classroom, school and playground. If you want to establish a new procedure make sure you teach it to the children.

PROCEDURE FOR GETTING THE CLASS TO LISTEN

Explain: This is what I want you to do when I want your undivided attention. You will see me standing by the board/light with my hand up (some teachers ring a small bell, because some children may not be able to see them). When you see my hand (or hear the bell), this is the procedure:
1 freeze
2 turn, face me, pay attention and keep your eyes on me
3 be ready to listen.
Then repeat and demonstrate, perhaps asking one child to be the demonstrator. Rehearse with the whole class.

Observing and challenging children's use of time

This is so obvious that it seems insulting to have to state it, but watching many trainee teachers over several years it is possible to see that children are not challenged because there is a lack of balance between allocated time, instructional time and learning time. Allocated time is the amount of time given over to learning, i.e. the timetabled time. This will vary from subject to subject, so that so many hours per day/week will be spent on different curriculum areas.

The instructional time is when the teacher is actively teaching. The National Literacy Strategy and National Numeracy Framework are both designed to increase instructional time. This is largely because it was felt that teachers were acting too much as 'facilitators of learning materials' rather than actively teaching.

The third area of time is academic learning time. This is when children demonstrate their understanding of a skill or knowledge of the content. In the past, the attraction of many curriculum programmes, particularly maths schemes, was that the use of a workbook-based or textbook-based scheme increased this academic learning time, because children appeared to be working hard at covering the materials at a steady pace and were therefore learning. This was not always the case.

The NLS and NNF are both intended to increase not just instructional time but also academic learning time. Several small research projects are going on to evaluate whether this is happening and whether all children are making more progress as a result of the increase in whole-class instruction. Literacy coordinators often choose to do this type of assignment as part of their dissertation for a higher degree.

Student teachers have the advantage that they can observe children carefully before teaching, and these observations can inform their planning. Good classroom observation prior to planning can inform planning to maximise academic learning time. This is a luxury the class teacher does not have.

 Observe and record how two children use (i) instructional time and (ii) academic learning time. The 10-minute or 20-minute learning sheet (see page 76) will structure this for you. Plan how you would increase the time they spent in active learning. What sort of challenges do they need? Choose two children in the class you feel are underachieving, although they are performing at an average level for the class.

Academic learning time is linked to achievement. Research in the USA on international differences in children's learning and achievement using standardised tests over a period of six years (Stevenson 1996) showed that Chinese and Japanese children (compared with American children) were making more progress and had higher rates of achievement in school because:

- their attendance was better
- they spent more time on homework and Saturday schools
- they paid attention to the teacher
- they spent less time day-dreaming
- they enjoyed academic work more.

Setting targets

Good target setting is a key element to planning and teaching challenging lessons. We make statements about target setting in all the chapters because it is seen as an important means of raising achievement in school. In this context, it is worth pointing out that there is a difference between a procedure and a target. A teacher uses a procedure to tell children what they are going to do. They 'target set' when they tell them what to accomplish. Clearly, children do need to be told what to do before they start on an activity; but it is equally important that they understand what they should accomplish or achieve by the time they have finished the task. Good learning objectives, set out in teaching plans, are essential for this. Targets may vary for different children and this is part of planning for differentiation. The challenge for the teacher is working out the appropriate level of task setting and, if the task is similar for all children, ensuring differentiated outcomes for children with different learning needs and abilities. Differentiation is also planned for when you set different tasks for children, provide different resources, and give more or less adult support. The major danger of poor differentiation is that some children are insufficiently challenged and presented with tasks which they complete, without having made any progress.

Questioning

Questions are seen as another teaching strategy to challenge children and maintain the pace of lessons. When the Leverhulme Primary Project analysed the findings of over 1,000 teacher questions they found they could be sorted into three main categories:

- **managerial** – to do with running the classroom, e.g. 'Have you got your books?'
- **informational** – involving the recall of information, e.g. 'How many legs does an insect have?'
- **higher-order** – if a child had to do more than just remember facts, and analyse or make generalisations, e.g. 'Why is a bird not an insect?'

If you return to Chapter 4 (p.27 on) and look again at the lists of verbs which can be used to identify learning objectives, you can see that different levels of thinking skills require different types of questions. These are linked, in turn, to the different levels required by learning objectives. If questions are simply managerial and informational, they will not provide children with challenge. Again, as we pointed out in Chapter 4, this is not a linear progression. Five-year-olds need evaluative-type questions just as much as eleven-year-olds. Indeed, more five-year-olds ask higher-order questions than do older children.

Many trainee teachers find it useful to write down the types of questions they want to ask. The advantage of doing this is that you can analyse what sort of category the majority of your questions fall into. As you become more experienced, you will find that you do not keep to the set pattern of questions, but adapt them in response to children's answers. This is the higher-level skill.

Example

1 KNOWLEDGE: These questions show how well children have remembered previously learnt material by recalling facts, terms, basic concepts and answers.

Key words:

who	omit	find	show	name
what	where	how	spell	relate
why	which	define	list	tell
when	choose	label	match	recall
select				

Questions
- What is … ?
- Where is … ?
- How did … happen?
- Why did … ?
- When did … ?
- Which one … ?
- Can you list the three … ?

2 COMPREHENSION These questions demonstrate understanding of facts and ideas by organising, comparing, translating, interpreting and giving descriptions.

Key words:

compare	interpret	illustrate	relate	summarise
contrast	explain	infer	rephrase	show
demonstrate	extend	outline	translate	classify

Questions
- How would you classify the type of … ?
- What facts or ideas show … ?
- What can you say about … ?
- Which is the best answer … ?
- Can you say that in your own words … ?

3 APPLICATION These questions solve problems in new situations by applying acquired knowledge, facts and rules in a different way.

Key words:

apply	construct	make use of	plan	utilise
build	develop	organise	select	model
choose	interview	experiment with	solve	identify

Questions
- How would you use … ?
- What examples can you find to … ?
- How would you solve … ?
- What would result if … ?
- What questions would you ask in an interview with … ?

4 ANALYSIS These questions examine and break down information into parts by identifying motives or causes. They make inferences and find evidence to support generalisations.

Key words:

analyse	contrast	divide	simplify	conclusion
categorise	discover	examine	test for	list
classify	dissect	inspect	function	take part in
compare				

Questions
- What are the parts or features of ….?
- Can you list the parts … ?
- How would you categorise … ?
- What ideas justify … ?
- What is the theme … ?

5 SYNTHESIS Bring information together in a different way by combining elements in a new pattern or proposing alternative solutions.

Key words:

build	construct	imagine	predict	discuss
choose	design	invent	propose	modify
combine	develop	make up	solve	elaborate
compile	estimate	originate	solution	test
compose	formulate	plan	suppose	improve

Questions
- What changes would you make to solve … ?
- What would happen if … ?
- Can you invent … ?
- How would you adapt … to create a different … ?
- What way would you design … ?
- Can you predict the outcome if … ?

6 EVALUATION Questions which present and defend opinions by making judgements about information, validity of ideas or quality of work based on a set of criteria.

Key words:

award	select	compare	estimate	prove
choose	support	judge	agree	disprove
conclude	estimate	value	mark	explain
justify				

Questions
- Would it be better if ... ?
- What choice would you have made ... ?
- What information would you use to support the view ... ?
- How would you evaluate ... ?
- Why was it better that ... ?
- How would you justify ... ?

Several of these questions appear in the writing frames material set out in the NLS. These higher-order questions can be used with young children as we tease out their ability to evaluate, judge and make choices.

In their book *Questioning*, George Brown and Ted Wragg work through six units (1993). They not only look at types of questions we ask but also why we ask them, the tactics that are involved in effective questioning, the sorts of lessons we teach, the process of learning, and key questions in relation to the objectives for a lesson.

They also touch on the type of questions asked by children. Children are in the odd position in school of answering questions when the questioner already knows the answer. It is not surprising that children have problems asking higher-order questions, if the models they are provided with are restricted. As most of us know, the vast majority of questions children ask are procedural, e.g. 'Is it home time yet?' If planning and teaching are to challenge children, they need to motivate, interest and enthuse them. Concrete evidence of this would be in the types of questions they then ask, both of the teacher and each other. Teaching children to ask questions is a skill in itself. It is possible to start the process by looking at the types of words which can be used to ask questions – 'who', 'what', 'why' and 'when'. Encourage children to ask questions starting with 'what' and then join them in looking at the different types of questions they have asked. Some they will know the answers to; others they cannot possibly know, e.g. 'What will tonight's lottery numbers be?', and for others the answer can be researched. Then look at the way in which sentence construction can be changed to phrase a question. This type of question-creating activity can take place in the word-level and sentence-level work of the literacy hour, and can be linked to the type of questions which you want children to be able to ask if they are following different subject areas.

Explaining

Another key pedagogical skill for challenging children lies in the effectiveness of the explanations given by their teachers. Wragg and Brown have also written this work into a useful distance-learning text, *Explaining*. They examine what is meant by 'explaining', strategies of explanation, analysing explanation, the need to know subject matter in order to explain it, and effective explaining.

'An explanation can help someone understand:
- **concepts** – including those which are new or familiar to the learner, like 'monarch'
- **cause and effect** – that darkness is caused by the absence of light
- **procedures** – classroom rules
- **purposes and objectives** – the purpose of the activity and what is expected to be learnt as a result of it
- **relationships** – between people, things and events
- **processes** – how people behave'. (adapted from Wragg and Brown 1993)

The section on explaining in relation to subject matter is particularly useful when related to the role of the subject specialist. The work of Bobbie Neate, *Finding Out About Finding Out*, also identifies some of the language involved in subject-specialist explanations (1999). She highlights those found in non-fiction texts, but oral explanations often use the same type of language, particularly when there is uncertainty about the content and the explanation is written down and read aloud to the children.

Using group learning so children can challenge each other

If you look back at your readings on children's learning, many psychologists have shown the importance of oral language as a means of cognitive development. This is not just true for children, but for adults as well. Many of the support mechanisms for people undertaking distance – learning courses are designed not just to give moral support, but also to advance learning. The onus for the distance – learner is on them to make the human contacts necessary to increase learning. The onus on the primary teacher is to plan for genuine collaborative and cooperative work, where children's learning is enhanced through group work. This is another strategy to increase learning time, and is not intended to replace instructional time.

The importance of group learning

Catherine McFarlane, of the Development Education Centre in Birmingham, suggests seven different reasons why group learning is important for children (McFarlane 1991):

- **for effective learning** – where it encourages the creative sharing and generating of ideas. Of course, this must be linked to good group organisation, and group sizes should not be so large that children can slip into inactivity and not be missed by other group members.
- **for working together** – learning can be too individualised if children work through textbooks and sheets by themselves. Through well-organised group work children can develop self-confidence and maximise opportunities for building skills.
- **for open-ended learning** – group learning allows children to take more responsibility for and control over their own learning. Of course this means acknowledging many of the other factors covered in this chapter, e.g. positive expectations of children's behaviour and motivation to learn.
- **for confidence-building** – it takes confidence to share opinions and ideas in a class discussion. Small-group work helps children test out their thoughts on others and clarifies their ideas. As we all know, talk is a valuable medium for sorting out our own ideas.
- **for building on enthusiasm** – group work involves children being active for a large proportion of the time.
- **for learning to value their own experience** – all children come to school with a wealth of experience, and group work gives them the opportunity to talk about and share this with others.
- **children with English as an additional language** – these children can benefit when they are working in a group with children who share the same heritage language, but whose English is stronger. They may also feel more confident about trying out words and sentences in a small group. It encourages them to talk in their own language and explore ideas at a more advanced level than they may be able to do in English.

Types of group

Groups may be self-selected, chosen by the teacher, or random. It is best to start in pairs and then move into fours. Some children can work well in groups of six, but effective participation is more strained and it becomes easier for a child to opt out if he or she is one of six. Some other points to think about to support challenging learning in groups are:

- **making sure that the group task is clearly defined** – this probably works best with older children, when the group task is written down and a concrete learning outcome is expected, e.g. a poster, role play.
- **roles** – when first starting to work in groups, it is easier to give each child a specific role so that they are clear what their purpose is in the group. For classes used to a very structured working environment, a task card with the roles on it helps.
- **rules** – small-group rules are much the same as class rules, e.g. only one person should talk at a time; but many children are tempted to see small-group work as family-type relationships, where everyone talks at once and snatching someone else's property is part of being in a

small group. As with whole-class management, set out the ground rules, practise, and keep the expectations that they will work. For the child who has real problems working in a group, make sure that he or she has a task which covers the learning objectives, but avoids them becoming disruptive to other children.

- **evaluation** – valuing children's evaluation of small-group work is important, and several recording checklists are available for children to complete after they have worked in a group. The plenary session can also be used to look at the success of a group activity and ways in which it can be improved next time.

- **use of circle-time activities** to promote skills useful for group work – there are many publications, both new and old, on activities for learning skills in group work. These are useful for any class as they raise cooperation as a discussion point and establish a series of behaviours to encourage it. Older publications tend to come under the heading of development education; more recent ones can be found under social education, citizenship and personal and social education. There are an increasing number of posters about co-operative working and a glance through most current educational publishers' catalogues will show how publishers are responding to the demand for more materials in this area. Hopscotch Educational Publishing (01926 744227), for example, produce a series of teacher resource books in this area.

Homework

Homework for primary school children has been a controversial issue for a long time. Below are some of the arguments made for and against it. Perhaps you can think of some more.

Some pros and cons

For	Against
1. Gives children something worthwhile to do in the evenings. 2. Consolidates work done during the day. 3. Provides an opportunity for parents to work alongside their children. 4. Raises standards of achievement. 5. Exploits resources for learning which may exist at home, local study centres and libraries.	1. Children work hard enough at school and need to have a break from academic work. 2. Homework tasks are often time wasting and children could be doing more worthwhile activities. 3. Many primary children have an active social life which takes in activities which are being cut out of the pimary school curriculum, e.g. gym club, swimming, dance, drama, music. Homework means they have less time to do these. 4. Causes conflict between parents and children. 5. Some children do not have facilities and resources for doing homework. Homework is discriminatory.

In 1998, the government published guidelines for primary schools on homework. These can be found on http://www.dfee.gov.uk/opps These guidelines encouraged schools which did not have a homework policy to have a written policy which 'is publicly available'. As a direct consequence of this most schools now have a policy. This must be followed to the letter – children should not simply be asked to 'finish off the work'. This is too vague, and will lead to some children having very little to do and others too much. In many schools homework is part of the lesson planning and challenging tasks need to be clearly structured so that parents, as well as children, can see their purpose.

The importance of good planning for homework is made more obvious by the government's recommended time allocation for daily homework activities. This starts at 20 minutes per day for children in reception classes to 50 minutes per day for children in Years 5 and 6.

In 1999, the government introduced statutory home–school agreements. These link closely into the government's parent–school partnership philosophy for the ways in which academic standards can be raised. The framework for these agreements can be found on http://www.dfee.gov.uk/has/thelaw.htm

The subject manager/specialist

The role of the subject manager in the improvement of teaching skills is often given high priority in OFSTED reports. This has resulted in more and more emphasis on teachers' own subject knowledge. Training institutions have been encouraged to look at the role of the subject manager or coordinator in relation to students' main degree subject. Many institutions training postgraduate students only take students with a degree in a primary National Curriculum subject. Undergraduate trainee teachers may only be allowed to take one Primary National Curriculum subject to degree level. This can create a very narrow perspective; for example, primary modern languages teaching is being identified as a key area for development, yet many training institutions would not train a linguist for primary teaching.

Fortunately, once inside school, there is more flexibility. There has to be, because the majority of trainees are on the arts and humanities side and many move – very successfully – into subject managers for mathematics and science. Students with degrees in the social sciences often find that their degree has enough history or science or mathematics within it to make them well qualified to take up a leadership post in these areas. Students who have worked in industry or offices frequently develop good skills in modern technology, which can be used very successfully to lead subjects such as ICT, design and technology and art in a primary school. The professional knowledge and understanding aspect of subject management has been aided by the publication of recommended schemes of work by the DfEE and QCA. Most schools adapt these to their own needs, but they do provide a starting point for trainee teachers to examine.

The TTA see their principal aim as 'promoting effective and efficient professional development for teachers and headteachers .... The cornerstone of this work is the development of national standards for the teaching profession to define expertise in key roles.' The key roles are identified as headteachers, subject leaders and special educational needs coordinators. In 1998, the Agency produced National Standards for Subject Leaders. These can be viewed on http://www.teach-tta.gov.uk/standards/index/htm or are available free from the TTA. They can be requested as a generic package on National Standards, or simply as the booklet for Subject Leaders.

The booklet published by the TTA for subject managers covers:
• The core purpose of subject leadership
• The key outcomes of subject leadership
• Professional knowledge and understanding
• Skills and attributes
• Key areas of subject leadership.

The booklets are short and look at fairly generic management areas. More helpful for subject management are subject leaders' handbooks produced by a number of different educational publishers.

What makes for effective teaching: a view from the children

Children's views about teaching and learning are informative. These examples come from one primary school where children's views were sought prior to the drawing up of a monitoring procedure.

Reception:
- A happy teacher
- Not being silly
- Being with friends
- Sitting nicely so we can listen

Year One
- We like it when we can do it by ourselves. We know the rules and where everything is.
- It helps us remember if we know WHY
- Lots of praise
- When it gets a bit harder
- When we are given reasons, not orders

Year Two
- When Miss brought in a skeleton
- Doing new things
- Working all the time – lots of work
- When everyone is working together, sharing and getting on
- Learning to do new things

Year Three
- Teacher talking to us and not shouting
- Getting stars
- Celebration of each other's achievements
- Listening to each other, helping each other. When we make mistakes, not laughing.

Year Four
- Energetic teacher
- Good resources

Year Five
- Everyone giving 100 per cent
- Good teamwork
- Being able to use equipment, more visual, hands on
- The teacher having a sense of humour
- Challenge
- Being able to trust the teacher
- No-one having a cold

Year Six
- Different perspectives and new ideas
- When we are inspired
- The use of demonstration and concrete examples
- We need to feel we can ask for help
- We need to feel secure
- Remember our names. A respectful attitude is important.
- Sweets

One very honest Y5 child wrote: 'I enjoy sitting down talking about things other than work'. This was well balanced by another child in the same class writing: 'I think it would be better if there would be more lessons in the day'.

Chapter 9

Special children

Learning objectives

- To develop skills in identifying children with special educational needs.
- To know the role of the Special Educational Needs Coordinator in order to get help in providing positive and targeted support.
- To be able to set high expectations for children with special educational needs and establish appropriate targets for them.
- To know the *Code of Practice on the Identification and Assessment of Special Educational Needs.*
- To develop skills involved in establishing effective working relationships with staff supporting children with special educational needs.
- To develop skills in identifying able and gifted children and knowledge of strategies to support, extend and challenge them across the curriculum.
- To know about the needs of children who are not yet fluent in English and ways in which they can be supported within mainstream classes.

Of course, all children are special, so before working through this chapter, look back at Sections 1 and 2 to remind yourself of specific aspects of children's learning (Chapter 2) and the ways in which achievement is measured (Chapter 6).

Each child's uniqueness

In Section 1, and Chapter 2 in particular, we looked at the uniqueness of each individual child, including the ways in which he or she learns. The background reading in that Section will have informed you about different learning theories and given an insight into different learning styles. Each child has special educational needs, so we need to look further at how the law defines particular children as having special educational needs.

Defining special educational needs through measuring achievement

In the UK an individual's achievement is measured as laid down by central government in terms of their English and maths ability. The government has identified the acquisition of specific levels in the Standardised Assessment Tasks (SATs) as being indicative of the attainment of that particular child. Children who do not have Level 4 in both English and maths at the end of Key Stage 2 are seen to be underachieving in relation to the 'national average'. The overall scores from a cohort of children are then used as a measure for the standard of education in the school. This, in turn, is put with other schools in the same LEA and used as a measure of the performance of that LEA. When schools and LEAs are inspected by OFSTED, these SAT results are seen as important indicators of the success of the school or authority.

As part of the situation analysis for your second school placement, look at the SATs results, which can be found in the school prospectus. Compare the school results with the national results which, by law, must also be included in the school prospectus. Is the school in line with other schools nationally, or is it above or below? Has the school analysed its results and looked for specific patterns? How are these being addressed?

Schools analyse and evaluate their SATs results and this is also done nationally. One pattern which has emerged from this analysis is the general underachievement of boys in all the core areas. Assessment coordinators look at possible reasons for this and strategies that can be adopted to improve performance. Nationally, the QCA (1998) has looked at raising boys' achievement in English, and has recommended specific strategies to improve it. What does the pattern look like in your school? Can you think of reasons for it? Setting high expectations in terms of behaviour, concentration and appropriate learning strategies may be an important element in raising attainment. Most LEAs cluster particular schools together, so that comparisons can be made with similar schools. There are several different ways of doing this, but one of the most common is that of free school meals. The percentage of children taking free school dinners in a school is seen as a measurement of the economic deprivation within its catchment area. The national average for free school dinners is 23 per cent. Other indicators used by OFSTED teams when inspecting a school and deciding whether it is giving value for money include the number of children on the special needs register and the numbers speaking English as an additional language. Can you think of any factors which might make free school dinners a questionable measure of economic deprivation?

Schools' definitions of special educational needs through attainment

Schools use three basic methods of measuring a child's performance against a 'national' average.

1 *Use of National Curriculum criteria*

Many schools use the levels in English and maths set out in the National Curriculum as a basic measurement for defining what is the 'average' for a particular age group. This is clearer at Key Stage 1 than at Key Stage 2. At Key Stage 1, the 'average' child should be reaching Level 1 in Year 1 and Level 2 in Year 2. In Key Stage 2, there is often a gap between what is expected of children in different year groups. This is one reason why an increasing number of schools are purchasing the government's SATs material for Years 3–5 and using this as a baseline for defining average, below average and above average attainment.

Schools gather data in different ways. One school has set up a Concerns Register in the nursery and records on this any 'deviant', i.e. not average, behaviour. This covers social, emotional, intellectual and developmental dimensions. This is reviewed and updated throughout the year and continues when children move into the reception class. It is not resourced because of lack of funds, but also because it is acknowledged that children mature at different rates. Indeed, many of the children who are identified as having indications of special needs on their initial entry into the nursery are later removed from the Register. Date of birth is often a key issue, as children born between May and August have had less time to mature before entering school. In Year 1, there are formal reviews of all children. Children's intellectual development is measured using the levelling process in the National Curriculum. They are asked to produce free writing, read their reading book and use early maths skills. A general decision is made that if the children are not working at Level 1 of the National Curriculum they are put on to a special programme. This involves working in groups, which are particularly carefully monitored. In Year 2, this National Curriculum levelling process is used to identify children who are only working in English at the 2c level or below. A child gaining Level 2 in English can do it at different points – 2a, 2b or 2c. It is now generally agreed that 2c is a very low level and children reaching this are at risk because they are unlikely to be able to reach Level 4 by the time they have finished in the primary school. The children most at risk are the older children in the Year 2 class.

2 *Measurement of attainment by textbook*

Schools also use published schemes as measures of child performance. English and maths schemes which contain textbooks generally arrange this into notional age ranges, so Book 1 is for Year 1, Book 2 for Year 2, etc. This makes good commercial sense as schools purchase 15 or 30 copies for each class. Teachers make very different use of such texts, but generally children are ability grouped when working through the texts. Some children are identified early because they cannot cope with the text at all. Others are identified only as they struggle with it and others as they work through at a slower pace than others. By the end of Year 3 it is usually possible to see that children who are still on the Year 2 or 1 text are those with particular learning difficulties.

3 *Standardised testing*

An increasing number of schools are using standardised tests to identify those children who have learning difficulties and those who are very able. Sometimes this indicates a concern about the validity of the SATs as an objective form of measurement, but often schools use these in addition to the SATs. One of the best sources of information about the range of standardised tests available is the National Foundation For Educational Research (NFER) catalogue. The NFER has a huge bank of tests covering many areas of learning, but schools will often use reading and maths tests from other sources as well. These tests are 'standardised' against a norm, i.e. they have been given to a large number of children of a specific age. This enables a distribution curve to be drawn up and children can be identified as being on the norm (average), below the norm and above the norm. Children who fall into the bottom sixth are generally those considered to be at risk. This does perhaps deflect attention away from children who may be underperforming, but are on the norm or above. An increasing number of schools are using standardised tests to identify underachievement amongst children who seem to be performing satisfactorily in class.

It is perhaps worth mentioning at this stage that much of the controversy about using standardised tests is that they have been used to label children and place them in particular programmes. Test developers argue strongly that a child's test scores should be just one of many different pieces of information contributing to placement and performance setting. They should never replace teacher judgement, although ironically they may be most useful when they disagree with such judgements.

Interpreting scores requires some understanding of statistics. Results are reported in different ways, including composite scores, scores in major skill areas, individual item analysis, etc. Some are more appropriate and useful than others. The test manuals are full of useful information and should be read or referred to before using the test. Test scores can reveal important discrepancies, and differences in average scores between certain groups of children reveal differences in opportunities to learn. Standardised tests are not all equally valid and reliable, i.e. measuring what they claim to measure and providing individual scores which remain consistent over multiple tries. Their increasing use suggests that more time should be spent during initial teacher training on their use and ways in which children can be supported in learning how to take such tests. The section on assessment in Chapter 6 suggested four major skill areas needed when taking such tests. Parents also need to be informed, so that they can provide the support children need before taking such a test and understand the results which come from it.

Some areas are very much easier to test than others, and in Chapter 2 we looked at Gardner's theories of multiple intelligences. The SATs in English and maths measure logical-mathematical and verbal-linguistic intelligences. This means that children who have strengths in other areas – musical-rhythmic, visual-spatial, bodily-kinaesthetic, interpersonal-social and intrapersonal-introspective – are unable to demonstrate their achievement formally through the SATs. McGrath and Noble (1997) provide some practical strategies to deal with this, although these have not been developed into standardised tests.

Children with special educational needs often have strengths in areas other than English and maths, and many children with learning disabilities have average or above average intelligence. Some may be gifted. Sadly, many people outside schools still associate learning disabilities with the word 'handicap'.

An official definition of special educational needs

'A child has special educational needs if he or she has a learning difficulty which may be a result of a physical or sensory disability, an emotional or behavioural problem or a developmental delay' (Education Act 1981, see Farrell, M. 2000 Appendix 1). The 1981 Act was pivotal in changing ideas about children with difficulties. It changed the focus away from labelling the child as 'physically handicapped', 'mentally handicapped', 'educationally subnormal' or 'maladjusted'. The Act also recognised that a learning disability creates a gap between ability and performance because the mind processes words and information differently. This makes it difficult to learn, particularly in a school context, where learning experiences have to be structured in certain ways. These may be unsuited to the learning-disabled child. The Act moves the focus from the child to the situation in which the child is placed. This results in teachers:

- looking at how a learning difficulty prevents a child from learning with other children of the same age
- examining ways in which special educational provision could help them to learn.

One of the major challenges facing trainee teachers when they meet children with special educational needs is that many of the children show high intelligence and creativity in some areas. Then, when they do not perform as well as others in English and maths, it is assumed that they are being lazy. Look at areas in your own life where you might be described as 'lazy'. How often is it because you have difficulties with these areas?

Today, children who have special educational needs are described in terms of learning difficulties, emotional and behavioural difficulties, physical disabilities, sensory impairment, language difficulties or communication impairment.

The Code of Practice on special educational needs

The Code of Practice on the Identification and Assessment of Special Educational Needs was produced by the DfE and the Welsh Office in 1994. All schools will have a copy of it, together with *The SENCO Guide* (1997). *The SENCO Guide* gives good practice for Special Educational Needs Coordinators and covers IEPs and developing special educational needs policies in school. The Code gives practical guidance to LEAs and the governing bodies of all maintained schools regarding their responsibilities towards all children with special educational needs.

The Code establishes:
- that there is a continuum of special needs and this must be reflected in a continuum of provision
- that the special educational needs of most children should be met in mainstream schools
- that additional specialist help would be provided for some children to enable them to stay within mainstream schooling
- that effective assessment and provision will involve partnership between children, their parents, schools, LEAs and other agencies, including district health authorities, social service departments and voluntary bodies
- guidelines to schools and LEAs on the identification of children with special educational needs
- that all schools should have a special needs policy and issue annual reports to show how it is being implemented
- a five-stage model (not all LEAs adopted this, and some have six stages):

Stage 1: class or subject teachers identify or register a child's special educational needs. They then consult the SENCO and initial action is taken. The child at this stage might need a little more attention from the teacher, or slightly easier tasks. (This is the stage that is most likely to disappear under the current review.)

Stage 2: the SENCO takes responsibility for gathering information and for coordinating the child's special educational provision, working with the child's teachers. This results in the creation of an individual education plan (IEP) for the child.

Stage 3: teachers and the SENCO are supported by outside specialists. This is recorded in the continued provision of further IEPs.

Stage 4: the LEA considers the need for a statutory assessment. This comprises reports from a range of agencies.

Stage 5: the LEA considers the need for a Statement of Special Educational Needs. This is reviewed annually.

Parents are involved at all stages, and most LEAs provide good guidance to the process. Parents have the right of appeal if the LEA does not issue a Statement for a child who has passed through the final stage of assessment.

Individual education plan

The individual education plan (IEP) is a teaching and learning plan for the child drawn up by the SENCO. The Code of Practice states that it should cover:
- the nature of the child's learning difficulties
- action – the special educational provision, the staff involved, the frequency of support, specific programmes, activities, materials, equipment
- help from parents at home
- targets to be achieved in a given time
- any pastoral care or medical requirements
- monitoring and assessment arrangements
- review arrangements and dates.

If possible, all target setting should involve discussion with the child and non-teaching staff who support children with special needs, e.g. learning support assistants, special needs assistants, teacher assistants, special school assistants or welfare assistants.

Statement of Special Educational Needs

This is the document issued by the LEA which details what the special educational needs of the child are considered to be and what should be provided in order to meet those needs. It is estimated that only two per cent of children would have such severe and complex difficulties that significant additional resources or special schooling would be necessary to meet their needs. There is growing concern about the number of children who have statements. One of the intentions of the current review of special educational needs is to cut down on the numbers of statements. Statements should only be issued for those children who have very severe and complex needs requiring ongoing multidisciplinary assessment. The Statement comprises six parts:
1 introduction
2 special educational needs
3 special educational provision
4 placement
5 non-educational needs
6 non-educational provision.

Reports about the child are collated from parents, the school, the school medical officer and the educational psychologist. Reports may also come from the social services, specialist teachers, education welfare services, speech and language therapists, physiotherapists, occupational therapists and child psychiatrists.

Parents have a right to appeal against any decision by the LEA, and the media have reported several such appeals.

Uniformity of provision

One of the intentions of the Code is to provide uniformity of provision. This has not happened. Many of the statements made in the Code sound relatively straightforward but they are open to different interpretations. This results in an inequality of provision between LEAs and schools. This is one reason why special needs provision is under review at the moment.

- Both the Code and the Green Paper (see below) emphasise the need for early identification of problems, but do not make this specific. This leads to huge variations between schools. Some schools identify a number of children at Key Stage 1. Other similar schools leave it until the child is almost at the end of Key Stage 2. In one LEA, children move on to the school's special needs register when they are four years behind their peers; in an adjoining authority they move on to the register when they are two years behind.
- This early identification requires using 'appropriate screening instruments', but there is little guidance as to what instruments these might be or at which point to intervene.
- LEAs have different types of facilities and resources available, and this inequality permeates possible support.

The Green Paper: Excellence For All Children: Meeting Special Educational Needs

This Green Paper was published in 1997 and sets out six main themes:

1 additional support for parents
2 improving and simplifying the special educational needs framework
3 developing a more inclusive education system
4 developing knowledge and skills
5 working in partnership to meet special educational needs
6 setting high expectations for children with special needs.

One of the major intentions of the Green Paper was to improve provision by cutting down on the bureaucracy involved. This is helpful, as many SENCOs are full-time class teachers and may have minimal non-class contact, which makes it difficult to visit other classrooms and carry out their responsibilities effectively. This is particularly true in schools where a large number of children with special educational needs are identified.

Identification of children with special educational needs

A checklist approach is often used and can include social, physical and intellectual dimensions. Here is checklist provided by one school, which provides some additional areas to address.

Social
- poor attendance and/or punctuality
- frequent moves of school
- nursery attendance
- socialisation problems
- chooses younger children to play with or prefers playing by themselves

Physical
- visual – near-sighted or far-sighted, wearing inappropriate glasses, failure to wear glasses, seated in poor position to see
- auditory – temporary (glue ear), permanent – with or without hearing aid
- medical conditions, including those involving medication which may make the child drowsy

Intellectual
- discrepancy between overall intelligence and achievement or performance
- difficulty with speaking, reading, writing and maths
- difficulty with perceptions of time and space
- poor hand–eye coordination

- low self-esteem
- poor organisation
- weak short-term memory
- concentration and attention problems
- overreaction to noise and/or changes in routines
- inability to follow instructions
- hyperactivity
- poor emotional control
- weak listening skills

Poor attendance and/or punctuality may be a very simple explanation for a discrepancy between overall intelligence and achievement or performance. Many schools spend a great deal of time encouraging reluctant attendees to make an appearance. This can include self-signing, certificates and awards. When a school is inspected by OFSTED, overall attendance below 90 per cent is seen as a matter of concern, particularly if the school does not seem to be trying to improve it.

 Do you think there are any areas which have been missed here?

Many of the indicators mentioned above seem to cover behaviours many of us exhibit at one time or another, and most children will exhibit one or more of these characteristics at different times in their lives. Children with learning disabilities show more of them and display them more frequently.

Policies for special educational needs in mainstream schools

LEAs and schools all have policies related to special educational needs. Many LEAs produce additional guidance for parents. These will be attractively presented, easy to follow and freely available. You may be able to find them in the local library as well as in school.

School policies are comprehensive and will explain the Code of Practice and distinct school procedures for ensuring compliance with it. Most school policies will cover:
- a policy statement showing how the philosophy of the school is linked with its special needs policy and with the requirements of the Code of Practice
- the name of the SENCO and governor responsible for special needs
- procedures for initial identification of special needs and the responsibilities of the class teacher for this initial identification
- assessment, monitoring and review arrangements
- a description of the five different stages (see above) set out in the Code of Practice. Some LEAs have a slightly differently staged process, e.g. six stages, but the school policy will make it clear what happens at each stage
- copies of forms to be filled in at stages 1–4
- referral and review procedures
- roles and responsibilities – LEA, governors, headteacher, SENCO, class teachers, subject co-ordinators, support teachers and assistants, outside agencies
- details of parental involvement
- resources
- descriptions of different types of special needs
- suggested targets and teaching strategies
- bibliography.

Working with a learning support assistant (LSA)

Children may have additional adult support provided as part of the provision for their needs. Also, many schools use both paid and volunteer adult help to work with groups of children with special educational needs. The Code of Practice states different kinds of special need which may require additional learning support:

- mild learning difficulties
- moderate learning difficulties
- specific learning difficulties (dyslexia)
- dyspraxia
- severe learning difficulties
- profound and multiple learning difficulties
- physical disability
- sensory impairment (visual or auditory)
- language impairment
- communication impairment, including autism and Asperger's syndrome
- emotional and behavioural difficulties (including Attention Deficit/Hyperactivity Disorder – AD/HD).

Michael Farrell's *The Special Education Handbook* (2nd edn, 2000) provides a guide to understanding definitions of autism and Asperger's syndrome. Robb and Letts (1997) in *Creating Kids Who Can Concentrate* take a more radical perspective.

There are different patterns of organising this additional support. One of the most common is to place the child in a group with other children who have learning difficulties but not necessarily IEPs. The additional adult is then used to support the whole group and ensure that the child to whom they are attached is part of the class and has an opportunity to take part in group and collaborative activities. This works with varying degrees of success. It is certainly better than the child and their adult support working in isolation outside the classroom in a corridor, but some children with special educational needs can be very isolated, even if they appear at first sight to be an integral part of the class. Playtimes and lunchtimes are key times to identify such isolation and then work to effect strategies which provide genuine inclusion.

Many LEAs have excellent training programmes for staff involved with special educational needs and student teachers can learn a lot from LSAs, many of whom have followed children throughout their school career. In addition, an increasing number of those working with children with special needs have formal qualifications in areas such as nursery nursing, early childhood studies and degrees in a variety of subjects.

Any adult working in the classroom needs
- to be clear about their roles and responsibilities
- if they are paid staff, to have an effective job description which covers their duties in relation to the child, teacher and school
- to be valued as part of the learning support team
- to be given regular opportunities for planning with teacher colleagues
- to be clear about learning objectives
- to be deployed efficiently, effectively, flexibly
- to be given opportunities for training and development.

Glenys Fox, in her excellent *Handbook for Learning Support Assistants* (1998), suggests that the teacher and LSA separately fill in a checklist like the one above. They give each statement a rating from 1 to 5 – 1 being 'not at all' and 5 being 'very much' – and then compare notes. Trainee teachers are not in a position to do this, but the use made of adult support staff is often an issue in OFSTED reports.

Find out who is the SENCO in your school and ask them about their role. Start to make a file about the provision of special educational needs in the school and identify your own role in this. Your file should include the school policy and an example of a completed IEP. Make sure that you take out the child's name.

Perhaps one of the most worrying aspects of the Example job decription shown opposite is that it does not mention responsibilities towards trainee teachers. As more and more teacher training takes place in school, such job specifications need to take on the responsibility for teacher education which was once the province of the initial teacher trainers.

Target setting and special educational needs

Targets for learning are mentioned in the Code of Practice. At stage 1 of the Code a record of the nature and aims of special educational provision might include 'targets to be achieved and monitoring arrangements'. At stages 2 and 3, an IEP should set out targets to be achieved in a given time. At stage 5, it is accepted good practice to have IEPs for children with Statements, and these should include targets.

As the assessment section of Chapter 6 identified, the writing and use of targets is difficult. Target setting, where possible, should involve the child and be attainable. Most LEAs provide guidance for target setting in IEPs and the vast majority of this guidance it linked to literacy and behavioural outcomes.

Example

LEA SUGGESTED TARGETS: READING

Recognise name
Recognise letters in name
Recognise labels in classroom
Recognise sight vocabulary – 12 common words; or from reader
Recognise 50 common words
Recognise words in different formats (upper-case/lower-case/italic)
Reconstruct jumbled sentences – from reader to dictated stories

Retell familiar stories
Read own dictated stories
Read current reader with 90 per cent accuracy
Be able to predict
Complete Cloze exercises
Explain simple motives
Describe characters
Demonstrate understanding of stories
Use picture cues to 'guess' unfamiliar words
Use syntactic cues to 'guess' unfamiliar words
Sequence sentences from current reader/familiar story with partner
Sequence sentences from current reader/familiar story independently
Name favourite authors.

> **Example**

The role of the SENCO

Below is a fairly typical job description of a SENCO.

1 The administrative/managerial role
- the interpretation of legal requirements for staff, parents and governors
- the day-to-day operation of the school's special educational needs policy
- the coordination of provision for children with special educational needs
- the maintenance of the school's special educational needs register and other confidential documentation
- attendance at meetings, case conferences, etc., as necessary
- acting as a consultant member of the School Senior Management Team

2 The assessment role
- identification of children with special educational needs in collaboration with staff, parents and other professionals
- the administration and interpretation of a range of assessment instruments in consultation with support agencies
- the preparation of IEPs in conjunction with support services
- the costing and budgeting of special needs delivery

3 A teaching/pastoral role
- cooperating in joint teaching approaches, i.e. collaborative teaching, when time is available

4 A school-supportive role
- supporting colleagues with advice, ideas, materials and techniques for in-class use

5 A liaison role
- liaison with parents and the encouragement of their equal participation in the education process
- liaison with agencies and support services
- liaison with the governing body, in particular with the governor responsible for special educational needs
- liaison with the broader community to their mutual benefit

6 Staff development role
- responding to staff needs and the initiation of development programmes in conjunction with the School Development Plan
- the dissemination of information, knowledge and research pertaining to special needs

7 A collaborative role
- collaboration with SENCOs in other local schools to facilitate joint policies, the maximisation of expertise and equipment, in-service training and other cooperative ventures
- facilitating the transfer of special educational needs children between the different phases of schooling.

The IEPs below are fairly typical and you should evaluate them in terms of their use to you as a teacher. Decide what other information you would need about the children before planning and teaching. How could these IEPs be improved?

STAGE 1 ACTION PLAN

Age: 5.8   Date Plan Started: 30th October   Date for review: January

Specific Targets	Review (with measured outcomes and comments on success of strategies)
Target 1 a) Development of book awareness and appropriate behaviour; left to right tracking; picture clues; words and pictures. b) Recognise first 5 key words/New Way names. **Strategy** 1. Daily reading opportunities. Home reading opportunities. 2. Structure sentence verbally, then write and read to me. 3. Flash cards, games and worksheets.	Anna can comment on each page of a story and is beginning to point to each word when encouraged. She recognises first 5 key words and is beginning to recognise characters from New Way.
Target 2 a) Write both names correctly. b) Write own sentence starting with 'I'. c) Form each new letter into sounds book. **Strategy** 1. Write name daily. 2. Practise sentence beginning with key words 'I'.... 3. Copy each new letter into sounds book.	Anna can write both names correctly on most occasions. She recognises and can write 'I' but needs help with the rest of sentence. Her letter formation is poor.
Target 3 a) Recognise and write first 10 single letter sounds from LEA list followed by next set of 5 when ready. **Strategy** 1. Use of magnetic, sand and sponge letters; flash cards; worksheets from phonic handbook; bingo. 2. One new sound in workbook weekly.	Anna can recognise and write 8/10 letter sounds.
Target 4 a) Participate more fully in group discussion. **Strategy** 1. Give opportunity in circle time.	Anna has grown in confidence in spelling and listening sessions but needs to develop her 'talk'. She tends to shout news.

STAGE 2 INDIVIDUAL EDUCATION PLAN

Age: 10.1   Date Plan Started: September   Date for review: October Half Term

Specific Targets	Review (with measured outcomes and comments on success of strategies)
Target 1 To develop comprehension skills, within level of Wellington Square. **Strategy** Use Wellington Square workbooks and extension books.	Lizzie has worked hard in the Wellington Square stories and listened to tapes. When she is familiar with script her comprehension work is much better.
Target 2 To increase Lizzie's ability to work independently and finish a task. **Strategy** 1. Redrafting 2. Use dictionary 3. Reward system 4. Work away from Terry	Lizzie has been finishing tasks this term, with much encouragement from her mum. Well done!
Target 3 To develop phonic skills – vowel digraphs 'ai' 'oa' 'ir' 'ou'.... **Strategy** 1. Use Spelling Made Easy. 2. Word families and dictation, L.C.W and plastic letters.	Lizzie does well on look, cover, write, but can't cope as well with the dictation.

Problems with target setting

There is clearly a conflict between target setting which is very mechanistic, e.g. 'recognise name', and that which is less focused and specific, such as 'demonstrate an understanding of stories'. The former targets clearly fulfil all the criteria of target setting, but when reading them through it is easy to see that IEPs covered with such reading targets could turn children off reading for meaning. So children could achieve the targets set, but never want to pick up a book and read it for themselves.

Tony Martin, in *The Strugglers* (1993), adopts two central strategies for helping struggling readers:
1 developing children's response to literature
2 seeing the difficulty from the child's viewpoint.

Martin's ideas include:
* seeking the child's feelings and perceptions about why they are not successful
* why can't he or she read?
* what are his or her views on the nature of reading?
* a relationship between child and teacher has to be formed which takes account of and tries to explore these feelings.

He suggests special needs work sessions should be:
short – for attention span
purposeful – for motivation
interesting – naturally
supported – apprenticeship approach.

Of necessity these constraints rule out
* copying other people's work (including the teacher's)
* exercises from the board or books
* purposeless worksheets for practice
* repeating shoddy work for little purpose other than to improve it
* giving written work as punishment.

Martin provides a checklist for helping the strugglers:

Teachers can
- give confidence and retain high expectations of success
- model reading and give access to written language and texts
- share reading with the child and set up other shared reading situations
- put reading material on tape and encourage reading along with tape
- make books based on the child's own language
- make an informed diagnosis resulting in a definite reading programme
- encourage parents to become partners in the reading enterprise
- have a range of reading texts, including magazines and non-fiction
- encourage writing as communication and teach a spelling strategy for learning a writing/reading vocabulary
- draw attention to sounds, rhymes, patterns, internal structure, initial sounds
- encourage children to write the 100 most common words, many of which are meaning-free and hence often difficult to read.

Mathematics

Page 23 in the introduction of the *National Numeracy Strategy* looks at 'catering' for pupils with special educational needs and individual education plans. It will be interesting to see if this results in IEPs targeting maths as well as English.

Children with emotional and behavioural difficulties

There are an increasing number of children with emotional and behavioural difficulties in our schools, and a glance through the national figures for exclusions and suspensions in primary schools shows that numbers have risen rapidly in recent years. The term 'emotional and behavioural difficulties' includes a very wide range of conditions. It is also a term which causes a high degree of controversy, as people try to refine it further by identifying specific categories within it.

 Make a list of 'problem behaviours' you have noticed in classrooms.

Sadly, you probably found this one of the easiest tasks to undertake.
Fox (1998) suggests 21 different forms of behaviour:
- pencil tapping
- humming
- kicking the table legs
- chair rocking
- constantly moving out of his/her seat
- poking, pushing, interfering with others
- shouting out
- constant talking, giggling
- taking others' equipment
- lashing out at others
- swearing or shouting
- defiance
- throwing equipment
- damaging equipment or property
- spitting
- bullying
- withdrawn behaviour
- frequent crying
- running away
- hiding
- stealing

Specific support strategies

Many books suggest strategies for supporting children with such behaviours, many of which are good teaching strategies for all children. These include improving self-esteem; tangible rewards (e.g. a wallchart with agreed targets); children taking responsibility for their own actions (i.e. they are making a choice to be disruptive, but they can make a choice to be well behaved); pointing out good role models and teaching good behaviour (do not assume children know what appropriate school behaviour is); anticipating trouble and trying to avoid it; dealing with 'bad' behaviour in a positive way; being realistic.

The IEPs for children with emotional and behavioural difficulties should try to identify where the problems are coming from. Targets should be SMART:

S – specific
M – measurable (and manageable)
A – achievable
R – realistic
T – time-related

Example

Fox (1998) suggests twelve different steps in planning a structural behavioural programme. The first four of these are outlined below as being particularly useful for trainee teachers. A newly qualified teacher with a class would need to work through all twelve.

Step 1

Record unwanted and wanted behaviours.

Unwanted behaviours	Desired behaviours
Shouting out	Listening and working quietly
Getting out of seat	Staying in seat

Step 2

Do a half-hour observation of the child.

Observation Sheet

Name:
Lesson:

	Shouts out	Out of seat	'On task'
10.00–10.05	3	2	3 mins
10.05–10.10	2	0	2 mins
10.10–10.15	2	1	1 min
etc.			

Step 3

Review the observed and recorded behaviour and compare this to the list in Step 1. Decide which behaviour you are going to encourage, e.g. staying in seat.

Step 4: environmental analysis

Identify ways in which this behaviour could be prevented in the first place, e.g. change seating, proximity to teacher, peer group, task, child's physical and/or emotional state, in order to eliminate or reduce unwanted behaviour.

Attention deficit (hyperactivity) disorder

This is probably one of the most controversial of all categories for special educational needs. It is now the most frequently diagnosed learning need in the USA and this pattern is likely to be repeated here. Children who are diagnosed with attention deficit (hyperactivity) disorder AD/HD) are seen to display specific behaviours such as being bossy, intrusive, disruptive, off-task and easily frustrated, so everyone suffers. Teachers spend more time coping with misbehaviour and less time on teaching, and the AD/HD child continually receives negative messages from everyone, including (generally) his or her peer group.

The disorder is often treated with a drug called Ritalin. This is used to stimulate the central nervous system and help the child become more responsive to feedback from his or her social and physical environment. The drug has a 70–75 per cent 'success' rate. It reduces disruptive behaviour and helps to improve relationships with parents, teachers and peers. It also helps the child to concentrate enough to complete academic work, thus improving achievement. The drug is given alongside a programme to teach the child acceptable behaviour, and he or she is kept on it from two to seven years. Anyone who has seen the difference between a child before and after taking Ritalin can understand why it is seen as some sort of solution to severe behavioural problems, but it is extremely controversial. There are negative side-effects, such as sleeping problems and weight loss.

The idea of drugging children into compliance is disturbing and there is little evidence about the long-term effects of such treatment. Robb and Letts work with children identified as having ADD and their book, *Creating Kids Who Can Concentrate* (1997), is an excellent read for anyone concerned about finding proven strategies for beating ADD without drugs. It is a comprehensive guide that shows how lack of concentration has become a medical condition. It then moves into do-it-yourself mode and uses children whom the authors have worked with as case studies to suggest solutions. The final section shows how adults helping such children can help themselves. This includes using relaxation to 'give you a tranquil moment as you work your way through the book'.

Children in crisis

Children in crisis were touched upon in Chapter 7, where we looked at what may be presenting behaviour in a classroom. Some children react to crisis with anxiety disorders or phobic problems. These may be expressed in different ways in the classroom – depression and withdrawal, aggression, phobic or obsessive behaviour.

Four common disorders can cause these behaviours – separation anxiety, generalised anxiety, specific phobias and post-traumatic stress. Few teachers are trained to deal with them and children usually need professional help, which is often difficult to obtain. Yet some children in crisis manage to overcome the odds. Trainee teachers who are made aware of a crisis in children's lives by the children themselves must inform the class teacher. The Green Paper published in 1997 'Excellence for All Children: Meeting Special Educational Needs' identified the need for a review. This is taking place at the time of writing.

Able children and giftedness

The definitions of able and gifted children are very vague, so this section looks at children who are at the opposite end of the 'learning difficulties' spectrum. Anyone who has been a parent of a very able child knows that such children have their own special needs and are frequently overlooked in school if their behaviour is satisfactory. They may be part of that very useful 'sub-teachers' group mentioned in Chapter 7, but they may also be isolated and quietly unhappy. The distinction between a gifted and a very able child is a difficult one to make. 'Gifted' tends to be used to describe very exceptional children, such as musical and mathematical prodigies. This has the advantage of making them relatively rare!. The federal government in the USA offers a much broader definition of the gifted child as one who 'gives evidence of high performance capability in areas such as intellectual, creative, artistic, leadership capacity or specific academic fields, and who requires services or activities not ordinarily provided by the school in order to fully develop such capabilities'. Most of our very able children would come into this category.

Lee-Corbin and Denicolo, in their work on recognising and supporting able children in primary schools (1998), examine key research on able children; look at the educational provision for them; explore case studies of achieving and underachieving able children and look at ways in which teachers can be more responsive to their needs. They note that teachers have different concepts about the very able – some defining them as those children who are excellent all-rounders, while others move towards the definition of seeing them as gifted in a particular area.

A workable definition of the intellectually very able child is that the child
- can think much faster than other children
- can identify and solve more complex problems
- thinks in unusual and diverse ways
- exhibits profound insights.

In the days of IQ testing, the very able child would be seen as one who had an IQ of 135 and over. Research on the human brain has demonstrated that such children are biologically different. There are cellular changes and biochemical processes setting them apart from others. This advanced brain function appears to result from both genetic and inheritance and environmental opportunities.

Special programmes for the very able/gifted tend to be low-key, as selectors of participants disagree over the definition of these terms. Saturday morning clubs for very able children held in Liverpool over twenty years ago attracted a wide range of children, including the siblings of those initially identified. There is also the fear of elitism and a general distrust of using scarce resources for the very able. In most schools, scarce resources are used to support those with learning difficulties because their needs are seen as being the greater. There is also the belief that very able children can get by themselves. If we are concerned about all children receiving a challenging education, then academically very able children cannot be left out. Gifted/very able athletes do tend to get more resources with extracurricular clubs, leisure centre and club provision; but even in this area the UK lags behind many other countries.

Sadly, intellectually very able children walk into our classrooms every day knowing 90 per cent of the content before they start. There are three types of programmed intervention which can be found in schools in the UK.

1 **Enrichment** – extending classroom work, either by using more in-depth material or adding topics to study. Enrichment programmes often build on the child's own interests and involve either the individual or small groups. They are often built into homework and after-school projects, e.g. foreign language teaching. Programmes may be general enrichment to extend the children's interests; special skills programmes to help children pursue an area of interest, and self-selected projects which will make a contribution to the school or community.

2 **Acceleration** – this offers content at an earlier age so that the child can complete schooling in less time. Technically, this can be done by early entrance to school, skipping classes, or moving through the curriculum at a more rapid rate. The private sector tends to be much more flexible about acceleration and it is rare to find children in the state sector in non-age-related classes. The increasing use of cross-age ability grouping for maths and English can provide the younger able child with opportunities for acceleration.

3 **Affective programmes** – these address social and emotional needs and focus on the special problems and concerns of very able children. Again, they tend to be found in the private sector in the UK and are often linked to small educational consultancies.

Specific support strategies

The six strategies below are simply good practice and are not elitist. Their use for very able children involves using teaching methods which sustain the momentum of their work by stimulating intellectual curiosity, matching approaches to the children being taught and exploiting opportunities to contribute to the quality of pupils' wider educational development. All these form part of the standards for Qualified Teacher Status. Teachers need to have high expectations for the very able and this is a challenging as well as a humbling task. Most of us meet children in our teaching careers who we know are intellectually more able than ourselves, but they still need our support.

1 Give children opportunities to make choices – about what they learn, how they learn and how they demonstrate their learning. Encourage self-directed behaviour. This sounds difficult at a time when the curriculum is more proscribed than it has ever been, and some subject areas lend themselves more easily to different teaching strategies.

2 Facilitate opportunities to enable high-ability children to work with other high-ability children. Cooperative learning situations that continually group very able children with the less able can lead to frustration. 'Sub-teaching' can be a useful learning device for the 'sub-teacher', but over a period of time children can become frustrated in this role.

3 Provide materials and resources which challenge children. If able children are never given such challenges they have trouble developing good study skills and learning how to learn. This is particularly true for those children who do not learn study skills at home and who are entirely dependent on school for their intellectual challenges.

4 Matching learning outcomes to children's needs. Give very able children credit for what they already know and can do. It is still possible to see young able readers plodding through a reading scheme which offers little challenge or interest and then see them happily reading far more complex texts when they have a choice.

5 Allow and plan for independent study projects. These may be after-school or homework projects, as well as projects within the prescribed curriculum. Areas like history and geography are particularly good for this type of study project because they harness literacy skills as well as extending children's investigative and study skills.

6 Provide opportunities to practise divergent and critical thinking. The Development Education Centre in Birmingham has produced some excellent material for primary teachers over the years which challenges children's thinking and encourages varied teaching strategies (see Further Reading).

Language arts and the gifted child: nine-point plan

1 **Teach study skills**
Teachers who equip their children, of all abilities, with study skills are contributing to the child's satisfaction in learning and making their own job much easier.

2 **Self-pacing**
Dead time occurs when children cannot control the direction and the next stage in their own learning.

3 **Self-marking**
Along with self-pacing, develop self-marking. This does not mean that the teacher is unnecessary but that they monitor the child's progress and set targets.

4 **Record-keeping**
When some children are pacing themselves and taking responsibility for their own progress, record-keeping and accountability become even more essential. Children, too, can keep their own records of achievement and set targets.

5 **Giving praise and sustaining quality**
Quality does not mean performing to the norm but improving one's own standard. Bright children still need competition. Try to find some way of setting goals. They will often set their own high standard.

6 **Fostering interests beyond school**
Chess club, Venture Scouts, computer club, choirs, orchestras.

7 **Special resources packs**
Collections of materials that the child helps to categorise and use for extra study.

8 **Sustaining long-term interests**
Bright children are tenacious. Discover these interests and provide a source of contacts who will act as mentors and supports.

9 **Learning at the teacher's own level**
Be prepared to discuss their interests with the child at the teacher's own level.

English as an additional language

English as an additional language (EAL) does not come under the provisions of the Code of Practice, although if English is not the child's first language he or she may have problems in school. There are huge variations between schools. In some schools all children are monolingual, in others, 14 or 15 different languages may be spoken. Schools qualify for additional funding if there are a significant number of children who have English as an additional language. These children present unique opportunities and unique challenges. The first challenge for the trainee teacher is to understand who these children are. Many, particularly at the start of Key Stage 1, have been born in the UK and their parents may also have been born in the UK. Make sure that you know which heritage languages are spoken. Some children may already be very skilled in speaking more than one language. Look at the histories of the local communities from which the children come. In some localities, the majority of families may have come from one area, but in another locality the families may come from a much wider range of countries. Reasons for the movement of people vary. There are many very settled communities, where children arrive at school with English as an additional language, but sadly wars, environmental and family disasters can force reluctant movement. Particular areas in cities such as Liverpool, London and Manchester have traditionally attracted different heritage groups, but it is also true that towns like Preston, Bolton and Bury have schools where a substantial number of children have English as an additional language.

Understanding a little of the way in which the heritage languages are constructed helps to identify possible misconceptions in early reading and writing, although children are very quick to identify different ways in which a book works and can often tell you how they read differently in different languages.

Stages of language acquisition

For readers who are monolingual, it might be useful to think back to learning a foreign language in primary or secondary school.

1 **Pre-production** – learners start to understand the new language, but cannot engage in conversations or respond to questions. Appropriate activities include listening and pointing to things. Words are repeated back to the speaker.

2 **Early production** – there is better understanding and learners respond to simple questions with one-word or two-word answers.

3 **Speech emergence** – comprehension starts to increase and learners can speak in simple sentences. There are plenty of errors, but children can be encouraged to retell, define, describe and explain.

4 **Intermediate fluency** – comprehension is very good and the learner can construct complex sentences and engage in higher-order speaking skills in the new language.

The teacher's role

There is a delicate balance between giving children challenging opportunities to demonstrate their knowledge and skills and giving them frustrating tasks that they are not yet equipped to deal with. Trainee teachers who are working with children who do not receive additional help could try some of the following strategies:

- provide a caring classroom environment which acknowledges the child's first language and culture
- seat the child near the teacher, where directions and instructions can be given with fewer distractions
- speak naturally, but slowly, to allow for comprehension
- use clear, simple language – short sentences, simple concepts.
- support instruction with visual materials such as pictures, diagrams, etc.
- provide manipulative materials to enable lessons to be meaningful
- do not call on the child for a lengthy response
- avoid correcting pronunciation, structural or vocabulary errors; either accept the response or say it again correctly, without comment
- do not expect the accuracy of a native English speaker
- assign a friend to provide additional instruction
- do not treat the child as if he or she is 'different'.

Children who speak English as an additional language have much to offer. Geography lessons, for example, come alive for all children when a classmate speaks about visiting a country and can show objects and evidence from the visit. They are often in a good position to identify bias and stereotyping in textbooks and provide valuable insights into the ways knowledge is constructed by such books. It is humbling to ask a child of 10 how many languages he or she speaks and be told of three languages in which they are fluent, then to ask about their favourite authors and be told about different authors in different languages. We must value diversity and we can also learn much from it. OFSTED has produced a potentially useful (and free!) booklet on raising the attainment of minority ethnic pupils. This looks at existing evidence and presents key issues for schools and LEAs. It is, however, limited to four specific groups – Bangladeshi, black Caribbean, Pakistani and gypsy traveller pupils. This results in a rather 'deficit' model of the attainment of minority ethnic pupils and this contrasts with the experiences of many schools where pupils are achieving well above the national average.

Pauline Gibbon's very practical book *Learning to Learn in a Second Language* (1993) is very much more positive.

The account below describes one child's experience of her first days in school and the support she received from her friends.

Speaking English as an additional language

THE FIRST TIME I WENT TO SCHOOL

The day came when I had to go to school. The awkward thing was I couldn't speak any English. The nursery door stood right in front of me. I trembled and my legs were like jelly. I hid behind mom's coat. Mrs Renodon opened the door. My mom had to drag me in. I was so frightened that I almost cried, but Mrs Renodon smiled at me so I followed her dragging my mom behind me. I saw so many different faces. Mrs Renodon asked me a question but I couldn't understand, and to this day I've never known what she had asked me. My mom was going and I began to walk to the door with her but she was telling me I was staying there. She walked out of the door and I was crying until my brother Andrew came and explained to me that I was there to learn. When I went out to play I just stood out and watched how the other children played. A girl walked up to me and told me something, her name was Danielle. Two other girls were behind her and their name's were Sarah and Hortense, I also told them my name. After about 4 weeks I knew how to speak English, now I was able to join in with all the games with other children. I wasn't perfect at English. Danielle, Sarah and Hortense tried to teach me more English. So I was able to show off to my sister and brother to say I knew more English than they did. By the end of the nursery I was able to speak ENGLISH! 100% That is how I remember the first time I came to school. What wonderful memories, and three excellent teachers too. Now your English is wonderful, have you remembered your home language?

Chapter 10

Home–school–community connections

Learning objectives
- To examine the skills required to liaise effectively with parents and other carers.
- To understand the changing role of parental involvement in school.

Parental involvement

Few issues enjoy such universal support as the idea that family and community involvement are essential for successful schooling and learning. Research over many years has shown that there is nothing more important to success in schools than the quality of relationships between and among children, parents and teachers. Jean Mills's (1996) *Partnership in the Primary School* gives a readable overview of whole-school approaches in relation to nurseries, children with special needs, reading and literacy, environmental education and school literacy partnerships in minority language families.

Studies of effective programmes for children at risk consistently identify parent involvement as a key component. Yet newly qualified teachers often identify their relationship with parents as one of their major concerns and an area about which they feel ill-informed.

The reason for this is quite simple. It is one area where it is very difficult, while a trainee teacher, to do anything more than follow the class teacher. Some students therefore have very positive and creative experiences with parental involvement, but many – particularly those working at Key Stage 2 – may see very few parents. This is particularly true when teaching practices occur at periods when parental involvement is less obvious – in the late autumn and spring terms, for example. It is not surprising, then, that they become anxious about how to plan for parental involvement in the classroom, discussions at parents evenings and writing reports. Key Stage 1 teachers tend to be less anxious as they see parents on a daily basis and are gradually able to build up a relationship. Newly qualified teachers who are parents themselves are over the first hurdle because they have been on the other side of the fence.

Cooperation between parents and teachers doesn't just happen; it has to be worked at. It needs good communication and interpersonal skills. These include good listening techniques, tact, kindness, consideration, empathy and an understanding of parent–child relationships. Never be confrontational, however much you are provoked! You also need to be positive to work effectively with families, particularly families which are very different from your own.

Remember:
- Parents are the first and primary educators. They are also children's most important teachers. Research and common sense have shown that intelligence is heavily influenced by the experiences a child has in his or her first years, i.e. well before they enter school. Teachers can encourage parents to continue playing a critical role by reading to their children, taking them on visits, talking and listening with them, giving them opportunities to engage in creative activities and modelling self-discipline and task commitment.
- Parents need to feel that their time is well spent, valued and useful. Formal contracts will never replace the friendly encouragement and support of a class teacher.

- Parents have important insights and understandings about their children.
- Most parents really care about their children.
- Schools and homes have shared goals. Parents and teachers are partners. Parents can share their special knowledge of their own children, volunteer in classrooms and encourage children to complete homework.
- All families have strengths, however oddly they may be constructed. Many family forms exist and are legitimate.
- Cultural differences are valid and valuable.
- Parents (and grandparents) have a wealth of talent, information, ideas, skills and hobbies to share. Parent instructors not only supplement the curriculum but also act as role models.
- Parents can learn new techniques.
- Communicate respect – through your tone of voice, choice of words, facial expressions and general courtesy. Keep to appointment times, however fascinating another discussion may be. Parents who are kept waiting feel undervalued. This can also be dangerous. In my first year of teaching, a child died when the babysitter went home because the parents had been delayed at school for over an hour. The child was not in my class, but I still have a mental picture of a toddler climbing over a balcony and falling to his death because an appointment time was not kept. This is also true at the end of the day, when children are going home. As a parent, nothing is more frustrating than dashing to school to find that the teacher delays the children coming out because the room is not tidy.

Parents as volunteers:
- **tutors** – with individuals and small groups, listening to children read; giving spelling words, playing literacy and numeracy games; reading aloud
- **aides** – supervising individual reading time, project time or setting other independent tasks, e.g. the 20 minutes of group work within the literacy hour
- **field-trip helpers** – either one-day or residential visits
- **lunchtime and playtime helpers** – sometimes parents may be students themselves, conducting projects looking into the pastoral side of the school's work
- **clerical helpers** – assisting in the library, photocopying materials, helping to produce class newsletters
- **presenters** – parents and other family members sharing their special expertise and knowledge.

After-school support:
- **in school** – extracurricular clubs, planning teams (e.g. parent governors)
- **at home** – reading to and with their children, supervising home and project work, collecting labels for computers and musical instruments, taking their children out to museums and art galleries, acting as learning models.

An increasing number of primary schools give parents the opportunity to gain formal qualifications through their work in school. There are several local initiatives all over the country which you may be interested in finding out about, or may even have been involved with yourself. There are also many initiatives which involve parents prior to their children starting school. These include playgroups and toddler groups held at the school, Portage groups, home visiting, and preschool packs.

Planning for parents

If parents are helping in the classroom, they must be included at the planning stage. Teaching plans must identify clearly which adults will be present and what their teaching role involves. Parents need to be met well before the lessons in which they are involved and their role and the children's learning objectives discussed. Therese and Jacquie Findley's cards (1996, see Further Reading) come directly out of this. They outline the purpose of the activity and the adult's role in it. The cards were built out of many years' experience of working with parents and other adults in a reception and Year 1 classroom, e.g.

Example

Maths	
Area	Fractions
Grouping	2–4
Learning objective	To introduce the concept of quarters
Activity	To fold squares and circles into quarters and colour them
Resources	Paper circles and squares, colouring pens

Achieved by

1 The helper gives out a circle and a square to each child and says: *'I want you to fold your circle exactly in half.'*
   The helper moves round to assist, where necessary. When every child has folded their circle the helper asks: *'How many parts does your circle have now?'*
2 The helper asks: *'Can anyone show me how to fold this in half again?'*
   The helper either uses a child's example or, if necessary, folds one to show the group.
3 The helper asks the group: *'How many parts does the circle have now?'*
4 Once the correct answer has been given, the helper explains that the four parts are called quarters.
5 The helper says: *'Now you are going to fold your square into quarters.'*
6 When all of the children have folded their two shapes, they can colour the quarters different colours.

Discussion should take place after the session as well, so that assessments can be made about the quality of learning which has taken place and children's progress. Parental help can be sought in making detailed observation notes; as, for example, in a 10- or 20-minute observational schedule on children's working patterns. The need for confidentiality must be stressed, both in terms of your shared assessment of the children's learning, but also in relation to stories and personal information that children share.

Note: if a child shares information which is related to Child Protection, this must be reported to the class teacher and the school procedures put into action.

 Find out who is responsible for parental involvement in your school and what sort of provision is made for volunteers who work in the school. How else are parents encouraged to feel part of the school community?

The most useful rule of thumb for parental involvement is whether you would feel comfortable as a parent volunteer in this school. Are parents planned for? Are their roles clear? Is there somewhere to put their coats and bags safely? Can they make a drink or heat up food for themselves? Does the school run an in-service programme with regard to parental involvement? Are there training programmes for parents? Do parents have a genuine role in decision making?

Do class teachers make time to speak with parents? Many of the factors involved with being a student visitor to a classroom are in evidence with parental and community involvement.

Improving listening skills

This may appear a rather odd subheading for this section, but researchers estimate that we only listen to about a quarter of the information fed to us. This listening inefficiency provides concrete proof to those of us with families who deny ever having heard us ask them to do something. We only hear what we want to hear. If we want to 'hear' what parents say to us we need to improve our listening skills.

Management courses suggest particular strategies, and these are just as useful in school life:
- maintain eye contact
- face the speaker and lean slightly forward
- ignore distractions
- make non-interrupting acknowledgements – nods and smiles
- when the speaker pauses, allow them to continue without interrupting – only add your comments once the parent has finished
- be alert for non-verbal cues: body language speaks volumes
- don't ignore off-hand comments – they often give an insight into personalities and family situations
- ask for clarification when necessary
- check your understanding of what the parent has said by summarising the essential points and reaching some agreement on them
- find out what parents know about what goes on in school and what expectations they have for their child.

It is important to remember that there are cultural differences, e.g. relating to eye contact.

Open-door policies

Most schools have policies on parental involvement, and there is a wealth of literature about projects involving partnership with parents. Trainee and newly qualified teachers need to follow such policies, but once you are an established teacher you can be proactive in bringing parents into schools.
- Invite parents into school to observe, participate and help. Parents who go out to work need plenty of notice, so they can take time off. Parents who visit and are involved are the school's strongest allies. Proof of this can be seen, over and over again, in the media. Parents quickly rush to support schools which are threatened with closure, fail OFSTED inspections and need emergency funding.
- Be prepared to meet parents before and after school and at lunchtime. Working parents often have real problems getting into school to visit their child's classroom and talk with the teacher. This can include parents who act as carers to their own parents and other relatives.
- Invite parents to special events – a class drama production at the end of the day, a special display of work.
- If your school has a newsletter, give information about your class and activities to whoever writes it. Teachers work hard, but are often weak on publicising their children's and their own achievements. Use community languages if you know parents of children in your class use them.
- Establish routines about visits. Both you and the children's parents benefit from guidelines about the most appropriate time to visit. Unannounced visits are disruptive as well as unproductive. Most schools provide guidance for parents about this, but if you find, once you are qualified, that you are receiving too many unannounced visits, discuss the problem with the headteacher. Often, a well-phrased sentence in the newsletter will sort out the problem.

Problems or challenges

It would be unrealistic to suggest that problems do not occur when you try to increase parental involvement. The following strategies will help to keep these to a minimum:
- make decisions about classwork and keep to them. The school's long- and medium-term planning will support you. One school puts these outside the classroom so that parents can study them
- keep to the school's policy on homework – OFSTED inspectors find it one of the most controversial issues among parents: some parents want more, some less
- mark all the children's work and ensure that it is not you who is making the spelling errors
- diagnose all the children's needs and be prepared to share with parents the next series of targets towards which their child should work, and ways in which they can help
- discipline and class management – children are quick to identify poor teaching strategies and report them to their parents. They resent this and will show their resentment by making it more difficult for the teacher. The vast majority of children want to achieve and see schooling as the way forward.

Relationships with parent volunteers

- Be proactive in recruiting volunteers; do not sit back and wait.
- Try to avoid parents tutoring their own child. Many children do best with volunteers other than their parents.
- Make sure volunteers with babies and toddlers have good childcare arrangements. It distracts everyone if a baby is crying or a toddler is running around.
- Ensure that volunteers understand the need for confidentiality regarding information about children.
- Make a special attempt to communicate with parents who have English as a second language. Identify someone who may be able to act as an interpreter and ask them if they would like to help; describe how their help is needed and discuss when they could come to school.
- Take time to get to know volunteers. This is particularly important if you are working with parents who speak English as an additional language.
- Make sure you can always see the volunteer and that they bring any discipline problems to the teacher's attention.
- Make sure there is something for volunteers to do. If they come in and there is nothing to do, they will not come again.
- Give volunteers a variety of things to do, so they do not get tired of doing the same thing each week.
- It is a matter of preference, but having volunteers call you by your first name makes people feel at ease. After all, you are equal partners.
- Ask volunteers to let you know when they cannot come in, so you can plan accordingly.
- Be appreciative towards volunteers – offer a word of thanks, a card, or a small present at the end of term.

Pointers for involvement

- There is no overall guidance on practice, although many books and research papers have been written on the subject. This has resulted in many different ways of involving parents and carers in the life of the school and the formal education of their own children.
- The word 'parent' is used, although it often means mother, or female carer. Despite the large number of fathers, stepfathers, grandfathers and uncles who bring their children to and from school, most parental involvement is female. Some schools have worked extremely hard to bring men into school, arguing that many of their children do not have fathers living at home and therefore need to see more men in caring roles. The literature about parents often assumes it is addressing mothers and very little work has been published about male involvement in schools.
- Trends in recent legislation show several government initiatives for more parental involvement. These include:
  - The Education Act 1981 – this gave parents the right to participate in assessment of special educational needs and the annual reviews, a right to information and to appeal.
  - Education Act 1986 – schools were required to give annual reports to parents and meet with them to discuss and record their child's progress. This Act also increased the number of parents on the governing body.
  - The Education Reform Act 1988 – this introduced parental ballots on opting out, and admission limits were relaxed to allow open enrolment and parental rights to information on programmes of work and progress.
  - The Education (Schools) Act 1992 – this gave parents the right to consultation before formal inspection, the right to reports on individual children, including examination and test results.
  - The Education Act 1993 – this gave more power to parents in relation to children with special educational needs. It established an independent tribunal to hear parents' appeals over children with special educational needs and the Code of Practice for special educational needs. In addition, the rules governing school attendance and exclusion were tightened and new rules created for opting out ballots.

- Circulars 2/96, 3/96, 6/96, 12/96 – these extended the legal requirements of schools to give parents more details about children's achievements, admission arrangements and the curriculum.
- The National Literacy Strategy 1998 – parents are encouraged to help to improve their children's literacy by signing home–school contracts which include supporting their children in learning to read. It is recommended this is done by spending 20 minutes or so each day either reading to their children or hearing them read.
- For regular updates, use the parents centre on the DfEE website www. parents.dfee.gov.uk/

OFSTED and parental involvement

OFSTED inspectors are required to evaluate and report on the effectiveness of the school's partnership with parents, highlighting the strengths and weakness in terms of:

- information provided about the school and about children's work and progress through annual and other reports and parents meetings
- parents' involvement with the work of the school and with their children's work at home.

Examination of the relevant sections of OFSTED reports show that judgements about parental involvement are made in terms of:

- parental involvement in the classroom and extracurricular activities – parents need to be properly briefed, and their involvement identified in the planning
- parental comment on the reports, reading records and records of achievement – this records the dialogue between teacher and parent and provides a source of evidence about the support the school has given parents in helping their own children
- parental involvement in whole-class events, e.g. assemblies, school productions, musical performances
- the language used by teachers about parents – this can be quite sexist ('Your mum can mend this'; 'Take this note home to your mothers'). It can also be very negative ('Our children come to school with very little language'; 'The parents don't care'). Criticisms can be made about non-traditional/conventional childcare, e.g. the child's poor behaviour is put down to 'both parents working', or a 'single-parent family'. This is a deficit model of childcare, which blames family circumstances for difficulties with the child in school. It fails to look at the many successful children who come from non-traditional and perhaps economically disadvantaged homes
- schools where there are formal structures to support closer links, e.g. home visiting prior to attendance, curriculum information meetings, etc.
- parental and community involvement in recognising parental work, for example by giving certification for courses undertaken in the school, linked with practical experience
- formal parents' associations, such as the PTA (Parent Teacher Association) or Friends of the School. This needs to be social as well as academic and it should be clear that the association is not solely to raise funds to buy resources for the school
- the involvement and evaluation of projects such as Portage (preschool), reading and numeracy partnerships.

Parents evenings/conferences

1 Know the school policy.
2 Be clear about the purpose of the meeting/open evening/conference. It may help to have a written report to discuss or provide yourself with a form to complete with the name of the child, the child's strengths, the child's needs and suggestions for action at home and at school. The latter can then be agreed at the meeting.
3 Be sensitive. For the vast majority of parents, their children are the most precious people in the world. If you criticise, withhold praise, their own self-worth is questioned. Self-esteem for a parent can be closely linked to the child's progress and attainment (social and intellectual) in school.
4 Defuse a difficult situation by remaining calm yourself and asking parents to be seated. Let them talk to you first, so you can find out exactly what is the matter. If you are in the least worried, make sure another adult is present. Let the headteacher know what has happened and if you have been unable to resolve the problem record it on paper as soon as you can.

5 Do not surprise parents with a big problem. Make sure they are kept up to date with the progress their children are making. It is helpful to send home classwork regularly and to have an open-door policy, which lets parents know that they can contact you easily.

Other ways to reach parents as a class teacher

These need to be discussed with whoever is responsible for parental involvement. Ways of communicating with parents include:

* the written word, electronic or otherwise, and using community languages where needed. E-mail in the classroom will make a big difference to home–school–community links. It becomes easy to type out a quick message and send it
* reading diaries or logbooks
* displays celebrating children's work and also explaining aspects of the curriculum, e.g. photographs showing the role of structured play in promoting intellectual, social, emotional and moral development
* letters to individual parents concerning their children or a class letter to all parents
* class newsletters
* volunteer request forms – giving name, availability, work preference (running machines, hearing readings, small group tutoring, storytime reading, monitoring small groups, typing, anything!)
* curriculum planning for half-term and suggestions for helping the children
* reports – these are now a legal requirement and schools will have their own procedures about completing them. Schools keep copies of reports, so look through a sample of these to get an idea of the genre. Good report writing is a skill and it is helped by informative record keeping over the whole year. It can include photographs, which can be displayed as a record of children's achievements. A video taken at the start and end of the year can also provide useful information about very young children's progress. The 20-minute schedule advocated in Chapter 7 (pp. 75/6), is another way in which you can be sure that you do not miss giving considered   thought to each child during the course of a year.

Building multicultural partnerships

Cultural, class and language barriers can inhibit partnerships and interactions between home and school. Often this affects the children who would most benefit from closer understandings. Some schools work extremely hard at involving the whole community in the life of the school and have community rooms and support workers to ensure that the communities are truly welcomed. If this is not true of the school you are working in, here are a few pointers.

* Learn more about the children's cultures and backgrounds.
* Watch for hidden cultural differences – relationships between parent and teacher, male and female; time seen as a simultaneous process rather than linear; ambiguous statements made rather than a clear, explicit complaint; different forms of eye contact, looking down, rather than directly into another's face; a smile used to express confusion rather than pleasure.
* Make a checklist for parental involvement – this can include a place for people to meet informally within the building; an open, friendly reception area; somewhere to make a drink; defined policies regarding parental involvement in the school; policies regarding homework; communications between home and school, clear, attractively presented and in the heritage languages represented by the school population; good communications between parents and teachers; local businesses and communities involved in the school; parents' opinions asked for and respected; all staff aware of cultural and language differences; parents in evidence in the school.

Community links

Schools vary considerably in their ability to draw in the local business community. Some schools, for example, are in areas where there is little or no business. However, all schools do have communities around them. Sometimes these may be very tightly knit, as in a small village community, where the school acts as the focal point for many community activities. In more urban areas, schools have the opportunity to make links with a range of different organisations, services and employers through which children can 'gain a greater understanding of society and the nature of citizenship' (OFSTED 1995). Primary schools have found it harder than secondary schools to persuade businesses to sponsor particular aspects of their work, but there have been many projects which have involved close links with specific businesses for a period of time.

When the National Curriculum was first introduced, a number of cross-curricular themes were identified. One of these was 'education for economic and industrial understanding'. This was identified as an essential part of every child's curriculum, whatever their age. The National Curriculum Council (NCC) said this would 'help pupils understand the world in which they live and prepare them for life and work in a rapidly changing, economically competitive world' (NCC 1989, NCC Circular 6: The National Curriculum and Whole Curriculum Planning). The NCC produced some useful guidelines on ways in which this could be taught through English, maths, science and ICT (NCC 1990, Education for Economic and Industrial Understanding, Curriculum Guidance 4). The younger the child, the more likely it was that education for economic and industrial understanding would involve local businesses and services. Colour photographs in the guidelines show children visiting the local vets; undertaking a shopping survey; role playing in the school post office and visiting a local farm. Most schools still have these curriculum guidance booklets hidden away somewhere. They do contain some useful ideas, as well as supplying a wide variety of learning objectives related to children's understanding of the world around them.

The section in the QCA's website headed 'Personal, social and health education and citizenship at key stages 1 and 2' (www.qca.org.uk) revisits many of these ideas in its citizenship section. The Citizenship Foundation on www.citfou.org.uk is likely to become more orientated to primary schools over the next few years as a direct result of government initiatives.

Chapter 11

Professional and legal issues

Learning objectives
- To be aware of the professional duties set out in the current School Teachers' Pay and Conditions document.
- To know teachers' legal liabilities and responsibilities and other professional requirements.
- To understand the need for constant updating with regard to the law and practice relating to professional and legal issues in schools.

Teachers' professional duties

At the time of writing, teachers' professional duties are set out in the School Teachers' Pay and Conditions document, issued under the School Teachers' Pay and Conditions Act 1991. These are under discussion at the moment. Most schools have very clear guidance for teachers about their professional duties, which are often set out in a job specification and may form part of the contract of employment.

The 1991 Act established a review body to consider schoolteachers' statutory conditions of employment, and made special provisions for grant-maintained schools.

Conditions of Employment 1993

1 Particular duties

A teacher shall perform in accordance with any directions which may be reasonably given to him/her by the headteacher.

2 Professional duties
- Planning and preparing courses.
- Teaching … in school and elsewhere.
- Assessing, recording and reporting on the development, progress and attainment of pupils.

3 Other activities
- Promoting the pupils' general well-being.
- Providing guidance on educational and social matters, making relevant records and reports.
- Making records and reports on the personal and social needs of pupils.
- Communicating and consulting with parents.
- Communicating and cooperating with persons or bodies outside school.
- Participating in meetings for any of the purposes described above.
- Assessments and reports – providing or contributing to oral and written assessments, reports and references.
- Appraisal – participating in arrangements for the appraisal of self and others.
- **Review, further training and development** – reviewing methods of teaching and programmes of work and participating in arrangements for further training and professional development.
- **Educational methods** – advising and cooperating with the headteacher and other teachers on preparation and development of courses, methods of teaching, assessment and pastoral care.

- **Discipline, health and safety** – maintaining good order, safeguarding health and safety on school premises and when authorised elsewhere.
- **Staff meetings** – participating in meetings at school which relate to curriculum, administration or organisation, including pastoral care.
- **Cover** – supervising children whose teacher is not available, provided that the teacher has been absent no more than three days, unless he or she is a teacher employed for this purpose and/or the relevant body has exhausted all reasonable means of providing supply cover without success.
- **Public examinations** – participating in, supervising and preparing children for examinations, recording and reporting assessments.
- **Management** – contributing to the selection for appointment and professional development of other teachers and non-teaching staff. Coordinating or managing the work of other teachers. Taking part in review, development and management of activities relating to the curriculum, organisation and pastoral functions of the school.
- **Administration** – participating in administrative and organisational tasks related to the above, including the ordering and allocation of equipment. Attending assemblies, registering attendance of children and supervising them before, during and after school sessions.
- **Working time** – 195 days: 190 days teaching; 1,265 hours directed time. In addition … work such hours as may be needed to enable him (sic) to discharge effectively professional duties, including in particular marking pupils' work, writing reports, preparation of lessons, teaching materials and programmes. The amount of time required for this … shall not be defined but shall depend upon the work needed to discharge the teacher's duties.

4 Teachers' legal liabilities and responsibilities relating to:
(i) The Race Relations Act 1976

Many LEAs and schools translate this requirement into whole-school anti-racist or equal opportunities policies. During the 1980s and early 1990s there were many in-service programmes designed to look at both the personal and school implications of this Act. The legal jargon makes it difficult to tease out the meaning, and discussion is needed to establish exactly what understandings are held about its provisions. Strong and active anti-racist policies and procedures are seen in many areas as essential for the safety of pupils, both inside the school and when getting to and from school. The Act also has implications for teachers working in the 'White Highlands' where the opportunities to examine cultural diversity and its practical implications are far more difficult.

The Race Relations Act states that: a person discriminates against another in any circumstances if
- on racial grounds he treats that other less favourably than he treats or would treat other persons, or
- he applies to that other a requirement or condition which he applies or would apply equally to persons not of the same racial group as that other but which is such that the proportion of persons of the same racial group as that other who can comply with it is considerably smaller than the proportion of persons not of that racial group who can comply with it, and which he cannot show to be justifiable irrespective of colour, race, nationality or ethnic or national origins of the person to whom it is applied, and which is to the detriment of that other because he cannot comply with it.
- segregating a person from other persons on racial grounds is treating him less favourably than they are treated.

Discrimination by victimisation is also covered. In educational establishments it is unlawful to discriminate against a person
- in the terms on which it offers to admit him to the establishment as a pupil or by refusing or deliberately omitting to accept an application for his admission to the establishment as a pupil, or
- where he is a pupil of the establishment, in the way it affords him access to any benefits, facilities or services, or by refusing or deliberately omitting to afford him access to them, or
- by excluding him from the establishment or subjecting him to any other detriment, or
  - aiding unlawful acts.

- Anything done by a person in the course of his employment shall be treated for the purpose of this Act as done by his employer as well as by him, whether or not it was done with the employer's knowledge or approval. A person commits the offence of incitement to racial hatred if he publishes or distributes written material which is threatening, abusive or insulting.

The table below identifies the 'responsible body' for differnt educational establishments.

ESTABLISHMENT	RESPONSIBLE BODY
Educational establishment	LEA or managers or governors according to which of them has the function in question.
Independent school	Proprietor
Special school not maintained by LEA	Proprietor
University	Governing body
Establishment not falling within paragraphs 1–4 of the Act providing full- or part-time education	Governing body

(ii) Sex Discrimination Act

As with the Race Relations Act, many LEAs and schools have translated the provisions of the Sex Discrimination Act into equal opportunities policy statements.

The Act states that it is to be read as 'applying equally to the treatment of men, and for that purpose shall have effect with such modifications as are requisite'.

A person discriminates against a woman
- if on the grounds of her sex he treats her less favourably than he treats or would treat a man, or
- if he applies to her a requirement or condition which he applies or would apply equally to a man but which is such that the proportion of women who can comply with it is considerably smaller than the proportion of men who can comply with it, and which he cannot show to be justifiable irrespective of the sex of the person to whom it is applied, and which is to her detriment because she cannot comply with it.

He may also discriminate against a woman
- in the arrangements he makes for the purpose of determining who should be offered that employment or in the terms on which he offers her that employment, or by refusing or deliberately omitting to offer her that employment, or
- in the way he affords her access to opportunities for promotion, transfer or training, or to any other benefits, facilities or services or by refusing or deliberately omitting to afford her access to them, or by dismissing her, or subjecting her to any other detriment.

Exceptions are:
- where being a man (or woman) is a genuine occupational qualification for the job, nor does it apply to opportunities for promotion or transfer to, or training for, such employment
- where being a man is a genuine occupational qualification for a job, only when the essential nature of the job calls for a man for reasons of physiology (excluding physical strength or stamina), or in dramatic performances or other entertainment, for reasons of authenticity so that the essential nature of the job would be materially different if carried out by a woman

- where the job needs to be held by a man to preserve decency or privacy (physical contact or states of undress)
- where the nature or location of the establishment makes it impracticable for the holder to live elsewhere and there is no separate sleeping accommodation and it is not reasonable to expect the employer to so equip premises
- where the job is to be held by a man because part of the establishment requiring special care, e.g. a prison or hospital, contains only men
- where the job is one of two to be held by a married couple.

Discrimination in education
- It is unlawful in relation to an educational establishment to discriminate against a woman – in the terms on which it offers to admit her to the establishment as a pupil, or by refusing or deliberately omitting to accept an application for her admission to the establishment as a pupil, or – where she is a pupil of that establishment – in the way it affords her access to any benefits, facilities or services or by refusing or deliberately omitting to afford her access to them, or by excluding her from the establishment or subjecting her to any other detriment.
- The establishments and the responsible bodies are the same as those for the Race Relations Act.

Exceptions to these rules are single-sex establishments.

(iii) Health and Safety at Work Act 1974 (Sections 7 and 8)

Sections 7 and 8 of the Health and Safety at Work Act 1974 state:

It shall be the duty of every employee while at work:

a) to take reasonable care for the health and safety of himself and of other persons who may be affected by his acts or omissions at work; and

b) as regards any duty or requirement imposed on his employer or any other person by or under any of the relevant statutory provisions, to cooperate with him so far as is necessary to enable that duty or requirement to be performed or complied with.

c) No person shall intentionally or recklessly interfere with or misuse anything provided in the interests of health, safety or welfare in pursuance of any of the relevant statutory provisions.

Teachers' common-law duty is to ensure the health and safety of pupils on school premises and when leading activities off the school site.

This is the common-law concept of someone acting *in loco parentis*, or 'in the place of the parent'. It dates back to 1893 when it was ruled that 'A schoolmaster was bound to take such care of his boys as a careful father would take of his boys.' The law does not recognise degrees of competence in parenting but assumes the best parental care, and takes into account the training a teacher has received.

Supervision in the classroom

Guidelines for ensuring your classroom is safe are:
- know and understand the health and safety policy for the school, in particular the requirements for particular subject areas. These should be written into lesson plans as well as short- and medium-term planning
- ensure tables, chairs are placed in an orderly fashion so that pupils can sit comfortably and that their movement is not impeded
- ensure that you can see all pupils
- avoid pupils sitting near dangerous equipment or features
- have clear and simple rules for behaviour, particularly over entry and exit
- regularly inspect the equipment in your class, including desks and chairs, to identify anything needing repair
- report and record potential risks. If necessary, do not use the equipment, and if nothing is done, inform the safety representative at the school.

General supervision

The notion of the careful parent applies, but:

- it cannot be expected that on and around playgrounds school pupils will be watched all of the time: to have sufficient staff patrolling is enough
- accidents will happen even in careful homes, and children should not suffer an impoverished curriculum because teachers are over-cautious. If in doubt, ask for advice.

Guidelines for school visits off site:

- study both school and authority regulations and ensure they are met
- investigate the terrain and facilities (including the qualifications of centre staff and numbers available for supervision), and check fire regulations and insurance certificates
- circulate details of the visit to parents – call a meeting if necessary
- gain written consent from parents to take children away from the school premises
- include a space for medical information, particularly if you are going to be away for a day or two, and check school records for any known health risks (e.g. asthma)
- arrange emergency contacts
- if free time (e.g. for shopping or unsupervised activities) is planned, make sure parents are informed of this so that they cannot claim they do not accept responsibility (they have the option to withdraw their child)
- see that adequate warnings and instructions are given to the children. It is wise to issue written guidance.

(iv) Section 3(5) of the Children Act 1989

This Act covers 'what is reasonable for the purpose of safeguarding or promoting children's welfare'.

Under Section 3(5), 'A person who does not have parental responsibility for a particular child but has care of the child may subject to the provision of the Act do what is reasonable in all the circumstances of the case for the purpose of safeguarding or promoting the child's welfare.' This can include:

1 **Welfare reports** – A court considering any question with respect to a child under this Act may ask a probation officer or Local Authority to arrange for an officer of the Authority or such other person (other than a probation officer) as the Authority considers appropriate, to report to the court on such matters relating to the welfare of that child as are required to be dealt with in the report. The report may be made in writing, or orally, as the court requires.

   Headteachers generally, but not always, undertake this duty, but the class teacher may be asked to do it and will certainly be asked to make a written report. Teachers are often the only other adults a child may come into contact with and the information they hold is extremely valuable. Children changing for PE, for example, have often been identified as being abused as a result of teachers seeing bruises and markings on the child.

2 **Residence Order 13(1)** – where a residence order is in force with respect to a child no person may cause the child to be known by a new surname, without the written consent of every person who has parental responsibility for the child or the leave of the court.

3 **Access to information by a court 48(1)** – Where it appears to a court making an emergency protection order that adequate information as to the child's whereabouts
   (a) is not available to the applicant for the order; but
   (b) is available to another person,
   it may include in the order a provision requiring that other person to disclose, if asked to do so by the applicant, any information that he may have as to the child's whereabouts.

4 **Privacy 97(2)**
   No person shall publish any material which is intended or likely to identify
   (a) any child as being involved in any proceedings before a magistrate's court in which any power under this Act may be exercised by the court with respect to that or any other child; or
   (b) an address or school as being that of a child involved in any such proceedings.

Notes

1 In any proceedings for an offence under this section it shall be a defence for the accused to prove that he did not know, and had no reason to suspect, that the published material was intended, or likely, to identify the child.

2 The rule of law that a father is the natural guardian of his legitimate child is abolished. Where parents were married at the time of birth each parent has joint responsibility, and where parents were not married the mother has parental right, unless the father has acquired rights in accordance with the provisions of the Act.

(v) The Role of the Education Service in Protecting Children from Abuse (DfEE circular 10/95)

- All schools have a Child Protection Officer, who has undergone specific training for this purpose. Schools have policy statements relating to procedures, and trainee teachers, as well as qualified teachers, should be alert to information and behaviour which may cause them concern. They should seek information from the child with tact and sympathy. It is not, however, the responsibility of teachers and other staff to investigate suspected abuse.

- Staff should be aware that the way in which they talk to a child can have an effect on the evidence which is put forward if there are subsequent criminal proceedings. They should therefore not ask leading questions which encourage the child to change his or her version of events in any way or impose the teacher's own assumptions.

Staff should not give undertakings of absolute confidentiality. *The child should be assured that the matter will be disclosed only to people who need to know about it.*

Staff who receive information about children and their families in the course of their work should share that information within appropriate professional contexts.

Good practice for keeping child protection records includes noting the date, event and action taken in cases of suspected child abuse or when the child is placed on the child protection register.

Reports prepared for child protection should focus on:
- the child's educational achievements
- attendance
- behaviour
- participation
- relations with other children
- where appropriate, the child's appearance.

Reports should be objective and based on evidence.

(vi) Appropriate physical contact with pupils (DfEE circular 10/95)

It is unnecessary and unrealistic to insist that teachers should touch pupils only in emergencies. It is important not to touch pupils, however casually, in ways or on parts of the body that might be considered indecent. In extreme cases a teacher might have to physically restrain a pupil to prevent him or her causing injury to him or herself, to others or to property.

(vii) Appropriate Physical Restraint of Pupils (Education Act 1997, Section 4 and DfEE circular 9/94)

Under the Education Act 1997 the 'Power to Restrain Pupils' is identified as follows:

550A(1)

A member of staff of a school may use in relation to any pupil at the school, such force as is reasonable in the circumstances for the purpose of preventing the pupil from doing (or continuing to do) any of the following, namely:

(a) committing any offence,

(b) causing personal injury to, or damage to the property of, any person (including the pupil himself), or

(c) engaging in any behaviour prejudicial to the maintenance of good order and discipline at the school or among any of its pupils, whether the behaviour occurs during a teaching session or otherwise, ... but it does not authorise anything to be done in relation to a pupil which constitutes the giving of corporal punishment.

Many schools have 'holding policies' which set out in detail the procedure to follow, including the position of hands to 'restrain pupils'.

(viii) Detention

The headteacher of the school must have previously determined and have

1 made generally known within the school, and

2 taken steps to bring to the attention of the parent of every person who is for the time being a registered pupil there, that the detention of pupils after the end of a school session is one of the measures that may be taken with a view to regulating the conduct of pupils.

Note The pupils' parents must have been given at least 24 hours' notice in writing that the detention was due to take place.

Detention must take account of:

- the pupil's age
- special educational needs
- religious requirements
- travel arrangements.

In addition, trainee teachers need to demonstrate that they:

- have established, during work in schools, effective working relationships with professional colleagues including, where applicable, associate staff
- have set a good example to the pupils they teach, through their presentation and their personal and professional conduct
- are committed to ensuring that every pupil is given the opportunity to achieve their potential and meet the high expectations set for them
- understand the need to take responsibility for their own professional development and to keep up to date with research and developments in pedagogy and in the subjects they teach
- understand their professional responsibilities in relation to school policies and practices, including those concerned with pastoral and personal safety matters, including bullying
- recognise that learning takes place inside and outside the school context, and understand the need to liaise effectively with parents and other carers and with agencies with responsibility for pupils' education and welfare
- are aware of the role and purpose of school governing bodies.

Look back at how you perceived the role of the teacher in Chapter 1. Identify how it has changed. What implications do these legal requirements have on the teacher's role?

By this stage of your course most of the professional requirements will be second nature to you and their legal implications will have permeated your understanding of the role of the teacher. The professional requirements identify the teacher as an extended professional, who has an important role in society as well as within the classroom.

Changing law and practice

Law and practice do not remain static. Teachers' unions and professional associations will keep their members up to date on the law, and most schools keep a copy of Croner's *Guide to the Law*. Nowadays schools and their governing bodies are very much aware of their legal responsibilities, making sure that their policies and practices are kept up to date.

Chapter 12

Thinking and growing professionally

Learning objectives
- To identify ways in which teachers can work with colleagues to improve their teaching.
- To create a career plan for effective professional development.
- To identify key skills such as partnership, assertiveness and time management to cope with stress.

Better skills

Newly qualified teachers

Continuing commitment to professional development should be at the heart of teachers' careers (DfEE 1998). It is very easy to feel overwhelmed sometimes, particularly when teaching in a self-contained classroom with little administrative support. Teaching can be a very isolated career, but it need not be, and your colleagues offer the best support for survival. At whatever stage of their career, all teachers need formal and informal networks for gaining and sharing information. A primary school with 15 teachers can represent hundreds of years of classroom experience with thousands of children. Tap into this experience.

Induction for newly qualified teachers varied considerably from one LEA to another but in 1999 a centralised formal induction programme was introduced. This is statutory and combines a general programme of monitoring and support, so that the NQT can 'develop further their knowledge and skills with an assessment of their performance'. The TTA has produced a free booklet which provides an overview of the induction arrangements and aims to help those with roles in monitoring, supporting and assessing new teachers to see how the elements of the process are interrelated. The booklet is available from the TTA on 0845 606 0323 or by downloading it from the TTA website.

The training institutions spend time preparing student teachers for this induction period, through the Career Entry Profile, which identifies needs and sets objectives. The NQT then shares their CEP with the induction tutor and headteacher of their new school as soon as possible after taking up their first teaching post. It provides the starting point for planning the professional development of NQTs and is intended to be used as a basis for setting objectives and developing an action plan for the induction period. Full details of the induction arrangements can be found in DfEE Circular 5/99. The teaching unions and professional associations also give excellent advice and help about the induction year and continuing professional development. The website for the National Union of Teachers, for example, supplies additional information about the role of the induction tutor and reports on its own surveys about conditions of service and new developments in the profession.

Future developments

The government has embarked on a series of other teaching reforms intended to enhance and reward professional development of teachers. The changes were launched by the 1998 Green Paper 'Teachers: meeting the challenge of change', which can be viewed on the DfEE teaching reforms website where there is an excellent summary. The reforms included:
- a new pay structure
- an appraisal of teachers' performance as the basis for professional judgements on pay and career development

- a performance threshold giving access to higher pay for teachers with consistently strong performance
- systematic career and professional development
- a National Fast Track.

The progress of implementation is rapid and the website provides useful updates. These should not be read uncritically. They are political statements and the teaching unions and associations often have excellent commentaries on their own websites.

New pay structure

This is closely linked with rewarding teachers for meeting national standards at a performance threshold. Initially the criteria for moving through a performance threshold was all those teachers who had taught for seven years (good honours graduates) or nine years (if they are not good honours graduates). Every teacher who met the standards of performance was entitled to a £2,000 pay rise and had access to a new upper pay range. Most schools encouraged all eligible teachers to apply as the additional payment came from central funds rather than the school budget. Teachers were encouraged to link their application with the growing wealth of statistical data about pupil performance in their school and in-service time was given to whole staffs to study this. Headteachers were given additional training on 'The Autumn Package' of data information, so that they could guide staff through it.

The Fast Track

The Fast Track is intended to recruit and develop 'top quality graduates and the most talented serving teachers; those with the highest potential for excellence in teaching'. The Fast Track teachers are expected to reach the performance threshold within five years and then move through to Advanced Skills Teacher (AST). This Fast Track is open to undergraduates; trainee teachers; those considering a change in career; serving teachers in the early years of their career and experienced teachers on passing the performance threshold. It is extremely controversial.

Good relationships

Good relationships don't just happen; they must be worked at. Even when you have finished your first year of teaching you will want to have good working relationships with experienced teachers because they can offer so much.

- Ask for help when you need it and work at getting along with your induction tutor.
- Communicate effectively, voice concerns, avoid being defensive.
- Acknowledge that being an induction tutor is not easy, particularly in formal tutor schemes where there is a set programme to follow and the tutor may be involved in teacher assessment as well as support.
- OFSTED inspectors, appraisers, support workers, parents and trainee teachers all observe experienced teachers. This process is much easier for teachers who continue to welcome people into their classroom

Peer coaching and/or appraisal

Teachers are more likely to be asked to observe their colleagues teaching than ever before. The National Literacy Strategy and Numeracy Framework require the literacy and numeracy subject managers in each primary school to observe and comment on the literacy and numeracy teaching in every class. Some appraisal schemes involve peer appraisal, including classroom observation. This is very much harder than it seems to those who devise the strategies. Ideally:

1 You should be able to pick your own partner, so that coaching is comfortable and non-threatening, involving someone you trust and who is committed to helping you.
2 You should be trained, because lesson observation and coaching is a skill. It involves gathering the relevant information and giving constructive feedback as well as observing and analysing teaching. Literacy and numeracy coordinators are provided with this training, but other co-ordinators may have to learn on the spot.
3 Focus on something specific. This can be identified jointly, and the type of observations and data collection can be agreed together. Many headteachers involved in peer appraisal have adopted this strategy.
4 Conduct systematic observations. A number of different checklists are available which can be developed and adapted to the particular needs of one partnership or school. The standards for QTS provide a good starting point. If, for example, the focus is 'paying careful attention

to pupils' errors and misconceptions, and helping to remedy errors', the checklist might read as follows:

- ability to identify errors and misconceptions
- use of questions to draw out pupils' ideas
- responses to pupils' comments and questions
- attentiveness to pupils' contributions in discussion
- attentiveness to misconceptions identified in written work
- ability to identify type of error, e.g. knowledge, skill, general confusion
- knowledge of ways these can be addressed
- skill in addressing them
- subject knowledge relating to errors.

Some of the data collected would arise from discussion with the teacher and children, as well as looking at books and displays.

Formal staff development

Nationally-based

In recent years, central government has given far more direction to staff development. Literacy, numeracy and ICT initiatives are three important examples. Comprehensive in-service packs have been written centrally and distributed to all schools. Local and regional in-service has been provided for named teachers with details of how to 'cascade' the information to others. These courses and the materials are generally free of charge. Much depends on the skills of local presenters to set these centralised materials into a local context.

LEA-based

LEA-based development mirrors central government directives, but also reflects perceived local needs. Some LEAs, for example, have been particularly vigilant in health education and citizenship programmes for primary teachers. All LEAs run courses for NQTs and encourage schools to release them to attend. The statutory induction programme now requires this. Sometimes this is done by providing funding to replace the teacher. Again, these courses are usually free of charge because schools 'buy into them', or there may be only a nominal charge for refreshments.

School-based

All schools have a staff development programme. Much of this is school-based and takes place in the evening after school, or at the start and end of term. The programme is linked directly to the needs identified in the School Development Plan, except when a new government initiative takes schools by surprise and they have to reorganise their programme. Many schools have a staff development officer or coordinator, who may draw up a 'needs identification' chart to determine the needs of individuals, groups and the whole staff. This can result in courses, peer coaching and in-service activity. Courses are evaluated in terms of their overall effectiveness and 'value for money'.

Personal programmes

Trainee teachers and newly qualified teachers have to complete a Career Entry Profile which identifies their own needs for professional development. The intention is to build these needs into a professional development programme. This may be school- or LEA-based. Sometimes the school may buy into a commercial in-service package for individual teachers by sending the teacher on a course run by a commercial concern.

Commercial in-service provision

There are a large number of different organisations which provide, for a fee, in-service programmes for teachers. Traditionally, the universities and other academic institutions have provided the route for higher degrees, certification and validation of courses. This is now a highly competitive and commercial business and a number of other agencies have moved into the area, including educational publishing companies.

A wide variety of short- and long-term courses are available – for a price. Many of these are advertised through mailshots sent to schools, or in local and national papers and educational magazines such as *Child* and *Junior Education*. Some headteachers and governing bodies are very generous in supporting individuals on courses they have asked to attend. Others are not.

Any teacher who decides to study for a higher degree which is seen as being in their own interests, rather than that of the school, is likely to have to fund it themselves. This makes an interesting contrast to some states in the USA, where it is expected that teachers will study for their Master's degree and complete it within the first seven years of teaching. It is also in teachers' financial interests in the USA, because undertaking a higher degree postpones the time when student loans have to be repaid!

In the UK, in-service provision, such as daytime courses during term-time, cost schools a considerable amount of money. Not only is there the cost of the course, but also the cost of the supply teacher needed to cover the class teacher's absence. Schools ask for evaluations of courses and evidence that the person going on the course disseminates course contents to colleagues. Quality in-service provision recognises this, and part of the input will look at ways in which course content may be cascaded to others.

Distance Learning Packages
Companies such as Chris Kington Publishing have a series of publications which build up into Professional Development Management, covering: Pre-entry to Initial Teacher Training; Beginning Initial Teacher Training; Block Teaching Practice; Pre-entry to First Teaching Post; The First Year of Teaching and Beyond the First Year of Teaching. This is a cleverly marketed package because each unit/booklet comes at a different career stage, and this makes the cost manageable.

Other publishers such as David Fulton Ltd have a very comprehensive range of texts which challenge as well as support current practices.

The Open University has a long tradition of providing distance learning packages, including Higher Degrees. The advertisements for these, and those from other higher education institutions, can be found in the educational press. It is now possible to study for a Doctorate as well as for a Master's degree in this way.

Madeleine Lindley Ltd
This is a specialist teachers' and children's bookseller based in Oldham which sells books direct, by telephone or the Internet. It has an excellent range of primary education materials housed in an attractive and welcoming centre. The staff are trained to give help and guidance, and visitors can even help themselves to a cup of coffee! In 2001, there is to be a new custom-built conference centre which will provide a unique opportunity for professional development, linked to resourcing.

Principles for professional development courses
Professional development courses should:
- provide opportunities to interact with colleagues – to discuss learning, teaching and classroom experiences
- give encouragement to adapt new teaching strategies to individual classrooms
- include opportunities to plan with others for improved practice
- use peer coaching to provide support and assistance
- offer sustained training, rather than 'one-shot' inputs – one-shot inputs are most effective when they relate to subject knowledge
- supply depth of content knowledge
- be rooted in and reflect the best available research
- contribute to measurable improvement in children's achievement
- expect teachers to be intellectually engaged with ideas and resources
- allow sufficient time, support and resources to enable teachers to master new content and pedagogy and to integrate these into their practice
- be designed by representatives of those who participate in them
- include different teaching and learning strategies.

Researching teaching
The act of teaching is an act of research. The first lesson plan you ever wrote was a research methodology paper: you stated what you wanted to happen, how you were going to make it happen, then evaluated what did happen. The next time you taught, you changed and adapted your experiment, so that the conclusion was more in line with what you expected.

The National Literacy Strategy and the Numeracy Framework are massive educational experiments to try and help children improve their performance in English and maths. Good evaluation of your own teaching helps you to target and plan more successfully the next time. Research should be a verb, rather than a noun. Teachers need to be active producers of knowledge about teaching, and this is acknowledged today by the growth of interest in teacher researchers.

Teacher researchers ask questions and look for answers. In the process they improve practice, grow intellectually and professionally, establish rewarding partnerships and sometimes even create new career opportunities for themselves. Action research involves studying your own teaching practice to solve individual teaching problems. It is cyclic in nature, involving a teacher or groups of teachers identifying a problem, collecting data, reflecting on the process and analysing the data, using their reflection and analysis to take appropriate action in the classroom. This is then monitored to see how well the action worked and the problem is redefined. There are three basic types:

1 **Individual teacher research** – this focuses on solving a problem in an individual classroom. You might want to help children work together more collaboratively and to devise a series of teaching strategies to promote this. After a period of time, you would need to evaluate what had been undertaken and how effective it had been. The advantage of doing this with a colleague is that the colleague could also evaluate it, and you could both discuss the success of the strategies used.

2 **Teacher research teams** – these can focus on problems in one classroom, several classrooms, or within a school or LEA. They involve the same investigative and reflective cycle as individual teacher research.

3 **School-wide research** – in the UK this is often carried out outside the formal school system with Family Literacy, Portage and Home-Link programmes. These programmes are often put in place when a problem area has been identified. Sometimes they receive considerable sums of money which enable additional personnel to be employed. Short-term evaluations are generally very positive, but the long-term effects are rarely looked at.

Judith Bell's *Doing Your Own Research Project* (1995) is a classic text in this field and Suzi Clipson-Boyles, in *Putting Research into Practice in Primary Teaching and Learning,* demonstrates some very practical ways in which teaching and research are interwoven. There are also a number of Internet links. What the Internet adds to the research is an opportunity to share and discuss the results without the formalities of academic publishing. Links with higher education can also be part of the process.

The government commissioned the *HayMcBer Report* on effective teaching. It was published in June 2000, at an estimated cost of over £4 million and was seen as controversial because teaching unions believed the findings would be linked to performance related pay. The report provides a menu of qualities such as high expectations, good use of resources, good classroom management and planning. A summary can be found at www.dfee.gov.uk/teaching reforms/ mcber.

Internet insights
The Canterbury Action Research Network can be reached at:
http://www.cant.ac.uk/depts/acad/teached/cantarnet/cantarnet.htm
The Educational Resources Information Centre (ERIC) is an information system sponsored by the US Department of Education. Each ERIC site is a clearing house for information and research on a certain aspect of education. For a brief description and direct Internet links to all clearing houses and adjunct clearing houses go to:
http://www.ed.gov/EdRes/EdFed/ERIC.html
The clearing house on Elementary and Early Childhood is:
http://ericps.crc.uiuc.edu/ericeece.html

Information gateways provide some of the support needed to find useful resources on the Internet. Here are three useful ones:
http://www.sosig.ac.uk
http://www.bubl.ac.uk/
http://www.niss.ac.uk

Rewards for those who share

- Join or organise a support group. This will be your best source of information and emotional support.
- Listen to others.
- Listen to tapes and watch videos. Invest in yourself, buy your own, or borrow, or record from the television.
- Read the literature. Subscribe to a professional journal. If your doctor did not know what was happening in his/her field, you would change doctors. You need to keep yourself updated.
- Observe effective teachers.
- Participate in conferences. Attend seminars and workshops. Don't sit at the back and say nothing: it is hot, crowded and uncomfortable and you cannot see or hear well; handouts tend to run out before they reach you; and you will be sitting with the less interested and less involved members of the audience.
- Learn how to use educational research. The Internet is a wonderful door to the research community. ERIC (see above) is an electronic library of all educational research and papers in the USA.

Most training institutions give online support to their students, either through library services and/or specialist websites for student teachers.

Career plan

Invest in yourself. Many professional educators invests in their careers. This helps the children they teach as well as themselves.

Career Evaluation Lifeline

 Imagine your life is a line. Draw it on a piece of plain paper. It can be any line you like: straight, curved or diagonal. Mark where you think you are. Make a list of some of the things you want to do before you reach the end of your lifeline. This can include paid work, non-paid work and personal aims.

This activity is best done with a group of people. It is then possible to talk about common experiences, effects on your career and where you are now.

ACTION PLAN

This is designed to help you identify the goals you wish to reach, or changes you may wish to make, at work or in your personal life. Again, it is useful to be able to discuss this with a friend.

Goals/changes/objectives	Action	Time-scale

Discuss action points, achievable goals and realistic time-scales. A personal action plan is likely to be different from the formalised induction action plan. Unlike the induction plan it is private and can be related to your own needs and aspirations.

Assertiveness

The implementation of a career plan requires assertiveness – at home as well as at work. There are many situations, both at work and at home, when we 'swallow' our own feelings and stay silent, even when we feel very angry inside. Being assertive is one way to stop this inner anger, which is destructive. It is destructive to ourselves, our families, our work colleagues and the children in our classrooms who watch and learn.

One way of looking positively at assertiveness is to compare it with being aggressive and being passive.

Being aggressive

This means getting your own way at the expense of other people, putting them down, making them feel small, incompetent, foolish, worthless or tricked. Humour can, and often is, used in an aggressive way. Can you think of someone who has treated you in this way? Aggressive behaviour by a line manager is now recognised for being what it is: 'bullying'. Several of the teaching unions, as well as the Trades Union Congress, have identified bullying as a key problem. Increased stress on some managers can make them bully their staff. Through assertive behaviour you can avoid being bullied.

Being passive

This means ignoring your own and your children's interests, needs and goals. It often means putting up with a situation which makes you very angry and burns you up inwardly.

Being assertive

This means being honest with yourself and with others. It means being able to say what you want, need or feel, but not at the expense of other people. It means being self-confident, positive and understanding of other people's points of view and being able to behave in a rational, adult way.

Example

VERBAL – words, tone, intonation		
Passive	**Assertive**	**Aggressive**
'I'm sorry'	'I believe ...'	Interrupting
		'You're only ...'
NON-VERBAL – body language		
Passive	**Assertive**	**Aggressive**
Covering mouth with hands	Physically at ease	Infringing others' bodyspace
		Finger-pointing

Teachers must be assertive so that they can act as positive role models for the children they teach.

Stress

If I do this, I won't get that done ...
If I do that, this will slip by ...
If I do both, neither will be perfect ...

Most of us feel like this sometimes. In Britain at least 40 million working days are lost each year owing to the effects of stress. Stress can affect health, performance, and relationships. Most of us can benefit from developing personal strategies to help us become more healthy, relaxed and effective. There are a number of publications for teachers about stress at work (see the Further Reading) and it often helps just to recognise what is happening at an early stage and to take remedial action quickly. Teaching unions give practical support and several produce leaflets on stress and other factors producing stress. www.teachers.org.uk has some of these online.

Symptoms of stress

Physical symptoms	Mental symptoms
Lack of appetite	Constant irritability with people
Craving for food when under pressure	Feeling unable to cope
Frequent indigestion or heartburn	Lack of interest in life
Constipation or diarrhoea	Constant fear of illness
Insomnia	A feeling of being a failure
Constant tiredness	A feeling of being bad or of self-hatred
A tendency to sweat for no good reason	Loss of interest in other people
Nervous twitches	Awareness of suppressed anger
Nail-biting	Inability to show true feelings
Headaches	Loss of sense of humour
Cramps and muscle spasms	Feeling of neglect
Nausea	Dread of the future
Breathlessness without exertion	A feeling of having failed as a person
Fainting spells	A feeling of having no one to confide in
Frequent crying or desire to cry	Difficulty in concentrating
Impotence or frigidity	The inability to finish one task before rushing on to the next one
Inability to sit still without fidgeting	An intense fear of open or enclosed spaces, or of being alone
High blood pressure	A feeling of ugliness

It is worth looking at children in your class who may exhibit any of these symptoms. Teachers are not alone in feeling stress, although if we are the stressed individual, it does feel lonely. As Jack Dunham (1992) states in *Stress in Teaching*, stress has important implications for teachers themselves, their families, the children they teach and the society of which these children are part.

Dunham notes that stress has different definitions because the stressed person has different perspectives. What stresses one individual will not stress another. One definition sees stress as external pressures, e.g. new central government initiatives like the Numeracy Strategy. Another definition sees stress as emotional reactions such as anger and physical reactions such as tension headaches. Dunham defines it as a significant excess of pressures over coping resources, which leads to the development of positive and negative reactions. His work looks at:
- the pressures in teaching
- children's behaviour and attitudes
- the pressures of poor working conditions
- role conflict
- staff reactions to pressure
- the identification of teachers' coping resources.

Learning to relax and helping children to relax

The literature identifies several different techniques for dealing with stress, and many tapes and videos on the subject are available. Robb and Letts (1995), in their book *Creating Kids Who Can*, devote an appendix to 'Turning can't do into can do through relaxation'. They explain why and how relaxation works. For children they explain that relaxation means:
- they learn faster
- they realise they are loved
- they become able to control how they feel

- they can enjoy other people
- they can make sense of the world
- they can use their imagination
- they become more likeable people.

Time management

Time management and stress are closely linked. How often do you feel 'I have to ... or else' and 'I can't ... because'. Stress is often linked to poor time management. Stress prevents the individual from organising his or her time rationally. Sadly, stressed managers create stress by being poorly organised, and a climate of stress then permeates the workplace.

 Write down ten statements which start with the words 'I have to' and finish with the words 'or else'.

> The 'I have to ...' statements represent some demand on your time or energy at work or elsewhere. 'Or else' statements represent a threat. If you work on this with someone else, you could ask them to challenge the statement 'I have to ... '. Does it really mean 'I want to'?

Teaching partnerships

One of the key features of successful teaching is teaching partnerships. We all need them, however long we have worked as teachers. In the past these were often natural partnerships, with people who:
- shared the same space as you, and/or
- shared the same views on teaching, and/or
- shared the same interests in professional development.

Thanks to technology, the opportunities for developing partnerships are global and almost infinite. Partnerships, electronic or otherwise, enable you to create your own culture. In the many schools I have visited over the past twenty years, what is very obvious is that it is not money, class size or resources which determine the success or respect of a group of teachers. It is culture. So make sure your teaching partnerships are positive. We all like a moan sometimes, but if this dominates partnerships it becomes destructive and makes it easier to create a 'blame culture' in schools.

Schools are blamed for faults which lie deeper within our society. As teachers we can defend ourselves against this by constructing a new and positive culture. This can build on the positive aspects of the profession.
- Remind yourself that all teachers are well educated. They have good degrees and often, higher degrees and qualifications. Yet how often do we see teachers advertise their education and training in the same way as we see framed certificates on walls in other professions?
- Teachers have influence. More teachers go into teaching because of the influence of another teacher. This is not so true of other professions.
- Teaching is the only profession which makes other professions possible.
- The majority of teachers have secure employment in a world where many people work on very short-term contracts.
- Most importantly, teachers play a key role in the lives of children:
  - they may be the only stable adult in children's lives
  - they may be the only people able to pass on culture
  - they may be the only models of success a child sees
  - they may be a child's only hope and dream for the future.

Chapter 13

Your first career move – finding your first appointment

This section, written by Les Hankin, has drawn on knowledge, experience and common sense from an updated range of professional career sources, to help you make confident, competent applications for the sorts of posts you want and for which you are best matched. The margin notes give direct front-line advice from the heads, governors, consultants and inspectors who are the gatekeepers to the system.

Market yourself by knowing yourself

Before you do anything else, write a complete broad profile of yourself, for yourself, to give you a clear picture of your strengths (and areas for development). Use the Standards to help you. The appropriate elements can then be selected from this profile when applying for a particular post.

Before wading through the appointments sections, write down what and where your ideal school would be. Exactly what type of job and school are you seeking? Advertisements are expensive, so schools spend hours composing them to make sure they attract exactly the people they need. The following two advertisement are typical. Read for the clues.

'Decide what jobs you want to consider before you start looking. You could trawl through the vacancies until you spot something you like the look of, but it is much better to draw up a checklist of parameters: north or south, town or country, large or small, strict or relaxed, etc.'

Rootless Community Primary School — Community
Key Stage 1 Teacher — Phase specialism
Common Professional Scale

Required September 1999, a committed and enthusiastic teacher for a Reception/Y1 class in this friendly school, with supportive staff and parents and active governing body. Fixed-term contract, — Governors initally for one year. You will be committed to a child-centred approach and work as part of a team. — Contract
Phone immediately for details and to visit the school.
Closing date: 31 April — Approaches

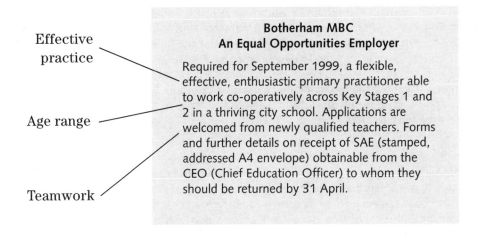

Effective practice

Age range

Teamwork

Botherham MBC
An Equal Opportunities Employer

Required for September 1999, a flexible, effective, enthusiastic primary practitioner able to work co-operatively across Key Stages 1 and 2 in a thriving city school. Applications are welcomed from newly qualified teachers. Forms and further details on receipt of SAE (stamped, addressed A4 envelope) obtainable from the CEO (Chief Education Officer) to whom they should be returned by 31 April.

> 'Pick out and stress different elements of your profile for different posts. Become familiar with the educational press, in which teaching posts are advertised: the *TES* on Fridays; the *Education Guardian* on Tuesdays, the *Independent*, the denominational press ..'
>
> The two ads shown were chosen randomly from a typical week in the *TES*.

Golden rules of job hunting

1 Find out about the school and education generally. Do your research. Think how you'll look at interview if you're unaware of the latest developments.

2 Know yourself. All employers are looking for competences (or Standards). Scour every corner of your daily life for examples of teamwork, the use of persuasive skills, leadership, verbal and written communication skills and general teaching awareness. Think of times when you were proactive and place less emphasis on spectator activities such as going to the cinema. Your future employers will want people who get things done and are involved.

Where do you look?

Jobs can appear at any time, from the beginning of the spring term. Most posts are advertised around May, when teachers in post must resign if they are moving on. As well as the national and local press, LEA vacancy bulletins and of course the Internet, there is the *hidden job market*. If there is a school where you long to work, consider sending them your CV and a covering letter (see later in this chapter). They may not have a job but they are part of a network of schools with often unpredictable staff turnover. You could chase up contacts such as your attachment school, or your old voluntary connections.
'Be businesslike, polite and to the point, and people will be impressed.'

Writing your profile of yourself

It is important not just to write down what you have done, such as being on a union society committee, but also **what you achieved** in that role. You are out to show why you are a better candidate than any other applicant for a particular job. This allows you more control in your relationship with particular employers. Instead of just responding to questions from them, it gives you the opportunity to offer something extra.

You need to convey your own philosophy of education, **either** in a separate paragraph **or** through the tone and emphasis of your overall statement.

> 'Schools like to think that prospective teachers have picked them out and taken the trouble to do some research about the school and its area.'

When you see a job you like, go through the details minutely before applying and make sure you answer every one of its points.
If details are vague, write down what you want to know and phone the school. Professional, polite enquiries make a good impression. If, say, a school requires a 'highly motivated teacher, preferably able to teach some music and games', it would be sensible to give some examples of personal projects which show motivation, as well as detailing your experience in music and games.

Finding information about the school or Authority in which you're interested is extremely useful as 'market research'. Make the effort to find out everything there is to know. Policy statements from the LEA give clues about the priorities of your prospective employers. Schools are now required to have a prospectus, so ask for one and read it closely.

> **Application is usually made by completing a detailed LEA form, but occasionally a CV is required. The CV is a useful check to make sure you have covered all aspects of the experience you have to offer.**

Referees

A detailed confidential report will be written by the tutors involved in your college career. This is often sufficient, as it is very comprehensive. The second referee is usually treated as a character reference, so choose someone who has known you for a long time. It is naturally a good idea to name someone of recognisable standing, such as a headteacher or past employer. You might consider asking the head of your school if your school experience went well. Some church schools require a priest to provide a reference.

Imperative

Make sure you clear any reference with the referee you nominate, not only out of courtesy, but also to alert them that they will be asked to provide one.

Your education tutor writes the summary report of your college career, so you are strongly advised to make sure they are made aware of any interests and/or achievements that you would like to be recognised or emphasised. Draw attention to your record and experience by contacting them regularly.

The paperwork: impressions, presentation

The purpose of the application is to secure an interview, so the medium is the message and first impressions are crucial! It just isn't acceptable to attach to the back of an A4 form a letter written on two small sheets of dinky coloured notepaper, or to write in blue ballpoint on both sides of the paper, or to send off application forms decorated with coffee-cup rings or biscuit crumbs. Heads and governors will turn cold at spelling mistakes, illegible handwriting, unanswered questions, any crossings-out, teardrops or perfume.

Writing the application form: standards

Keep the application papers looking tidy. This isn't always easy. You may make a number of applications and the temptation to cut corners or avoid rewriting a damaged form is strong. But you have to do it, because so much is at stake.

Standardise all letters and papers as A4, the size of the form. Make them easy to photocopy. Keeping on top of the task may mean writing the details elsewhere and having them checked before transferring them to the printed form.

> **Get more than one form so there is a spare if disaster strikes, and/or photocopy/draft everything in detail before copying it on to the original.**

Don't try to type on the form: alignment is always a problem. Also, some schools like to see your handwriting.

Make sure your envelope is big enough. Paper that has been folded too much looks ghastly and is awkward to photocopy. Use an envelope that can take the papers without any folding at all and slip the papers inside a simple, clean transparent pocket file. In any event, one fold across the middle is the limit.

Please use the exact address to ensure that the Records Office is able to respond immediately to reference requests. www.royalmail.co.uk/paf/home.htm provides help if you are unsure of postcodes, or if you know the postcode and wish to check the accuracy of the address.

'The hard fact is that when there are sixty applications for one post (and that is quite common these days) the untidy ones will be thrown out on the first sifting.'

Grammar and spelling!

A pristine set of papers gets you past one hurdle, but there are more to come. Heads and governors believe spelling and grammar are important.

Check and check again!
Check the apostrophes!
Check the small details (like getting the name of the school right).

Things like this matter to people who are proud of their schools.

Common misspellings include:
- it's/its (it's = it is)
- practise/ practice (practise is the verb, practice is the noun)
- curricula/curricular (as in 'extra-curricular activities')
- liaison; commitment; professional

Fill in the form and write the application letter (if handwritten) in black ink. They'll be photocopied so that several governors can see them. Use a fountain pen or good-quality fibre or rollerball. Keep a copy of the completed form, so you know what you said!

> 'Views on whether applications should be handwritten or typed differ, although I've never heard anyone complain that an application was too legible. Either way, I cannot emphasise enough the importance of drafting out your application first and getting some other trusted person to comment frankly on it.'

The application material

Most posts advertised have **job descriptions** stating the exact responsibilities and duties that the job entails. You may also get a **person specification**, which sets out the qualifications, skills, knowledge and experience needed to carry out these duties. Your application must refer to these closely, so that you demonstrate clearly just how suited you are to the job. The place for this is usually in the letter or supporting statement. It is useful to send off for some person specifications before you start applying, so that you know what to expect.

The letter or supporting statement

Usually there is a space for the letter on the form, but doing it separately looks neater and reduces the chance of spoiling the whole form. Write in the box *'Separate application letter attached'*. To make sure the letter and form can be kept together, head it with your name, address and reference to the post for which you are applying. It is now generally agreed that in this day and age handwritten covering letters give a rather sloppy and unprofessional image.

What separates shortlisted candidates from the rest is the quality of their letters of application. Your aim is to show concisely that you match the selector's requirements, and to emphasise abilities and experience that may not be fully apparent from the application form. The easiest way to structure your letter is to work from the job details you will have been sent. Job descriptions vary enormously and you may need to do some reading between the lines of less well-prepared examples.

You must personalise the letter to take account of the details the school has given you! Don't address yourself to thin air by starting 'Dear Sir or Madam' when you could easily find the name and put it in. Such touches cause offence. There is nothing more off-putting than getting a production-line letter. It appears cynical.

Some schools ask you to apply by letter rather than application form. In this case you need to include all the information about yourself that would normally be included in a form. The same points below apply.

The letter

What the head and governors want is a letter that picks up clearly, one by one, the points in the advertisement and in the published details. Avoid repetition, padding and jargon. Make it sound as original as possible. If you read 120 letters which sound exactly the same, you stop reading. Remember also that your application will be read by lay governors.

'Never put anything into the application that you are not ready to substantiate. The panel is bound to draw on it at the interview and you may well be asked to elaborate or explain what you have written.'

Prepare by listing the main requirements of the post on a blank sheet. This must go beyond parroting the points made in the application documentation. Aim to tease out the critical underlying qualities. Think also about any attributes not mentioned that are likely to be important. Then set out examples of activities and achievements that demonstrate your strengths in each of the areas you've listed.

Put the most recent relevant information about yourself at the beginning of the letter, rather than being strictly chronological. **Say what you have done rather than what you are going to do!**

The letter needs to highlight your experience, achievements, and professional and personal skills, to include:

Experience in school

'Check that there are no unaccountable gaps in your history.'

Details of types of school (area, urban/suburban, open-plan, community school, community comprehensive, mixed ability, etc.); classroom experience; age ranges taught and types of organisation experienced (vertical grouping, team teaching, resource-based activities, etc.); teaching practice and school attachment; examples of successful curriculum work (such as history visits).

Your main subject and specialisms

Emphasise what you feel you could offer the school in this area. See yourself as a potential subject specialist. You will have done a full course on this as well as other school experience, special needs and science attachments.

Your prospective employers will expect you to have covered the range of the curriculum in your college courses, but will be impressed to learn of any special study you have carried out. Include studies from your degree course if relevant. Don't waste space by repeating the details of your course.

Other experience and qualifications

These could emphasise music, ICT qualifications, first-aid qualifications, sports coaching and swimming certificates – indeed, any transferable skills that enrich your palette, such as jobs/roles that have involved responsibility, punctuality and initiative.

Church schools

Church schools are entitled to ask about a candidate's attitude either to Christianity in general or, perhaps, to the individual denomination which looks after the school. If the advertisement asks for this, then write something. Be honest, though. Vicars and parish priests will have heard evasions before, but will respect honesty. Also, think about what it is that makes a church school different (and have an answer ready for the interview).

The letter's importance

'Goldilocks principles apply to the letter: not too hot or cold; not too hard or soft; not too long or short. Keep to one A4 side and check it at least three times.'

If you take a careless approach to application writing in the belief that what really matters is the interview, remember: you can't interview brilliantly if you are not invited to attend. Selections have to be made and the application is all there is to go on. References are important but heads and governors have been known to place as much importance on the candidate's application letter.

Make sure your letter conveys a recognition that teamwork is an increasingly important factor in teaching, an ability to relate to children, an understanding of how they learn and an enthusiasm for teaching, as well as an appreciation of the need to differentiate work.

A common fault in NQT applications is the use of an excessively formal style. Try to pitch your writing at a level just light enough to let your personality shine through.

Useful expressions

Action words and phrases such as these may help you put yourself over professionally and present your considerable experience in the best light:

In carrying out this role, I had to ...
This was achieved by ...
Typical projects included ...
Against this background ...
To this end ...
Important achievements were ...
In the past year/years I have ...
In addition, I ...

My achievement may be summarised as ...
To do this involved ...
In this short period, I accomplished the following ...
The main activities that made this possible were ...

ACCOMPLISHED	CULTIVATED	IMPROVED	PARTICIPATED	SHAPED
ACHIEVED	DEFINED	IMPROVISED	PERFORMED	SIMPLIFIED
ACQUIRED	DEMONSTRATED	INCREASED	PERSUADED	SOLVED
ACTED	DESIGNED	INITIATED	PIONEERED	SPECIFIED
AMPLIFIED	DETERMINED	INSPIRED	PLANNED	STARTED
ANTICIPATED	DEVELOPED	INSTIGATED	PREDICTED	STIMULATED
APPLIED	DEVISED	INSTRUCTED	PREPARED	STREAMLINED
ARRANGED	DOCUMENTED	INTEGRATED	PRESENTED	STRUCTURED
ASSISTED	EDITED	INTERPRETED	PRODUCED	STUDIED
ATTENDED	ENABLED	INTRODUCED	PROGRAMMED	SUCCEEDED
AUGMENTED	ENACTED	INVENTED	PROMOTED	SUPERSEDED
BUILT	ENGAGED	INVESTED	PROPOSED	SUPERVISED
COLLABORATED	ESTABLISHED	INVESTIGATED	PROVED	SUPPORTED
COMBINED	EVALUATED	LAUNCHED	PUBLISHED	SURPASSED
COMPILED	EXERCISED	LED	RECOMMENDED	SURVEYED
COMPLETED	EXPLORED	MAINTAINED	REDESIGNED	TAUGHT
COMPOSED	FORMED	MANAGED	RELATED	TESTED
COMPUTED	FORMULATED	MEASURED	REPORTED	TIGHTENED
CONCLUDED	FOSTERED	MERGED	RESOLVED	TRAINED
CONDUCTED	GENERATED	MOTIVATED	REVIEWED	TRANSLATED
CONSOLIDATED	GUIDED	OBSERVED	REVISED	TREATED
CONSULTED	HANDLED	OBTAINED	REVITALISED	UNIFIED
CONTRIBUTED	HELPED	OPERATED	SAVED	UTILISED
CONTROLLED	IDENTIFIED	ORGANISED	SELECTED	VITALISED
CREATED	IMPLEMENTED	ORIGINATED	SET UP	WROTE

'Never send a standard letter to schools. Match the contents to the vacancy and be sure to answer any specific issue requested. Standard letters are easily spotted and quickly rejected. Only a properly constructed letter that either matches or is sympathetic to the school's philosophy, the degree of experience, the knowledge and the skills required, will suffice.'

adapted from prompt lists used by NAS/UWT and The British Council

Six tips for an effective application letter

John Caunt, writing in the *TES* of 17 April 1998, suggested:

1 Demonstrate your qualities by examples of experience and achievements rather than unsupported statements and vague generalisations.

2 Don't bore the reader with every last detail of your achievements. Aim for a maximum of six to eight main points and a page and a half of text.

3 Make life easier for the selector. Your opening paragraph needs to engage their attention and make them want to read on. Attributes they are looking for should be clearly illustrated.

4 Put your draft letter aside for a day and then review it. Invariably you will find things that you can express more persuasively.

5 Get somebody else to proof-read your final draft. We all have our presentational blind spots.

6 Don't include anything that you will not be able to demonstrate or justify at interview and remember to keep a copy for pre-interview revision.

> 'When schools start looking urgently for last-minute vacancies, you have to be around.'

The letter: example to accompany CV or form

A permutation of the following example letter should enable you to make a comprehensive, professional and businesslike application. The letter should emphasise your strong and relevant capabilities and experience, but not be so written to a formula that your own personality cannot shine through. You may not need some of it if an application form is involved. If in doubt, ask your tutor to read it through.

Keep the letter sharp. Never write more than two sides of A4. If you give your own opinions you will have to be ready to support them at your interview. Avoid sexist or discriminatory terms such as 'headmaster'.

> 'I feel we reject many worthwhile applicants because they don't do themselves justice in their letters. So: Think very hard about strengths and seek evidence to support these (previous jobs, college, other activities). Read the job description, person specification and other details properly. Explain briefly how you meet the requirements, giving evidence. Make the letter readable and personal. Cut out jargon. This is not a college essay!. Aim at lay people. Set it out carefully and legibly. Time is very important. We're wary of Goody Two Shoes. Everyone is still learning'.

your address and telephone number

Mrs/Mr P. Straw
Headteacher/Chair of Governors/other [whichever is specified]
school name and address

date [16 March 2001]

Dear Mrs Straw *[always address the recipient by name whenever possible]*
[Start enthusiastically with something like] I have pleasure in applying for the post of assistant teacher (Common Pay Scale) at your school, as advertised in the Guardian of 12 March *[include reference number, if any]*. In support of my application I would like to draw your attention to aspects of my personal education, professional training, talents and other relevant interests which I feel equip me for the post.
[Make the tone of the letter positive and dynamic.]

Professional training paragraph — At (training institution) I have followed a ...

School experience paragraph — During my school experience I have been able to practise my developing skills in a range of schools. *[Develop this.]* I have achieved ... *[Be specific on achievements in school and give a brief range of examples from across your school placement. Give yourself the opportunity to suggest what you would like to develop if – no, better make that, when – appointed.]* If you have worked in schools prior to your ITT course, give that information here.
[Make reference here also to your religious leaning, if appropriate.]

Other experience and qualifications — Sport, music, first aid, Catholic certificate ...

Interests and previous experience paragraph — My leisure activities and interests are mainly concerned with ... but I also enjoy ... *[Mentioning an unusual or particularly interesting experience gives the interviewers a hook and something about which you can expand enthusiastically and implant yourself in their collective short-term memory.]*

In my previous job as a legal officer I gained transferable skills in ... *[and elaborate those aspects useful for teaching].*

I include the names and addresses of two referees in my CV and shall be pleased to give further details or to attend for interview.
Yours sincerely
[Use 'Yours faithfully' if you are able only to address the recipient as 'Madam' or 'Sir'.]

> 'We notice how well a letter is written and organised. Organisational skills or the absence of them are well demonstrated in a letter.'

The CV

Note that if the advertisement specifies an application form then you would not normally include a CV.
It is still always worth having a bang up-to-date CV to hand. The purpose of this *curriculum vitae* (the Latin phrase means 'course of life'; a brief account of someone's education, qualifications and previous occupations) is to secure an interview by presenting a clear, organised and factual summary of your life.

> 'Your CV should be plain and simple, concise and include only relevant information. Here is not the place to extol the virtues of child-centred learning as your philosophy of education'. 'When is a CV not a CV? When it's a book!'

A CV would include:

Name and address
Telephone number and e-mail address
Age
Date of birth
Nationality

> 'The general CV should be immaculately word-processed but not excessively desktop-published, on one side of A4. It should contain facts, but not beliefs or philosophies. Be explicit about how you can be contacted.'

Status	married/single [whether you add this information is your choice]
Education	University(ies) Sixth-form college [?] and years Secondary school attended and years
Qualifications	GCSE, GCE A level or equivalents Degree PGCE expected (if appropriate)
Course information	List briefly your main school block experiences in terms of age range taught, type of school, etc.
Teaching experience	If you have taken part in additional school experiences, put that in as well. [It is worth indicating experience that would equip you to teach across the breadth of the age range in which you have specialised.]
Academic work	Outline your first degree course – not in great detail, unless it is strictly relevant to primary teaching.
Curriculum and professional studies	Again, add extension taster and school-based in-service courses, if you have attended these.
Previous paid employment and personal experience	Indicate such important details as other work in schools, voluntary work in the community, school or college leadership, etc.
Interests and activities	These could include musical talent, sport and games, hobbies, etc.

149

Referees	The following have kindly agreed to provide references: [see earlier in this chapter]
Edit your letter!	Before you finalise the document you should ruthlessly remove any verbiage. Pay particular attention to clichéd expressions and empty buzz-words. Shorten sentences where you can. Remove repetitions and redundant words and don't spell out what is already implied. To describe achievements, use strong active verbs that convey energy and enthusiasm wherever possible.

When you get that interview

Make sure you can be reached, as the school may phone you at short notice. When granted an interview you must confirm as soon as possible that you will be pleased to attend. If phoned, repeat the time details of the interview back to the caller to be sure you have them correctly and follow this up with a letter of acceptance!

Preparing for the interview

Before the interview, list the sorts of questions you think might be asked and those you ought to be able to answer. Then decide how you'd answer them. It is important to be tough with yourself: include questions such as *'Why did you retake your A levels?'*

It is also a good idea to list the questions you want to ask. Use them to indicate your preparation for the interview and concentrate on the area's education provision and issues relevant to newly qualified teachers (NQTs). You should also rehearse for interviews. Ask a friend to help. Mental preparation is vital: the interview should be treated with a meticulous eye for detail. Rehearsal will also help to reduce your nerves on the day. Develop a positive image of yourself by 'seeing' yourself doing well. Try out your style in front of a mirror. Experienced and seasoned interviewees always do this.

> 'Heads' common concerns are mostly about how well candidates have prepared themselves for the particular circumstances of their school.'

Before the interview

Read the job description fully. Note your strengths and areas for personal development.
- Take along copies of your application form, CV and covering letter.
- Reread your Personal Philosophy of Education (see earlier).
- Decide what you will wear and the timing and route to the interview.
- Try to visit the school and locality before the day.
- Work through a mock interview before the real one.
- Anticipate the questions you might be asked.
- Feed your self-confidence in the days before the interview.
- **Just remember, you're the best!**

> 'Clothes are crucial, and the camouflage approach is best. The rule is to apply the UN commanders' tactic of studying local warlords' dress code and wearing something just slightly more chic.'

What should you wear?

Confidence in yourself is so important in convincing your interviewers that you can take up the reins of the job immediately. But how do you convince yourself that you are confident? Selection consultants such as Rebecca Cornfield *(Successful Interview Skills,* Kogan Page 1997) believe that you almost need to kid yourself of your confidence. It really comes from knowing that you've prepared well, anticipating the questions, researching your employer and the tasks expected of you. Feeling good about your appearance is crucial in psyching you up and reinforcing the message that you're the person for the job.

These are general rules, which sound sexist but are essentially common sense:

- Dress to look the part! Keep it simple; anything frivolous detracts from your authority.
- Go for darker colours that suit your colouring; women should avoid dangly earrings, which distract attention from their face.
- A jacket is good for women: the square shape boosts their authority.
- Men should consider cream or ivory rather than white shirts, and socks that are long enough to cover their legs when they cross them.
- Men should choose ties with medium-sized, regular patterns and wear no more than one pattern on their suit or shirt. If you are going after a maths post, be prepared to say how your tie pattern could be used. Yes, it has happened!

The pre-interview

You should always ask to be taken round the school beforehand. You need to know whether the place is right for you. And don't be naive about encounters which take place before the interview. If you visit the school a week or two earlier to look round, or are invited with the other candidates to lunch on the day, be aware that the interview clock starts running as soon as you step through the gates. You can make a really positive impression and make this process work for you. Dress as if for interview.

Talk to the children and take an interest in what they are doing

Some candidates go way over the top in the 'pre-interview', laughing like drains, talking loudly about the depth of their experience, name-dropping, commenting on items on the noticeboard. If someone is obviously flipping in this way, deliberately set out to give the opposite impression. If you are drinking coffee with the staff, keep calm, smile, ask polite questions and give off an air of modest, good-natured confidence. Don't seek to dominate.

> 'The 'pre-interview' is the hidden interview that inevitably happens when you come and people size you up. There are many ways to skin a cat, after all, and all's fair in love and war. We watch to see if you're really interested in how the school teaches reading, for example.

The moment of truth

In the interview, sit in a relaxed, but poised and attentive manner. Answer questions concisely but not too briefly. Smile, try not to giggle, fidget or put your hand to your face. Sit up straight, look them in the eye without staring. Don't fold your arms in defensive mode, clench your fists or scratch your nose. Be ready for obvious questions – about your motives, about the curriculum – but remember that no interview panel is likely to take that kindly to new entrants who seem to know it all.

If you're at all nervous:

- breathe more deeply
- be yourself, but yourself on a good day!
- make it clear that you like teaching children
- enjoy it. It's a nice day out, whatever happens
- humanise the interviewers. They may be nervous too.

The interviewers should introduce themselves. Their role often indicates the type of question they are likely to ask. A teacher governor may well ask about curriculum interests and expertise. A parent might question you on homework, discipline and control and about how you feel about parents working in the classroom. Remember, parents have the greatest vested interest in the choice being made. Value all the questions and answer them with respect.

It is important to establish eye contact. With a panel this can present the problem of who to look at. It is best to answer mainly the person who has asked the question, but to try to include the rest of the panel as well. Don't just relate to the person on the panel who you think is the most important.

The questions

A school interview panel will include such luminaries as the headteacher, governors (parent/ Foundation/LEA/teacher), and possibly a representative from the LEA. Remember, they have all been through the pain of these sudden-death interviews to get where they are today!

The opening remarks will probably be ice-breakers to put you at ease, such as 'Tell us about your course'. You can't tell them everything, so be selective. Choose the relevant areas.

Interviewers almost always want to know 'why': 'Why did you take that course?' 'Why did you apply to us?' 'Why do you think you are suitable?'

'Why have you applied to our Authority/school?' Be sincere and indicate that you know something about the Authority and/or school.

Questions after this may centre on the curriculum, your particular interests, and your subject specialism.

> 'If you have listed reading and theatre as your interests, it would get you off to an embarrassing start if you could not name the last book you read or play you saw.'

Intrusive questions

In the (unlikely) event that inappropriate questions are asked such as 'Do you plan on having children soon?' or 'Do you have any religion?' politely ask the head or chair whether they wish you to answer such a question. This will make the point that it is intrusive and should be headed off.

During the interview

> 'Be ready for a question about the most exciting or interesting thing you did on your school experience. The most impressive newly qualified teacher I ever interviewed produced a file of colour photos in response to such a question, showing exactly what she had done in one class and, in the process, how gifted a communicator she was.'

- Hold on to your self-confidence and self-belief. Never assume that the other candidates are any better than you, however confident they appear.
- Enter the room calmly and seat yourself comfortably. Take the opportunity to answer fully questions you are happy with.
- If you don't understand the question, ask them to repeat or rephrase it. This is quite acceptable.
- Seek to illustrate some of your answers from your own experience in schools (such as on discipline: *'I remember on school experience when ...'*).
- If you find yourself wittering, round off your answer!
- When in a hole, stop digging!
- Make use of the chance you'll be given to ask positive questions about aspects of the post and the school.
- Be prepared for a sudden, awkward question from the quiet grey-suit in the corner!
- Remember that there is rarely a 'right' answer. The panel want to explore **your** attitudes and interests, reliability, commitment and enthusiasm.

Church or denominational schools

For church schools, you must be prepared to answer questions on the particular nature of such a school (Roman Catholic, Church of England or other).

Example questions

- Tell us something about your experience in schools (ages taught, where, kind of area, some aspect that you think was particularly successful).
- What kinds of learning experiences do you think are important for nursery/infant/junior/ secondary children?
- What steps need to be taken to ensure effective learning experiences for children? (This seeks your views on planning and presentation, differentiation of work, regular assessment to monitor progress, evaluation of the activities you provide and regular review of the work you've undertaken.)
- How do you plan for and organise the learning environment? (Give examples.)

- How do you know the children are learning and developing through these provisions? (Assessment and target setting usually come up, as your cue to talk of assessing the effectiveness of teaching, assessing progress, evaluating teaching strategies and providing evidence for sound professional judgement of a learner's progress.)
- Give examples of records you have kept.
- What do you feel is important about working as a teacher in a team?
- How should parents be involved in their children's learning?
- How would you put Equal Opportunities into practice in your class?
- How would you promote good discipline in the classroom?

Remember, you have so much to offer

You were accepted for your teaching course from a cast of thousands. You will complete the course when many do not. Your institution has a good name and interviewers will recognise this.

Learning and teaching styles

Refer to school experience where appropriate. Classroom organisation may be a source of discussion. *'Which age groups have you taught?'* *'What about discipline in the classroom?'* Get an idea of the school (or LEA) policy from brochures. Identify current educational issues in the media and be prepared to talk about them in relation to your teaching.

Church schools will ask about RE. Many state schools are very concerned about the legislation on RE. If you have any interest or expertise in this area you might find that this will distinguish you.

At the end

To mark the end of the interview you should be given the chance to ask any questions you have. You could say *'All the questions I had have now been answered'*, but this may be the opportunity to clear things up or score points.

Always ask about arrangements to support you through your first year in teaching. This ties in with the information on your Career Entry Profile (see below).

Do use this opportunity to express an interest in the job and your career. Don't dwell, at this stage, on pensions, holidays or other conditions of employment that don't relate directly to the responsibilities you are hoping to be entrusted with.

Contractual questions you should ask at interview or when you have the job

It is quite reasonable and sensible in the present climate to ask about the starting salary you might expect. The teachers' union, the NUT, advises that it is essential to discuss thoroughly the question of the starting salary at the interview: *'It is advisable, if possible, to obtain a written offer stating the starting salary before accepting the post.'*

Some Authorities in areas of teacher shortage might offer help with accommodation.

Acceptance

Once you have accepted a post a legal contract immediately exists on both sides, even if there is nothing in writing. It is quite unacceptable and unforgivable to decline the post later. You must also withdraw all other applications that you have made.

'The experts say that interviewers unknowingly set great store by first impression and other body language, 38% tone of voice and 7% of what you say.'

'Listen carefully to what questions are asked and look at the person addressing you. Eye contact is important, but don't stare: when you answer begin by talking to the questioner, then open it up and glance around the panel. Don't exclude them from your replies. Don't be familiar but don't be shy.'

'Don't forget that an interview is always a two-way process and both you and the school need to find out about each other.'

Non-acceptance

You may realise at some stage during the day that the post is not what you want. You can withdraw tactfully before the interview. But usually at the end of the interview you will be asked if you are 'still a serious candidate'. If you don't want the job, you must let the panel know this before they reach their decision or you will have wasted their time. It often happens that you could have another interview looming for a job you prefer, so you could ask the panel if they will hold the job open. This will depend on how badly they want you.

Type of contract

With all this in mind, you must be clear about the status of the post you have been given. If this isn't a **permanent** post, then what is your contract?

Fixed-term contracts are for a stated period. **Temporary contracts** may be offered when the contract is for a certain period of time, such as to cover long-term staff absence. You need to be clear about the implications of the contract you are offered in terms of job security. The headteacher should be prepared to clarify this.

Securing the post

When you get a job you will be asked to arrange to visit the school before starting and you may also get a form to claim travel expenses. This is a good time to meet the staff and also take away materials to help gird yourself for work there. You should later receive a letter confirming your appointment which you will be required to acknowledge. Open a file and keep a copy of this and of any documents, such as the Career Entry Profile.

Career Entry Profile

Every provider of teacher training and education is now required to provide you with a CEP, a profile folder conveying summary information about your particular strengths, and priorities for further professional development during your induction as an NQT. This relates to the work you will have done on Standards.

Job description

You are likely to be given a written job description along the following lines.

Responsible to: the headteacher of the school.

Main purpose: to provide an effective education for children by teaching within the framework provided by the Governing Body, and with regard to all statutory requirements.

Main duties:
- To fulfil the conditions of employment for school teachers as laid down in the Pay and Conditions Act 1987.
- To promote the development of the Equal Opportunity Policy throughout all aspects of school life.
- To work towards continuity of the curriculum at times of transition.
- To provide an interesting and effective learning environment for the children.
- To attend staff development initiatives.
- To involve parents in their children's learning.
- To be part of the staff team.

This makes it doubly important for you to look at the school's prospectus, policies and other documentation, to inform you for the interview and beyond.

Reflection

Just supposing you don't get the first job you go for. This might feel like the end of the world. It isn't, but you can learn from the experience. Always accept the decision with good grace. You may have been very close to getting the job: there is a network of heads and you may encounter some of the interviewers again!

Take the opportunity of a debriefing if it is offered. This will give you pointers on your performance. If you are being interviewed regularly this suggests that your applications are reasonable but that you may need to hone your interview technique.

You can ask for advice at any time from the Careers Tutor and from other professionals.
The following advice from inspectors of one LEA might help you review what went on. They recommend the appointment of applicants:
- whose communication skills are well developed
- whose professional thinking and knowledge of their phase and subject specialism are evident in their handling of ideas in discussion and their ability to see possibilities
- who have developed a clear personal philosophy about education
- who show that they have gained from the professional experience of school placements/ teaching practice through an appraisal of the curriculum of their TP schools, through observing behaviour and through analysing the variety of roles of the teacher.

> 'The choice the governors make is rarely based on one factor alone, so don't worry too much about the answer that seemed so daft once you get out of the room .... Painful though it may seem, don't pass up the offer of debriefing on your interview performance. It will boost your confidence.'

Sparkle!

Even where you are not offered a job instantly, a good interview can lead to another opportunity. *'Would-be teachers should expect to make more than one application before they find a place'*, according to the National Employers' Organisation for Schoolteachers.

When you have the job you want, what next?

The world of work is changing dramatically and the old paternalism of schools and LEAs, where the system took care of teachers' planned career progression, is no longer guaranteed. Instead of the 'familiar envelopes of jobs', we are said to be moving back to how it was before the Industrial Revolution, when we take on clusters of tasks, according to William Bridges, in his book *Jobshift*. These tasks will include study and homework. Everyone will have to take responsibility for their own career development. We must equip ourselves for a new culture of self-reliance where we each determine our own goals and development and training needs.

Career progress and continuing professional development

Leading career writers such as Charles Handy say we must each run our careers as though they were a business. Bridges calls it *You & Co*. You need to maintain the abilities and attitudes that education needs at present, but remain true to who you are. You need to find a balance so that your working life is nourished by your personal life. You need to decide what you ultimately want from life and work and find the training you need. Career opportunities will follow.

Appendix 1

Exemplification of standards

The standard is printed in bold and the exemplification follows it. These are not definitive statements, but are designed to help you look more deeply into the standards statements. Soon you'll be able to add to them. They cover Section B (Planning; Teaching and class management) and Section C (Monitoring, assessment, recording, reporting and accountability). Standards relating to the early years are included, although many primary courses only cover the Years 5–11.

Section B4 Planning

Objectives

(a) Plan their teaching to achieve progression in pupils' learning through:

(i) identifying clear teaching objectives and content, appropriate to the subject matter and the children being taught and assessed

Clear teaching objectives are an essential component of good planning in schemes of work, lesson/activity plans and target setting for groups and individual children. Objectives should be sharply focused to identify what children will know, be able to do and understand as a result of the session, lesson, or sequence of lessons. The content of good planning shows how these objectives will be achieved. Both teaching objectives and content will be informed by good knowledge of subject and phase. Precise teaching objectives should be used as a basis for assessing pupils' progress and attainment and for evaluating the effectiveness of lessons.

(ii) setting tasks for whole-class, individual and group work, including homework, which challenge children and ensure high levels of child interest

By carefully considering the use of whole-class, individual and group work, the planned allocation of tasks should be arranged to provide for a range of learning styles and suitable challenge for all children. These may, for instance, involve specific directed questions during whole-class activities, different tasks for groups of differing attainment, alternative ways of accessing the same learning, allocation of different roles within mixed-ability groups, or individuals working through personalised activities aimed at specific targets. Gender, ethnic and social mix should also be considered when planning group work.

Planning should identify when homework is set and any likely resource implications. Teachers should be aware of and follow the school policies relating to homework. Some homework may be more informal and involve children completing tasks set in school time and preparing themselves for their future learning. Planning should take account of the efficient and effective use of support staff, who should be consulted and informed about teaching objectives and involved in planning.

(iii) **setting appropriate and demanding expectations for pupils' learning, motivation and presentation of work**

Teachers must plan tasks that require all children to make significant progress, and produce work of appropriate quantity and quality. The work planned must take into account the need to motivate all children by capturing their interest, offering intellectual challenge and the opportunity for all to learn. The teacher must plan how to communicate the purpose, method and quality of presentation and the criteria for judgements to the children.

(iv) **setting clear targets for pupils' learning, building on prior attainment, and ensuring that children are aware of the substance and purpose of what they are asked to do**

Learning targets should be sharply focused and shared with children, as must be the purpose of the work. Planned work must take into account prior learning and attainment and set goals that are appropriate to each child. Effective target setting requires a good knowledge of how children learn, the levels of work and progression required by the National Curriculum, and of the pupils' current attainment. Child records, previous teaching plans and discussion with children provide good starting points for assessing current attainment.

(v) **identifying children who:**
- **have special educational needs, including specific learning difficulties**
- **are very able**
- **are not fluent in English**
- **and knowing where to get help in order to give positive and targeted support**

Planning should include differentiated teaching objectives and approaches that cater for children with particular needs that are not addressed by the objectives set for the majority of children. Teachers need to be aware of the school procedures for identifying and supporting those children with special needs, of very high ability and who have English as an additional language.

(b) **Provide clear structures for lessons, and for   sequences of lessons, in the short, medium and longer term, which maintain pace, motivation and challenge for children**

Lesson structures should show the effective and efficient use of time to promote learning, and an appropriate sequencing of content. Teachers need to inform themselves of how the school plans its teaching programmes and ensure that their short-term lesson plans are securely placed within agreed medium- and long-term plans. Schools vary in their definitions of long-, medium- and short-term planning, and often long-term planning is a collective responsibility within a school or department. Planning over a period of time should give evidence of progression and continuity. Planning for pace, motivation and challenge involves a good understanding of how the next sequence of lessons and activities will enable children to progress and raise their levels of attainment.

(c) **Make effective use of assessment information on pupils' attainment and progress in their teaching and in planning future lessons and sequences of lessons**

Assessment information on all children should be taken into account when planning the style of teaching and learning strategies, and the content to be taught to each child. Particular attention needs to be given to the use of assessment data in planning a response to the needs of individual children. This may result in grouping children according to their attainment or their preferred learning style for a particular lesson.

(d) **Plan opportunities to contribute to pupils' spiritual, moral, personal, social and cultural development**

Most schools have stated aims that relate directly to these areas of personal development. For effective spiritual, moral, personal, social and cultural development to take place and to permeate throughout a school it has to be planned and assessed. Teachers should plan opportunities for spiritual, moral, social and cultural development through the content and processes of their lessons, the interpersonal relationships between their children, and by them learning about the world in which they live.

(e)   **Where applicable, ensure coverage of the relevant examination syllabus and National Curriculum programmes of study**

Long-, medium- and short-term planning will normally be firmly based on these curricular requirements, and it must be evident that they are fully covered. Planning should make it obvious where schools have adopted national frameworks – for literacy and numeracy, for example – or have introduced vocational qualifications.

Teaching and class management

(f)   **Ensure effective teaching of whole classes, and of groups and individuals within the whole-class setting, so that teaching objectives are met, and best use is made of available teaching time (e.g. time for monitoring/helping specific individuals)**

The teacher must organise and structure his or her teaching so as to have time to address the class as a whole, deal with groups when the class is so organised, and pursue teaching points with individual children. Drawing together groups of children or the whole class during the course of the lesson is an efficient way to move pupils' learning forward. The planned use of the additional adult support in the classroom can help in providing a suitable method of working. Effective teaching may involve grouping children according to attainment or other criteria, and encouraging children to work together and to learn collaboratively.

(g)   **Monitor and intervene when teaching to ensure sound learning and discipline**

The teacher must be aware of what is happening throughout the whole class. Monitoring may involve moving around the classroom, observing children, listening to their comments and inspecting their work. The teacher can then address anyone who is not working appropriately, to further clarify the task, help with difficulties, maintain discipline and ensure that children are working and making progress.

(h)   **Establish and maintain a purposeful working atmosphere**

The teacher must communicate the expectation that children work thoughtfully and conscientiously, ensuring that children understand they are working to achieve the specified objectives to raise their attainment. Teachers must also maintain a good pace to the lesson and set appropriate targets for children to achieve during the lesson. Provision of meaningful continuation and extension work for those who complete the set tasks early, and presentation of pupils' work, can also help achieve an appropriate commitment to work. The physical environment and resourcing of the classroom will provide the background for a purposeful working atmosphere.

(i)   **Set high expectations for pupils' behaviour,   establishing and maintaining a good standard of discipline through well-focused teaching and through positive and productive relationships**

This standard relates closely to (h). The need for a high level of co-operation between child and teacher, and children and their peers, to achieve well-defined tasks with a clear purpose is paramount in encouraging good behaviour. This will help children enjoy the lesson and feel they are making progress. The teacher must also encourage high standards of behaviour and discipline through consistent implementation of a behaviour code and clear approval of good discipline. Teachers should be aware of whole-school policies which ensure a consistent approach to managing pupils' behaviour.

(j)   **Establish a safe environment which supports learning and in which children feel secure and confident**

The teacher must ensure pupils' physical safety by using recommended resources and following safe practice, including any legal requirements. The pupils' emotional security must also be ensured by making them feel at ease, avoiding threatening questions, confrontational attitudes or inappropriate tactics such as sarcasm. Pupils' intellectual security must be ensured through an environment which supports learning and may often provide children with visual aids to develop independent learning. The teacher must also be sensitive to pupils' personal circumstances, gender, and ethnic relationships.

(k) **Use teaching methods which sustain the momentum of pupils' work and keep children engaged through:**

(i) **stimulating intellectual curiosity, communicating enthusiasm for the subject being taught, fostering pupils' enthusiasm and maintaining pupils' motivation**

Teachers must engage pupils' interest and enthusiasm by using interesting topics and examples, employing relevant and stimulating resources, using eye-catching presentations and demonstrating links to other subjects. It can also be helpful if teachers communicate their own enthusiasm for the subject and show that they are learners themselves and have respect for pupils' independent learning.

(ii) **matching the approaches used to the subject matter and the children being taught**

Teachers must choose a variety of teaching strategies that acknowledge pupils' different methods of learning and are effective in developing pupils' understanding. They must ensure the resources and examples used take account of pupils' age group and interest. The pace of the lesson, the organisation, style and vocabulary used must match pupils' abilities and prior attainment.

(iii) **structuring information well, including outlining content and aims, signalling transitions and summarising key points as the lesson progresses**

Teachers must ensure that children know the purpose of the lesson, what they are expected to learn from it, and what they are actually expected to do. The ordering of activities or stages in an explanation can be an important factor in helping children understand a concept or procedure. The explained purpose, structure and sequence are likely to be more complex with older children. Teachers' own subject and phase knowledge will help them to structure the information appropriately.

(iv) **clear presentation of content around a set of key issues, using appropriate, subject-specific vocabulary, and well-chosen illustrations and examples**

Teachers must be able to provide a clear explanation of key concepts and use examples that make the ideas accessible to all children being addressed, and may well require a different approach with different groups. The different learning objectives must be clearly emphasised. Task setting needs to be closely matched to the consolidation and extension of concepts, knowledge and understanding of the key issues.

(v) **clear instruction and demonstration, and accurate, well-paced explanation**

Clear instruction is closely linked to a good understanding of the purpose of the activities and the variety of ways in which these can be explained, described, illustrated and demonstrated to children. The teacher needs to have an assessment of each pupil's existing knowledge and an awareness of possible misconceptions in learning. Instruction and demonstration should be at sufficient pace to keep children interested, but slow enough to encourage and check their understanding.

(vi) **effective questioning which matches the pace and direction of the lesson and ensures that children take part**

Teachers use questions for a wide variety of purposes. Questions can be directed at confirming pupils' prior understanding, drawing on their experiences, sharing their ideas, drawing their attention to a specific subject area, checking whether they have grasped the concept being considered and giving direction and purpose to the following activity. Pupils' progress is often the result of well-judged, open-ended questioning.

(vii) **careful attention to pupils' errors and misconceptions, and helping to remedy the errors**

This applies to pupils' answers to questions, their contributions to discussion and their written work. Teachers must identify pupils' difficulties and help to remedy any misconception, lack of knowledge or confusion through analysis and subsequent discussion or instruction. In some subjects there are recognised areas of difficulty for which there are well-documented strategies teachers can use to help children.

(viii) listening carefully to children analysing their responses and responding constructively in order to take pupils' learning forward

This covers both adult–child and child–child dialogue. Direct responses to open-ended questions are particularly useful in identifying pupils' thinking. Questions are also useful in helping identify less satisfactory elements of teaching; for example, if children are unable to complete a task, need far more support than expected, or fail to build on progress already made. Child–child dialogue provides an equally important insight into learning, motivation and progress.

(ix) selecting and making good use of textbooks, IT and other learning resources which enable teaching objectives to be met

The term 'learning resources' covers anything which can be used to enhance pupils' knowledge and understanding. In order to be effective, such resources must be identified prior to the teaching session and should include items that children use to promote independent learning. Displays, for example, in key vocabulary and activity areas, should also be seen as a learning resource. Teachers should be aware of the National ICT scheme of work and how this informs their teaching across the curriculum. All resources should be linked to learning objectives and should extend pupils' attainment and progress.

(x) providing opportunities for children to consolidate their knowledge and maximising opportunities – both in the classroom and through setting well-focused homework – to reinforce and develop what has been learnt

In order to maximise learning, children need to revisit information in a variety of ways, and not simply repeat an exercise or exercises they have already completed successfully. The words 'consolidate', 'reinforce' and 'develop' all come into play here. Opportunities should be sought to advance pupils' understanding by drawing on previous knowledge and skills. Homework should be used to reinforce school-based learning, but also can give opportunities for learning that are not easily provided in school.

(xi) exploiting opportunities to improve pupils' basic skills in literacy, numeracy and IT and the individual and collaborative study skills needed for effective learning, including information retrieval from libraries, texts and other sources

The cross-curricular skills of language and literacy, numeracy and IT are involved in all subjects at all ages. Where these form a natural part of the lesson the opportunity should be taken to explore and explain their role and importance in this context. This may be a quick reference to knowledge obtained during a previous lesson, or a much more lengthy use of numeracy skills in presenting and analysing a graph in a science lesson. Children need to develop independent learning skills, including finding and using information from libraries.

(xii) exploiting opportunities to contribute to the quality of pupils' wider educational development, including their spiritual, moral, social and cultural development

Teachers must be aware that opportunities for spiritual, moral, social and cultural development can be drawn from almost all subjects and from working methods and relationships within the classroom. They should discuss these aspects sensitively and purposefully within an overall policy of continuous development.

(xiii) setting high expectations for all children notwithstanding individual differences, including gender and cultural and linguistic backgrounds

For all children to achieve their potential, teachers must expect high, achievable standards. These can be demonstrated through providing suitably challenging work that has a clearly defined purpose in advancing each pupils' understanding, knowledge and skills from their current achievement by matching the needs of different levels of attainment and ability in the class. It is clearly unacceptable to make any assumptions concerning individual pupils' potential based on their social, cultural or linguistic background.

(xiv) providing opportunities to develop pupils' wider understanding by relating their learning to real and work-related examples

Learning is often more successful when it is embedded in a context which children understand. This includes the world outside school. Teachers need to have a good understanding of the local communities which the school serves and which inform pupils' understanding of what goes on inside school. Teachers need to build on this and extend pupils' experiences so that their learning is enhanced by the links between what goes on in school and what goes on outside, including the world of work.

(l)   Are familiar with the *Code of Practice on the Identification and Assessment of Special Educational Needs* **and, as part of their responsibilities under the Code, implement and keep records on individual education plans (IEPs) for children at Stage 2 of the Code and above**

Teachers need to know the procedures operated by the school to ensure the Code of Practice is carried out. They need to inform themselves of the ways in which particular special needs manifest themselves in terms of pupils' learning and ways in which children with special educational needs can be identified and supported. Together with the school special needs co-ordinator (SENCO), they should look at recommended ways of providing attainable targets for children with special educational needs. These should be written in the appropriate language and fulfil the requirements of the Code of Practice. It is essential that, where appropriate, they should be comprehensive and avoid a narrow focus on basic skills. All lesson and activity planning should incorporate the needs of these children and their progress and attainment should be monitored systematically.

(m)   Ensure that children acquire and consolidate knowledge, skills and understanding in the subject

This standard gives direction to almost all of the other standards. All the components of planning, teaching and monitoring must be judged according to their effectiveness in helping children make progress and raise their attainment.

(n)   Evaluate their own teaching critically and use this to improve their effectiveness

Teachers must consider their own teaching and make realistic judgements against QTS standards. Over a period of time they will identify which areas of their teaching they could most profitably work on to improve the attainment of the children they teach. Mentors will help in considering and helping improve teachers' practice.

Additional requirements relating to under-fives

(a)   Plan activities which take account of pupils' needs and their developing physical, intellectual, emotional and social abilities and which engage their interest

Plan effectively and sensitively to promote the early learning goals, making it clear what children should learn; group and deploy other staff effectively.

(b)   Provide structured learning opportunities which advance pupils':
- **personal and social development**
- **communication skills**
- **knowledge and understanding of the world**
- **physical development**
- **creative development**

Learning opportunities need to be structured carefully to combine a variety of different teaching strategies to advance children's learning and experiences of the world around them. Plans should include ways in which staff work directly with children, provide first-hand experiences and be well-balanced, purposeful and varied. All activities must have an explicit purpose.

(c) Use teaching approaches and activities which develop pupils' language and provide the foundations for literacy

All those working with under-fives should give high priority to language development and communication skills. Teaching and activities should enable children to develop, practise and gain experience of the four elements of language and literacy – speaking, listening, reading and writing. The emphasis should be on learning through talk. The planning and teaching programme should allow children to:
- regularly take part in conversations, speaking confidently and clearly
- communicate with others in imaginative play
- use talk that is related to their own investigations
- listen to and make up stories, rhymes and discuss their own experiences
- handle and look at books and share reading
- write, draw and paint with increasing control.

(d) Use teaching approaches and activities which develop pupils' mathematical understanding and provide the foundations for numeracy

Mathematical understanding should be planned within broad areas: number, shape, space and position and comparison of measurements. High priority should be given to developing children's awareness and use of mathematical language during practical activities, for example, expressions such as 'more', 'less', 'fewer' and 'how many'. Teaching approaches should support mathematical development through exploration of everyday materials and equipment. Planning should allow children to:
- develop their mathematical vocabulary
- sort and match objects, compare them and put them in order
- count objects and recognise and use the numbers 1 to 10
- learn about the number system
- think, talk about, solve and record numbers for simple mathematical problems
- develop spatial awareness through movement and handling objects
- learn about the properties of shape and relationships between shapes
- make and describe mathematical patterns.

(e) Encourage children to think and talk about their learning and to develop self-control and independence

This includes important aspects of spiritual, moral and cultural development, including the development of an understanding of self and of others and the ability for children to articulate their feelings. This is linked closely to work on language and literacy. High expectations for behaviour should be set; for example, stories can often be used to discuss incidents that arise and help children to distinguish between good and poor behaviour. Independence can be encouraged through providing a pattern of activities so that children are encouraged to develop personal independence in matters of dressing, hygiene and health. Planning should include opportunities for children to:
- take initiative
- select an activity or resource
- work well independently, in pairs and in small groups
- have personal independence.

(f) Encourage children to concentrate and persevere in their learning for sustained periods, to listen attentively and to talk about their experiences in small and large groups

Many young children can concentrate and persevere in their learning for sustained periods if they are properly motivated. Task setting and the overall learning environment for the under-fives need to stimulate, motivate and enthuse children so that they do listen attentively, talk about their experiences and show sustained concentration when working/playing independently or in small groups.

(g) **Use teaching approaches and activities which involve planned adult intervention, which offer opportunities for first-hand experience and co-operation, and which use play and talk as a vehicle for learning**

It is critical that all those working with under-fives have a clear understanding of the learning needs and potential of these children. The staff need to collaborate in planning so that adult support is used effectively. Other adults working with young children need a good understanding of the theory underlining good early-years practice.

(h) **Manage, with support from an experienced specialist teacher if necessary, the work of parents and other adults in the classroom to enhance learning opportunities for children**

The involvement of all adults should be planned. Ideally, any adult working with under-fives should receive basic training in child development and be helped to develop an understanding of the best ways in which adult support can be given. It is critical the adult support is not limited to monitoring safety and behaviour.

Section C Monitoring, assessment, recording, reporting and accountability

(a) **Assess how well learning objectives have been achieved and use this assessment to improve specific aspects of teaching**

At the end of any teaching session, a teacher should evaluate what learning has taken place and whether the planned learning objectives have been achieved. In assessing the extent to which these objectives have been achieved the teacher should evaluate the effectiveness of the teaching methods and strategies adopted, which will inform subsequent planning.

(b) **Mark and monitor pupils' assigned classwork and homework, providing constructive oral and written feedback, and setting targets for pupils' progress**

It is essential for continuity that school policies concerning marking are understood and that teachers share with the children the criteria used for assessing their work. Children should be involved in the assessment of their own work and be able to discuss the assessment with their teacher. Marking and monitoring should be largely formative and aimed at improving child attainment with oral and written comments relating to progress and giving specific suggestions for improvement. Some marking and monitoring will be summative and used for formal recording and reporting purposes.

(c) **Assess and record each pupil's progress systematically, through strategies including focused observation, questioning, testing and marking, and use these records to:**
(i) **check that children have understood and completed the work that is set**

Teachers should use a range of assessment tools, including focused observation, questioning, testing and marking, to diagnose whether children have understood, as well as completed, the work and tasks that are set.

(ii) **monitor strengths and weaknesses and use the information gained as a basis for purposeful intervention in pupils' learning**

Assessment of pupils' learning involves recording their progress over a period of time. Teachers need to establish a range of strategies to ensure systematic assessment for all children, including those that do not require written evidence of learning. Time needs to be set aside to reflect on individual strengths and weaknesses and plan targets and strategies for intervention.

(iii) **use different kinds of assessment appropriately for different purposes, including National Curriculum and other standardised tests and baseline assessment, where relevant**

Baseline assessment refers to the statutory requirement to assess all children on entry to school at the age of five. It also means identifying the starting point of understanding when any new subject area is introduced or at other points of transition. Assessment needs to take place before and after teaching in order to identify when and where progress has been made and as a means of evaluating the teaching. Standardised tests provide a useful means of comparing results between cohorts of children within and between schools, and provide the basis for making judgements about the effectiveness of the teaching. Assessment information is also used for reporting to parents on the progress and attainment level of their children.

(iv) inform planning

Evaluating pupils' learning involves having a good insight into the effectiveness of different teaching strategies and the learning outcomes they produce for different children. Good-quality assessment, which provides a clear view of what children know, can do and understand forms a basis for effective planning which enables the teacher to match task, content, and presentation style to the pupils' needs.

(v) check that children continue to make demonstrable progress in their acquisition of the knowledge, skills and understanding of the subject

An effective monitoring system using precise objectives and well-focused feedback helps to ensure that all children maintain their learning momentum. It is also important for teachers to use informal assessments and child discussions to combat underachievement in all children, so that they continue to be motivated to work hard and make good progress.

(d) Are familiar with the statutory assessment and reporting requirements and know how to prepare and present informative reports to parents

This refers to the National Curriculum statutory requirements for assessment, recording and reporting at selected points, such as the end of a Key Stage. Teachers need to be aware of the statutory reporting requirements for particular subjects and Key Stages as well as the format and style for reporting to parents.

(e) Where applicable, understand the expected demands of children in relation to each relevant level description or end of Key Stage description, and in addition, for those on 11–16/18 and 14–19 courses, the demands of the syllabuses and course requirements for GCSE, other KS4 courses, and, where applicable, post-16 courses

This standard refers to examination syllabus content and National Curriculum level descriptions. Government bodies such as the Qualifications and Curriculum Authority (QCA) produce exemplifications of standards and annual reports which can be used to support written descriptors.

(f) Where applicable, understand and know how to implement the assessment requirements of current qualifications for children aged 14–19

Assessment requirements vary, and teachers need to be thoroughly versed in the techniques appropriate to specialist subjects and be aware of the changes which new curriculum developments bring. 'Understand' emphasises professional knowledge. The 'know how to' refers to putting knowledge into practice.

(g) Recognise the level at which a child is achieving, and assess children consistently against attainment targets, where applicable, if necessary with guidance from an experienced teacher

This standard is closely related to (e) above. It requires the teacher to obtain and interpret evidence of a pupil's attainment, and to develop, with help, his or her ability to compare this evidence with National Curriculum level descriptions and similar statements in order to assess the pupil's progress.

(h) Understand and know how national, local, comparative and school data, including National Curriculum test data, where applicable, can be used to set clear targets for pupils' achievement

This standard requires teachers to be aware of how external criteria are used to make judgements about the progress and attainment of the children they teach. Teachers need to be aware of information, such as the 'Panda' data, which enables the necessary comparisons to be made and hence to develop appropriate targets for specific groups of children within the school. These provide a means of moderation and can be refined through good internal targeting.

Appendix 2

Child profiles

There is no 'right' way to construct a profile, but you will need to collect relevant evidence from an early stage. When beginning child profiles, we suggest you prepare a record sheet for each child on which you can gather information in note form.

These records can be used when you write up a child profile. You may find it useful to attach relevant examples of a child's work to this record. Records will be in three broad areas:

1 relevant background information which has relevance in terms of the child's ability (or otherwise) to benefit from the teaching situation and from the curriculum being taught
2 strengths and weaknesses (Is a child able to discuss ideas well, but slow or reluctant to write them down? Is a child gifted mathematically, but less able in English?). The section of Chapter 2 on multiple intelligences is useful here (see p. 11)
3 your own observations to inform judgements about the child's development.

These observations may be general, posing such questions as:
- Does this child relate well to others?
- Does he or she communicate well?
- Is he or she active or assertive in the group?
- Does he or she understand instructions?
- Does he or she need a high level of support and reassurance?

or they may be specific, relating to areas of the curriculum: maths, English, science, etc.

You will need to consult the class teacher to obtain general and background information to inform on the first two sections. The third section offers you the opportunity to develop skills of observation and to effectively record evidence of children's abilities. As the profile develops, information may be structured as on the following page.

Whenever you gather evidence, you need to ask yourself about the database: How do we know this? How secure are we about the evidence?

Intellectual development

This involves more than listing test scores. Try to observe the child engaged in different activities in different contexts. Comment both on the quality of the end product and the learning processes. Remember to look at all four modes of language: speaking, listening, reading and writing. How does the child cope with problem solving or investigation activities? What are the child's talents and interests?

Physical development

Comment on the child's build. How does he or she compare with others of the same age? You will also need to consider fine motor skills (writing, colouring in, using scissors, drawing, etc.) and gross motor skills (general movement, PE, dance, in the playground).

Emotional development

Is the child confident, self-assured, able to organise others, happy, secure, etc.?

Social development

How does the child get on with other children? Does he or she have lots of friends/mix freely/ have a few steady friends/exist on the fringe of the class/seem to be a loner, etc.? How does the child relate to you, the teacher, and other students?

You may include examples to illustrate your comments where appropriate. Include any observation schedules you have used. The 2-minute observation schedule is particularly useful.

Target setting

Discuss with the class teacher three learning targets for the child. Make sure that they link with the data you have already collected.

NOTE All child profiles should include only the first names of children in order to ensure confidentiality of information.

Appendix 3

Discipline policy and procedures: School A

Support for staff

Teachers need to feel that they are supported by senior management when they are facing difficulties in the classroom, but it must be the right kind of support. We have suggested that taking responsibility for discipline away from classroom teachers is the wrong kind. It simply undermines their authority and confidence. The primary aim of management support should be to increase teachers' capability to solve their own classroom problems.

Behaviour policies

(a) *The effectiveness curriculum.* Schools teach values as well as knowledge and skills. There must be a consensus among staff on the effective curriculum.

(b) *Models of behaviour.* Most sets of rules are written for children. The behaviour of teachers must be consistent with them. If children are told, for example, to be polite and respectful to others, teachers must provide good examples of such behaviour in their dealings with adults and children.

(c) *Consistency with religious education and personal and social education.* Tolerance and self-discipline are common themes in these areas. The values which underlie the rules must be consistent with them.

Applying the principles of good classroom management

Well-organised and well-delivered lessons help secure good standards of behaviour. Some of the clearest messages are that teachers should:

(a) know their children as individuals. This means knowing their names, their personalities and interests and who their friends are

(b) plan and organise both the classroom and the lesson to keep children interested and minimise the opportunities for disruption. This requires attention to such basics as furniture layout, grouping of children, matching work to pupils' abilities, pacing lessons well, being enthusiastic and using humour to create a positive classroom atmosphere

(c) be flexible in order to take advantage of unexpected events rather than being thrown off balance by them

(d) continually observe or 'scan' the behaviour of the class

(e) be aware of and control their own behaviour, including stance and tone of voice

(f) model the standards of courtesy that they expect from children

(g) emphasise the positive, including praise for good behaviour as well as good work

(h) make the rules for classroom behaviour clear to children from the first lesson and explain why they are necessary. The rules must be consistent and simple

(i) make sparing and consistent use of punishments. This includes avoiding whole group punishment which children see as unfair. It also means avoiding punishments which humiliate children by, for example, making them look ridiculous. This breeds resentment; and

(j) analyse their own classroom management performance and learn from it. This is the most important message of all.

Do all you can to avoid:

humiliating.......................................it breeds resentment
shouting... it diminishes you
overreacting............................... the problems will grow
blanket punishments ....the innocent will resent them
over-punishment.................keep your powder dry; never
punish what you can't prove
sarcasm...it damages you!
use humour..it builds bridges
keep calm...it reduces tension
listen..it earns respect

- Be positive and build relationships.
- Know your children as individuals.
- Carry out any threats you have to make.
- Be consistent.

Maintaining discipline

The majority of children conform and are co-operative. Deal immediately with the few who present problems.
- Establish your authority firmly and calmly.
- Separate the problem from the person.
- Only if you cannot resolve a problem, refer it on to one person. Make sure it is pursued to a satisfactory conclusion.

Procedures around school

As there are regularly new teachers on the staff, it would be beneficial to outline some of the procedures for supervising children around school.

Before school

1 Staff meeting at 8.50 a.m. each day.
2 Member of staff on bus duty supervises the children out in the yard at 8.50 a.m.
3 Children collected from the yard at 9.00 a.m.

If it is raining at 8.50 a.m. the staff meeting will be cancelled. Teachers to supervise their children in their classrooms whilst the head and deputy ensure orderly entry into the building.

Playtime

1 Teacher on duty makes sure that they are ready to lead their class out for the start of play.
2 Teacher on duty stands in the yard so that they can observe all areas of the yard, e.g. where the juniors line up.
3 All teachers ensure that their class is seen out of the building in an orderly manner.
4 At the end of playtime, teacher on duty blows the whistle, waits for silence and asks the children to line up with their teachers. Please do not whistle until the teachers are there to support you. This places a responsibility on all staff to be there to
   (a) take responsibility for their class; and
   (b) support their colleague on duty.

If playtime is wet, teachers should divide the duty between them and their year colleague. The teacher on indoor duty must remain in the corridor between the two classes, ensuring reasonable behaviour and giving permission for the toilet, etc.

Dinnertime

Teachers must supervise sending the children out to the welfare staff at 12 noon and ensure that the classroom and corridor are cleared. If it is a wet dinnertime, please ensure that your welfare person knows where comics, games, etc., are stored.

Junior teachers meet their children on the playground by 1.00 p.m.; infant teachers by 1.15 p.m.

Home time
It is each class teacher's responsibility to monitor the children leaving the school through the correct exit and in an orderly manner.

Principles for classroom procedures

There are no hard and fast rules, as teaching styles vary, but there are basic principles which need to be considered. The principles are generally school-based and classroom-based.

1 The class is a community with standards.
2 The teacher identifies with the class.
3 Poor or disorderly behaviour is unacceptable to the class.
4 Each member is privileged to be a part of the class.

If disruption is severe:
1 Whatever initial sanctions you adopt should be known and agreed.
2 Exclude a child from the class within the classroom.
3 If grossly unacceptable, then see Deputy Head, or if worse, the Head.

(Children should not be sent to the Deputy or Head, but taken there. If this is impractical, then send for the Deputy, then the Head: if not available, inform senior teacher, i.e. 'B' allowance holder or, if an emergency arises, inform S, who will interrupt P or I.)

When a child has been excluded, either within the classroom or with Head or Deputy, it should be done with an attitude of sorrow, not anger. The child then returns to the fold when they can or are willing to conform. Demanding an apology is not recommended – perhaps suggest one.

1 Much of the social activity of children takes place outside the classroom and the children's reactions to these situations are vital in their social development. For this reason, adequate and conscientious supervision of corridors, cloakrooms, playground and hall are vital.

   When a child enters school at 9.00 a.m. he or she is the responsibility of the school from then until he/she, and inevitably the class teacher, leaves.

2 It is important that whatever procedures the children are asked to follow, whether academic or behavioural, time is spent ensuring that nothing below expected standard is accepted. The children must learn that every detail, however trivial it may seem, is worth any time spent on getting it right. Eventually it becomes a good habit.

3 We are teaching in an area where, generally speaking, the children have certain language deficiencies. The importance of the spoken word as a means of control may be alien to the child; therefore it has to be taught and constantly reinforced.

   Therefore we must convey to the children the importance of what the teacher is saying and so they must be made to listen. It is what is being said that is important, so never speak over children speaking. Wait for them to listen, e.g. 'I am waiting – I am waiting – I am waiting' – and wait.

Anti-Bullying Policy: School A
Philosophy

School A will provide a safe, secure, pleasant and stimulating atmosphere which cares and meets the needs of all abilities and interests.

The school will develop positive attitudes to all people regardless of gender, race, age, creed and disability.

In order to achieve this we will encourage communication through relationships based on mutual respect.

Bullying is a word which can often be misused and misunderstood. For the purpose of the school's policy and practice it is defined as:

- a negative act or series of actions which are premeditated, intended and these actions are often frequent and covert
- these actions can further be defined and designed to hurt, threaten or frighten someone
- bullying may also directly relate to family influences and out-of-school situations.

This definition needs reinforcing both at class and whole-school level in order that children understand how seriously this is regarded.

Aims

1 The issue of bullying for the purpose of this policy will be considered in three ways:
- physical bullying
- verbal bullying
- bullying which focuses on a person's race, gender or disability.

2 Any incidence of bullying will be considered seriously. It should be recognised that although the effect of physical bullying is more visible, the effects of bullying in other areas often is more damaging to the victim, the bully and the school community.

3 Bullying will not be tolerated and will be confronted until a satisfactory resolution of the matter is confirmed.

4 Any incidence of bullying will be recorded.

Structure

1 Each member of staff will be given a copy of *Bullying: A Positive Response* and encouraged to read and refer to it.
2 Copies of the book are available from the headteacher for loan to parents. A copy will be retained in the library.
3 The assessment and treatment of bullies will be seen as equally necessary as the protection of victims.
4 Children will be encouraged to report incidences of bullying.

Procedures

Prevention is better than cure.
A member of staff should decide:
1 the degree of deliberation
2 the nature of the act of bullying
3 the severity of the act
4 the frequency of the act
5 the effect of the act both to victim and bully
6 the age, and understanding – premeditated and intended – of the parties concerned.

The member of staff may decide, after discussion with both parties, that the incident can be satisfactorily dealt with by a reprimand. If the member of staff is concerned that the effect of the act may be more serious, then the matter should be referred to the Headteacher or Deputy Headteacher.

The Head/Deputy will decide, after reports from the member of staff, upon the seriousness of the effect following discussion with the parties concerned. If the effect or the action is thought to be serious then:

- The parents of the victim and the bully will be called into school to discuss the situation.
- The bully's name will be entered in the bullying record. This means that one further incident will result in exclusion.
- Both the victim and the bully will receive counselling. The situation will be monitored to prevent recurrence.

Behaviour Policy: School B

Aims

- To encourage a calm, purposeful and happy atmosphere within the school.
- To foster positive caring attitudes towards everyone where achievements at all levels are acknowledged and valued.
- To encourage increasing independence and self-discipline so that each child learns to accept responsibility for his or her own behaviour.
- To have a consistent approach to behaviour throughout the school, with parental co-operation and involvement.
- To make boundaries of acceptable behaviour clear and ensure safety.
- To raise awareness about appropriate behaviour.
- To help give children, staff and parents a sense of direction and feelings of common purpose.

Children's responsibilities are:

- To work to the best of their abilities, and allow others to do the same.
- To treat others with respect.
- To obey the instructions of the school staff (teachers and welfare staff), and parent helpers.
- To take care of property and the environment in and out of school.
- To cooperate with other children and adults.

Staff responsibilities are:

- To treat all children fairly and with respect.
- To raise children's self-esteem and develop their full potential.
- To provide a challenging, interesting and relevant curriculum.
- To create a safe and pleasant environment, physically and emotionally.
- To use these rules and sanctions clearly and consistently.
- To be a good role model.
- To form a good relationship with parents so that all children can see that the key adults in their lives share a common aim.
- To recognise that each person is an individual.
- To be aware of each person's (special) needs.
- To offer a framework for social education.

Parents' responsibilities are:

- To make children aware of appropriate behaviour in all situations.
- To support the school in the implementation of this policy.
- To encourage independence and self-discipline.
- To show an interest in all that their child does in school.
- To foster good relationships within the school.
- To be aware of the school's rules and expectations.
- To offer a framework for social education.

What we do to encourage good behaviour

- We make clear our expectations of good behaviour.
- We discourage unsociable behaviour by promoting mutual respect.
- We encourage children to take responsibility for their own actions and behaviour.
- We set standards of behaviour through example.
- We praise and reward good behaviour both publicly and privately.

What we do if the child misbehaves

- We ask them to stop misbehaving.
- When necessary, we discuss incidents with the children involved.
- Where possible, we encourage children to try to resolve disagreements themselves.
- We encourage children to take responsibility for their own behaviour.

Repeated or persistent misbehaviour

Where there is repeated or persistent misbehaviour (e.g. bullying, insolence, swearing, fighting, defiance, name-calling), the following will apply.

Nursery

- If a child's behaviour in the nursery proves to be extremely disruptive it may be necessary to request:
  - A parent/guardian to stay and shadow the child.
  - The child to stay for a limited period only, e.g. he or she goes before a story.
  - The child's starting date is delayed until the child is more mature.

Infant/Junior

- The child's name is written on the blackboard.
- Movement within the class is restricted (for a limited period).
- Privileges, e.g. playtime, are withdrawn.
- An entry is made in the class teacher's behaviour file and the child fills out an ABC form to be retained in the file. A central record is kept of incidents. Playtime detentions, supervised by a staff member by rota, result from repeated inclusion in behaviour files.
- The teacher contacts the parents (face to face, by letter or by phone). A record is kept, and contact is mentioned to the Head/Deputy Head.
- The Head/Deputy Head is involved.
- A designated teacher is involved, and temporary withdrawal to another class is considered (the parents are informed).
- Formal contact is made with parents.
- Central Support Services are contacted.
- Exclusion – either temporary or permanent – may be made at lunchtime, with parental agreement.

Supporting guidelines

- We believe that children are less likely to misbehave if they are on task.
- Tasks should therefore be meaningful.
- They should be neither too hard, causing the child to be overwhelmed, nor too easy, leading them to be bored.
- Children should have a clear sense of short-term and long-term goals and receive positive feedback, leading to a growing sense of confidence.
- Children should have a high self-esteem through being valued and the development of a growing sense of competence.
- Children need to feel safe and secure, both physically and emotionally.

A positive approach

- We aim to ensure that children experience success through their efforts in the National Curriculum and broader school experiences.
- We aim to ensure that our children feel valued as individual and unique people who have things to offer as well as learn.

Strategies for positive encouragement

Nursery: Stickers for good work and behaviour.
Sharing assemblies.
Infants: Stickers for good work and behaviour.
Certificates for consistent good work and behaviour.
Sharing assemblies to reinforce expected standards of work and behaviour.
Juniors: Class star systems.

Team points to be allocated within a 'house' system. Progress of teams to be a feature of assemblies.

Example

	Behaviour	**Sanctions**	**Comments**
STAGE 1	AGGRAVATIONS Wandering about, calling out, interrupting teacher when talking to whole class, interrupting other children, ignoring minor instructions, talking with other children, making silly noises, pushing in line.	NAME WRITTEN ON BLACKBOARD Minimal. Eye contact. Frowns. Proximity. Reminders. Change of seating.	Not recorded. After several repetitions within a certain time period, e.g. 3 incidents in a morning, a warning is given that the next time it will change to Stage 2 and will be recorded.
STAGE 2	LESS SERIOUS Eating sweets, not responding to teacher's requests to work. Being more disruptive, deliberately creating a disturbance. Accidental damage through carelessness. Dallying. Cheek, off-hand comments. Minor challenge to authority. Swearing. Annoying other children.	Separation from the rest of the class group. Writing a letter of apology. **Withdrawal of privileges, e.g. playtime. Child to fill in a consequences report to go into class behaviour file.**	**Reminder that the incident is recorded in the behaviour file.**
STAGE 3	Deliberately throwing small objects with intention of breaking them. Harming someone. Damaging school or pupils' property. Leaving class without permission. Repeated refusal to do set tasks. Continued or more serious cheek/challenge to authority. Harmful/offensive name-calling. Bullying.	**Detention at break time. Mention made to Deputy/Head. Contact made with parent.**	**Use of a designated teacher.**

	Behaviour	Sanctions	Comments
STAGE 4	VERY SERIOUS Repeatedly leaving classroom without permission. Fighting and intentional physical harm to other children. Throwing large, dangerous objects. Serious challenge to authority. Verbal abuse to any staff. Vandalism. Stealing. Persistent bullying.	Head to be involved. Head contacts parent.	Possible involvement of outside agencies.
STAGE 5	EXTREMELY SERIOUS Extreme danger or violence. Very serious challenge to authority. Verbal/physical abuse to any staff. Running out of school.	Probably means immediate exclusion. Fixed term – up to … days.	Parallel procedures for official out-of-school activities.

Anti-Bullying Policy: School B

Introduction

We regard bullying as particularly serious and always take firm action against it. We encourage children to work against it and to report any incidents of bullying. Children should not suffer in silence. The golden rule should be: always tell, and do it the moment it happens. Tell a responsible adult in school. Don't leave it until you get home.

What is bullying?

Bullying can be physical, verbal or emotional and carried out by a single person or a gang.

Incidents of bullying can include:
- name-calling
- gossip, 'skitting' or belittling
- damage or stealing property
- coercion into acts they do not wish to do
- pinching or kicking
- lying to isolate an individual
- jostling
- teasing
- intimidation
- extortion and petty blackmail
- ostracism
- damaging school work and equipment
- manipulation.

Why are some children bullied?

Reasons for being a victim may be:

- differences in race, sex, class, appearance or disability
- being a new child in school
- social standing
- family crisis
- having special needs
- being easy to provoke
- not fitting in ('odd')

The bullied child may well be somebody who is not assertive (timid), unlikely to fight back, a loner with few friends, anxious or fearful, a younger child, or somebody outside the group.

Why do some children bully?

Reasons for being a bully may be:

- being themselves a victim of bullying or violence
- enjoyment of power, or creating fear
- problems in their family background ('spoilt', lack of rules or structure at home, being 'bottom of the pile')
- copying behaviour
- low self-esteem
- macho self-esteem
- personality defects
- transferral of blame.

Bullying occurs in children from all backgrounds, cultures, races and sexes, from nursery to the sixth form and to adults.

General statements about bullying

References

Bullying: a Positive Response, Cardiff Institute of Education.
Action Against Bullying, Scottish Council.
Bullying: the Child's View.

- Boys often bully younger children of both sexes.
- Girls often use verbal abuse and ostracise others from the peer group – usually other girls.
- Some victims are also bullies.
- Some victims are treated as culprits.
- Onlookers are, even unintentionally, condoning bullying and become part of it.

How to spot bullying

- Solitary or withdrawn behaviour.
- Deterioration of work.
- Spurious illness or erratic attendance.
- Desire to remain with adults (asking for jobs, etc.).
- General unhappiness, anxiety or fear.
- Late arrival.
- Bed-wetting.
- Anti-social outbursts.
- Avoidance of games and PE.

A school anti-bullying approach

Prevention is better than cure, so:

- we will encourage the caring side of children
- we will work for a caring, co-operative ethos (see Behaviour Policy)
- we will locate personal and social education issues in the curriculum

- we will work closely with parents to discourage bullying, and welcome their full support
- we will ensure adequate supervision of playgrounds and the dining-room
- we will positively encourage caring and discourage bullying.

Informal procedure

When faced with an incident of bullying the class teacher or assigned person should ask the children involved and any witnesses to give their account of events without interruption from other children. The discussions can be held with the children separately. Writing an account may help the older children put their point of view across better. The discussions may well be at a time when it is possible to hear the complaint in full, e.g. breaks or the lunchtime interval. The listening teacher should show patience and display clearly that they take the victim's complaint seriously.

Anti-bullying procedure

1 All complaints should go to the class teacher, teacher on duty, assigned person, Deputy Head or Headteacher. Welfare staff should report all allegations of bullying to the teaching staff.
2 All incidents and discussions with all the children involved should be recorded in a bullying file held by the assigned teacher.
3 Children will be entered at Stage 3 of the Behaviour Policy for proven or admitted incidents of bullying.
4 Parents will be involved in discussions over consistent bullying and will be given an explanation of any action taken. They will be asked to support the school in addressing bullying.
5 If the bullying persists the perpetrator will be entered at Stages 4 or 5 of the Behaviour Policy, depending on the seriousness of the incident.

Bibliography

Chapter 1

Coles, M. (ed.) (1999) *Professional Issues for Teachers and Student Teachers*. London: David Fulton Publishers.

Hayes, D. (1999) *Planning, Teaching and Class Management in Primary Schools: Meeting the Standards*. London: David Fulton Publishers.

Hayes, D. (1999) *Foundations of Primary Teaching*, 2nd edn. London: David Fulton Publishers.

Headington, R. (2000) *Monitoring, Assessment, Recording, Reporting and Accountability*. London: David Fulton Publishers.

Meighan, R. and Siraj-Blatchford, I. (1997) *The Sociology of Educating*, Chapter 19 'Social Systems, Structure and Functions'. London: Cassell.

Pollard, A. and Tann, S. (1994) *Reflective Teaching in the Primary School*. London: Cassell.

Teacher Training Agency (1997) *National Standards for Qualified Teacher Status*. London: Teacher Training Agency.

Trend, R. (1997) *Qualified Teacher Status: A Practical Introduction*. London: Letts.

Chapter 2

Cashdan, A. and Overall, L. (eds) (1998) *Teaching in Primary Schools*, Chapter 4: 'Schools, pupils and parents: Contexts for learning'. London: Cassell.

Desforges, C. (ed.) (1996) *An Introduction to Teaching: Psychological Perspectives*, Chapters 4 and 5 'Learning in classrooms', 'Learning out of school'. London: Cassell.

Fontana, D. (1995) *Psychology for Teachers*, (ensure latest edition), Chapters 1, and 3–7 'Early Social Development', 'Concept Formation and Cognitive Development', 'Language; Intelligence; Creativity; Learning'. London: Macmillan.

Hurst, V. (1997) *Planning for Early Learning*, Chapters 1 and 2. London: Paul Chapman.

Moyles, J. (1992) *Organising for Learning in the Primary Classroom*, Chapters 1, 2, 3. Milton Keynes: Open University Press.

Chapter 3

Pollard, A. and Tann, S. (1994) *Reflective Teaching in the Primary School*, Chapter 9 'How Are We Organising the Classroom?'. London: Cassell.

Proctor, A. *et al.* (1995) *Learning to Teach in the Primary Classroom*, Chapter 2, 'The Contexts for Learning'. London: Routledge.

Rosenthal, R. and. Jacobsen, L. (1968) *Pygmalion in the Classroom*. Eastbourne: Holt.

Chapter 4

Cashdan, A. and Overall, L. (1998) *Teaching in Primary Schools*, Chapter 8 'The National Curriculum: Background, Approach, Content'. London: Cassell.

Fontana, D. (1995) *Psychology for Teachers*, (Chapter 3 'Concept Formation and Cognitive Development'. London: Macmillan.

Pollard, A. and Tann, S. (1994) *Reflective Teaching in the Primary School: A Handbook for the Classroom*, Chapter 7 'What Are the Aims, Structure and Content of the Curriculum?'. London: Cassell.

Proctor, A. (1995) *Learning to Teach in the Primary Classroom*, Chapter 3 'Planning for Learning'. London: Routledge.

Chapter 6

Cashdan, A. and Overall, L. (1998) *Teaching in Primary Schools*, Chapter 15 'Assessment in the Primary Classroom'. London: Cassell.

DfEE (1998) *From Targets to Action* DfEE.

Headington, R. (2000) *Monitoring, Assessment, Recording, Reporting and Accountability.* London: David Fulton Publishers.

Stringer, J. and Powell, R. (1998) *Raising Achievement in the Primary School*. Robert Powell Publications (75a King Street, Knutsford, Cheshire WA16 6DX).

Chapter 7

Ayers, H. and Gray, F. (1998) *Classroom Management.* London: David Fulton Publishers.

Canter, L. and Canter, M. (1992) *Assertive Discipline.* Santa Monica: Lee Canter Associates.

Docking, J. (1996) *Managing Behaviour in the Primary School*, 2nd edn. London: David Fulton Publishers.

Fontana, D. (1995) *Psychology for Teachers*, Chapter 13 'Class Control and Management'. London: Macmillan.

MacGrath, M. (2000) *The Art of Peaceful Teaching in the Primary School.* London: David Fulton Publishers.

Pollard, A. and Tann, S (1994) *Reflective Teaching in the Primary School*, Chapter 10 'How Are We Managing Learning and Coping with Behaviour?'. London: Cassell.

Wragg, E.C. (1993) *Class Management.* London: Routledge.

Chapter 8

Brown, G. and Wragg, E. C. (1993) *Questioning.* London: Routledge.

Wragg, E. C. and Brown, G. (1993) *Explaining.* London: Routledge.

McFarlane, C. (1991) *Theme Work: A Global Perspective in the Primary Curriculum in the '90s.* Birmingham: Development Education Centre.

TTA (1998) *National Standards for Subject Leaders.* London: TTA.

Chapter 9

DES (1994) *The Code of Practice on the Identification and Assessment of Special Educational Needs.* London: DfEE (free).

DfEE (1997) *The SENCO Guide.* London: DfEE (free).

Farrell, M. (2000) *The Special Education Handbook,* 2nd edn. London: David Fulton Publishers.

Fox, G. (1998) *A Handbook for Learning Support Assistants: Teachers and Assistants Working Together.* London: David Fulton Publishers.

Gibbons, P. (1993) *Learning to Learn in a Second Language.* Milton Keynes: Open University Press.

Chapter 12

Bell, J. (1995) *Doing Your Own Research Project.* Milton Keynes: Open University Press.

Clipson-Boyles, S. (ed.) (2000) *Putting Research Into Practice in Primary Teaching and Learning.* London: David Fulton Publishers.

DfEE (1998) *Teachers Meeting the Challenge of Change.* London: DfEE.

Robb, J. and Letts, H. (1995) *Creating Kids Who Can.* London: Hodder & Stoughton.

Further Reading

Chapter 2

Farrell, M. (2000) *The Special Education Handbook*, 2nd edn. London: David Fulton Publishers.

Gardner, H. (1993) *Multiple Intelligences: The Theory in Practice*. New York: Basic Books.

Gibbons, P. (1998) *Learning to Learn in a Second Language*. New South Wales: Primary English Teaching Association

Hayes, D. (1999) *Foundations of Primary Teaching*, 2nd edn, Chapters 5–7, 'Organising for learning and Teaching', 'Strategies for effective teaching and learning', 'Teaching approaches'. London: David Fulton Publishers.

Hughes, P. (1991) *Gender Issues in the Primary Classroom*. Leamington Spa: Scholastic

Lee-Corbin, H. and Denicolo, P. (1998) *Able Children in Primary Schools*. London: David Fulton Publishers.

McGrath, H. and Noble, T. (1997) *Seven Ways at Once*, Books 1 and 2. Harlow: Longman.

Robb, J and Letts, H. (1997) *Creating Kids Who Can Concentrate*. London: Hodder and Stoughton.

Chapter 3

Dean, J. (1992) *Organising Learning in the Primary Classroom*. London: Routledge.

Findley, T. and Findley, J. (1996) *Briefing Resource Cards: 1, Number 2 Language and Literacy*. Wisbech LDA.

Fox, G. (1998) *A Handbook for Learning and Support Assistants*. London: David Fulton Publishers.

Ghaye, A. and Ghaye, K. (1998) *Teaching and Learning Through Critical Reflective Practice*. London: David Fulton Publishers.

Moyles, J. (1994) *Organising for Learning in the Primary Classroom*. Oxford: OUP.

Riding, R. and Rayner, S. (1998) *Cognitive Style and Learning Strategies*. London: David Fulton Publishers.

Wragg, T. (1993) *Class Management*. London: Routledge.

Chapter 4

Aldrich, R. (1982) *An Introduction to the History of Education* (1982). London: Hodder and Stoughton.

Chambers, A. (1993) *Tell Me*. Thimble Press.

Lang, P. (1988) *Thinking about Personal and Social Education in the Primary school*. Oxford: Blackwell.

Purvis, J. (1991) *A History of Women's Education in England*. Milton Keynes: Open University Press.

Selley, N. (1999) *The Art of Constructivist Teaching in the Primary School*. London: David Fulton Publishers.

Tattum, D. and Tattum E. (1992) *Social Education and Personal Development*. London: David Fulton Publishers.

Chapter 5

Drummond, M. J. (1993) *Assessing Children's Learning*. London: David Fulton Publishers.

Littledyke, M. and Huxford, L. (eds) (1998) *Teaching the Primary Curriculum for Constructive Learning*. London: David Fulton Publishers.

Pollard, A. and Tann, S. (1994) *Reflective Teaching in the Primary School*. Chapter 7, 'What are the Aims, Structure and Content of the Curriculum?' and Chapter 8, 'How Do We Plan and Implement the Curriculum?'. London: Cassell.

Rodger, R. (1999) *Planning an Appropirate Curriculum for the Under Fives.* London: David Fulton Publishers.

Chapter 6

Clarke, S. (1998) *Targeting Assessment in the Primary Classroom.* London: Hodder and Stoughton.

DfEE (1999) *The National Numeracy Strategy,* pages 33–37 Introduction. London: DfEE.

First Steps (1997) *International Edition: Reading Continuum; Writing Continuum; Spelling Continuum; Oral Language Continuum* Oxford: Heinemann.

ILEA (1987) *The Primary Language Record.* London: Center for Language in Primary Education

Lindsay, G. and Desforges, M. (1998) *Baseline Assessment: Practice, Problems and Possibilities.* London: David Fulton Publishers.

McNamara, S. and Moreton, G. (1997) *Understanding Differentiation,* London: David Fulton Publishers.

QCA (1999) *Target setting and Assessment in the National Literacy Strategy.* London: QCA.

Reeves, G. (1995) *Reporting to Parents.* Primary File Publishing.

TGAT (1987) *National Curriculum: Task Group on Assessment and Testing.* London: DES.

Tymms, P. (1999) *Baseline Assessment and Monitoring in Primary Schools.* London: David Fulton Publishers.

Chapter 7

Brophy, J. and Evertson, C. (1976) *Learning from Teaching: A Developmental Perspective.* Needham Heights, MA: Allyn and Bacon.

Canter, L. and Canter, M. (1992) *Assertive Discipline.* Santa Monica: Lee Canter Associates.

Clarke, D. and Murray, A. (eds) (1996) *Developing and Implementing a Whole-School Behaviour Policy: A Practical Approach.* London: David Fulton Publishers.

David, K. and Charlton, A. (eds) (1996) *Pastoral Care Matters in the Primary and Middle School.* London: Routledge.

Kounin, J. (1970) *Discipline and Group Management in Classrooms.* New York: Holt, Rinehart and Winston.

Kyriacou, C. (1997) *Effective Teaching Skills.* Oxford: Blackwell.

Lang, P. (ed.) (1988) *Thinking about Personal and Social Education in the Primary School.* Oxford: Blackwell.

Maslow, A. (1954) *Motivation and Personality.* London: Harper and Row.

Mosley, J. (1998) *Quality Circle Time in the Primary Classroom.* Cambridge: LDA.

Robb, J. and Letts, H. (1995) *Creating Kids Who Can.* London: Hodder and Stoughton.

Robb, J. and Letts, H. (1997) *Creating Kids Who Can Concentrate: Proven Strategies For Beating ADD Without Drugs.* London: Hodder and Stoughton.

Roffey, S. and O'Reirdan, T. (1998) *Infant Classroom Behaviour: Needs, Perspectives and Strategies.* London: David Fulton Publishers.

Rogers, W. (1990) *The Language of Discipline,* London: Falmer.

Tattum, D. and Tattum E. (1992) *Social Education and Personal Development.* London: David Fulton Publishers.

Walkerdine, V. (1992) *Democracy in the Kitchen.* London: Virago.

Chapter 8

Butterfield, F. (1986) 'Why Asians Are Going to the Head of the Class', *New York Times,* 3 August.

Neate, B. (1999) *Finding Out About Finding Out.* London: Hodder and Stoughton.

Purkey, W. and Schmidt, J. (1990) *Invitational Learning for Development.* Ann Arbor: University of Michigan.

Steiner, M. (1993) *Learning from Experience.* Stoke-on-Trent: Trentham.

Stevenson, H. (1996) 'Why Some Students are ahead of the class', *New York Times,* 3 August.

Wragg, E. C. (1993) *Primary Teaching Skills.* London: Routledge.

Chapter 9

DfEE (1997) *Excellence for All Children: Meeting Special Educational Needs.* London: DfEE

Lee-Corbin, H. and Denicolo, P. (1998) *Able Children in Primary Schools.* London: David Fulton Publishers.

Neate, B. (1999) *Finding Out About Finding Out.* London: Hodder and Stoughton.

Male, J. (undated) *Children First: A Guide to the Needs of Disabled Children in School*. RADAR (Royal Association for Disability and Rehabilitation).

Martin, T. (1993) *The Strugglers*. Oxford: OUP.

McGrath, H. and Noble, T. (1997) *Seven Ways at Once, Books 1 & 2*. Harlow: Longman.

NFER (1998) *The Directory 1998: Tests, Assessments, Training and Information Services in Primary Education*. Windsor: NFER-Nelson.

OFSTED (1999) *Raising the Attainment of minority ethnic pupils*. London: OFSTED.

QCA (1998) *Can Do Better: Raising Boys' Achievement in English*, see especially pp. 39 and 41. London: QCA.

Robb, J. and Letts, H. (1997) *Creating Kids Who Can Concentrate: Proven Strategies For Beating ADD Without Drugs*. London: Hodder and Stoughton.

TTA (1998) *National Standards for Special Educational Needs Co-ordinators*. London: TTA.

Warin, S. (undated) *Implementing the Code of Practice: Individual Education Plans*. Tamworth: NASEN

Development Education Centre catalogue (Development Education Centre, Selly Oak Colleges, Bristol Road, Birmingham B29 6LE).

Chapter 10

Cashdan, A. and Overall, L. (1998) *Teaching in Primary Schools*, Chapter 4 'Schools, pupils and parents: contexts for learning'. London: Cassell.

Home and School – A Working Alliance Series. London: David Fulton Publishers.

Mills, J. (1996) *Partnership in the Primary School*. London: Routledge.

OFSTED (1995) *Guidance on the Inspection of Nursery and Primary Schools*. London: HMSO.

Waller, H. and Waller, J. (1998) *Linking Home and School*. London: David Fulton Publishers.

Useful resources

Findley, T. and Findley, J. (1996) *Briefing Resource Cards: Number*. Wisbech: LDA.

Findley, T. and Findley, J. (1996) *Briefing Resource Cards: Language and Literacy*. Wisbech: LDA.

NCC (1990) Curriculum Guidelines:
1. A Framework for the Primary Curriculum
2. A Curriculum for All
3. The Whole Curriculum
4. Education for Economic and Industrial Understanding
5. Health Education
6. Careers Education and Guidance
7. Environmental Education
8. Education for Citizenship
9. The National Curriculum and Pupils with Severe Learning Difficulties

Chapter 11

Cole, M. (ed.) (1999) *Professional Issues for Teachers and Student Teachers*. London: David Fulton Publishers.

Croner's Guide to the Law (also available on CD-ROM; updated yearly). Kingston-on-Thames: Croner.

Chapter 12

Cook, R. (1992) *The Prevention and Management of Stress: A Manual for Teachers*. Harlow: Longman.

Dunham, J. (1992) *Stress in Teaching*. London: Routledge.

Frost, D. (1997) *Reflective Action Planning for Teachers*. London: David Fulton Publishers.

Jones, K. *et al.* (1990) *Staff Development in Primary Schools*.

Tolley, H., Biddulph, M. and Fisher, T. (1996) *The Professional Management File*. Cambridge: Chris Kingston Publishing.

Useful source of publications

Madeleine Lindley Book Centre, Broadgate, Broadway Business Park, Chadderton, Oldham, OL9 9XA. Tel: 0161 683 4400.

Index